WONDERS OF
THE MODERN WORLD

FOREWORD

To celebrate the turn of the century and the new millennium, **THE EVENTFUL CENTURY** series presents the vast panorama of the last hundred years—a century which has witnessed the transition from horse-drawn transport to space travel, and from the first telephones to the information superhighway.

THE EVENTFUL CENTURY chronicles epoch-making events like the outbreak of the two world wars, the Russian Revolution and the rise and fall of communism. But major events are only part of this glittering kaleidoscope. It also describes the everyday background—the way people lived, how they worked, what they ate and drank, how much they earned, the way they spent their leisure time, the books they read, and the crimes, scandals and unsolved mysteries that set them talking. Here are fads and crazes like the Hula-Hoop and Rubik's Cube . . . fashions like the New Look and the miniskirt . . . breakthroughs in entertainment, such as the birth of the movies . . . medical milestones such as the discovery of penicillin . . . and marvels of modern architecture and engineering.

WONDERS OF THE MODERN WORLD looks at major architectural and engineering feats of the 20th century. Architects have created homes that vary from the functional white cubes of Modernism to glittering palaces such as Hearst Castle and the Sultan of Brunei's Palace, while city skylines have become dominated by the skyscraper. Buildings as diverse as the Louvre Pyramid, the Sydney Opera House and the Empire State Building have surprised and thrilled the public. Monuments such as the Atomium in Brussels and the Moscow Rocket Museum have been built to celebrate the milestones of human progress, while others, such as Mount Rushmore and the Vietnam Memorial, proclaim the indomitability of the human spirit. Thanks to human ingenuity and skill, at the end of the century skyscrapers reach higher and bridges farther than ever before; huge dams, such as the Aswan Dam and Itaipú, harness the power of mighty rivers, and a giant solar oven captures the energy of the Sun.

WONDERS OF
THE MODERN WORLD

The Reader's Digest Association, Inc.
Pleasantville, New York/Montreal

WONDERS OF THE MODERN WORLD
Edited and designed by Toucan Books Limited
Written by Antony Mason
Edited by Helen Douglas-Cooper
Additional research by Mary Emma Baxter
Designed by Bradbury and Williams
Picture research by Julie McMahon, Marian Pullen
and Mary Emma Baxter

FOR THE AMERICAN EDITION
Produced by The Reference Works, Inc.
Director Harold Rabinowitz
Editors Ross Mandel, Lorraine Martindale,
Doug Heyman
Production Antler DesignWorks
Director Bob Antler

READER'S DIGEST PROJECT STAFF
Group Editorial Director Fred DuBose
Senior Editor Susan Randol
Senior Designer Judith Carmel
Production Technology Manager Douglas A. Croll
Art Production Coordinator Jennifer R. Tokarski

READER'S DIGEST ILLUSTRATED REFERENCE BOOKS
Editor-in-Chief Christopher Cavanaugh
Art Director Joan Mazzeo

First English edition copyright © 1998
The Reader's Digest Association Limited,
11 Westferry Circus, Canary Wharf,
London E14 4HE

Copyright © 2000
Reader's Digest Association, Inc.
Reader's Digest Road
Pleasantville, NY 10570

Copyright © 2000
The Reader's Digest Association (Canada) Ltd.
Copyright © 2000
The Reader's Digest Association Far East Limited
Philippines copyright © 2000
Reader's Digest Association Far East Limited
All rights reserved

Library of Congress
Cataloging in Publication Data

Wonders of the modern world
        p. cm – (The eventful century)
    Includes index.
    ISBN 0-7621-0271-3
    1. Architecture, Modern–20th century. 2.
Engineering–History–20th century. 3. Structural
engineering–History–20th century. I. Title: Wonders
of the modern world. II. Reader's Digest Association.
III. Series

NA680.A145 2000
724'.6–dc21   99-049604

FRONT COVER
From top: Mount Rushmore;
Keck Observatory; Empire State Building

BACK COVER
From top: Sydney Opera House; Petronas Twin
Towers; Hoover Dam

Page 3 (from left to right): Chrysler Building, New
York; Mount Rushmore, U.S.; Sagrada Familia,
Barcelona, Spain; De La Warr Pavilion, Bexhill,
England.

Background pictures:
Page 15: Fallingwater, U.S.
Page 27: Lloyd's of London
Page 57: Guggenheim Museum, Bilbao, Spain
Page 79: Sydney Harbor Bridge, Australia
Page 99: Thames Flood Barrier, London
Page 117: Great Hassan II Mosque, Morocco
Page 139: Futuroscope, Poitiers, France

Printed in the United States of America

CONTENTS

WHAT MAKES A WONDER?

ARCHITECTS AND ENGINEERS HAVE USED THEIR IMAGINATION AND DARING IN DESIGNING AND CREATING THE 20TH CENTURY'S LANDMARKS

Lists were almost as popular in ancient Greece as they are today, and by about the 2nd century BC writers and commentators had drawn up a list of what they considered to be the greatest man-made marvels of their time. They could have selected dozens, but they settled on just seven, each one truly astounding in scale, technological daring and an artistic achievement.

Some 2,000 years later, this fascination for selecting the great marvels of the day has not diminished, and the criteria remain much the same. The sheer scale of the Aswan Dam or the CN Tower or the Mount Rushmore sculptures incite wonder—and admiration, too, for the courage and belief of their creators in seeing the projects through.

HARD LABOR German builders excavating foundations in 1910 are a reminder that the main engine of the construction industry at the start of the century was the muscle power of its workers.

One of the main differences between the modern and ancient worlds lies in the technology available. During the 20th century, architects, engineers and artists have had at their disposal a huge and powerful array of machinery and materials that were unimaginable in the 19th century, let alone 2,000 years ago. In the ancient world, craftsmen had to make do with wood, stone, tools of bronze and iron, and muscle power. At the end of the 20th century, there are giant tunnel-boring machines, cranes, computers, prestressed concrete, plate glass, aluminum panelling, steel cables and glass fiber, to name but a few.

It is the rapidly changing technology that has driven the 20th century, and has given architects and engineers the power to take on ever greater challenges and ever more daring leaps of the imagination. Technology has dictated the scale of the endeavors, from the statue of Christ overlooking Rio de Janeiro to the Louisiana Superdome. It has also led to the development of new sources of energy, as seen at the Odeillo Solar Oven, the Altamont Pass Wind Farm and the Chinon A1 Nuclear Power Station; as well as

POWER LIFT By the time London's Canary Wharf was under construction in the 1990s, an array of machinery such as diggers, pile drivers and tower cranes was being used on building sites.

to the technical finesse of the W.M. Keck Telescope on Mauna Kea, capable of looking so deep into space that it observes events that took place billions of years ago.

The look of technology

Technology also influences style, and throughout the 20th century, architects have been investigating how new technology can be adapted to construction, and how this can or should be reflected in the look and shape of the buildings that result.

At the start of the century, Art Nouveau was all the rage. It was called "New Art" because it took no references from the past. Florid, curvaceous, even suggestively degenerate, it used new forms, shapes, colors and decorative gestures that spoke of an entirely new imaginative freedom. Technology also played its part in the equation. Victor Horta,

the Belgian architect who designed the first-ever Art Nouveau house in 1893, used iron and steel structures to create new kinds of spaces, but he also made a decorative virtue of these materials, seen noticeably in his department store, the Grands Magasins A L'Innovation (1901) in Brussels.

But there were others at the turn of the century who believed that this kind of stylistic elaboration was frivolity, a distraction. This was the line that the architects of the Vienna "Sezession" were beginning to evolve, as witnessed, for example, in the stridently rectilinear Palais Stoclet in Brussels, designed by Josef Hoffmann. However, it was the pioneering Chicago architect Louis H. Sullivan who declared that true architectural elegance derives from a harmonious marriage between new technology and the building's usage. The skyscraper—a new concept in architecture that came of age in the first three decades of the century—offered architects the perfect

BREAKING THE MOLD The Art Nouveau architect Victor Horta achieved novel effects by incorporating steel into his structures, as in the central well of the Maison van Eetvelde, completed at the turn of the century.

opportunity to put this theory to the test. Following Sullivan's adage, the Chicago school worked at seeing what kind of skyscraper would emerge if the architect minimized the stylistic adornments. By contrast, the Beaux-Arts school, which predominated in New York, took entirely the opposite view, using the skyscraper as an opportunity to reinterpret historical styles of the past. As a result, many of the great New York skyscrapers of the first two decades of the century were dressed up as Greek temples, medieval town halls, Napoleonic palaces, or a mixture of all of these. The Woolworth Building was the greatest of the Beaux-Arts skyscrapers, surging upward from Broadway like a modern version of a medieval Gothic cathedral.

It was the Chicago school, however, that won out in the end. By the late 1920s the classic skyscrapers made a virtue of their soaring, clean-edged, rectilinear shapes. Art Deco may have had an impact on the Chrysler Building, and even in some of the detailing on the Empire State Building, but minimalism was on its way, culminating in the ultimate statement of sheer verticality in the twin towers of the World Trade Center completed in the early 1970s.

All the while, the very same battle was being waged over domestic housing. Radical architects in the early years of the century wanted to abandon all references to historical style and grab the opportunities offered by new materials. The Swiss-born French architect Le Corbusier saw reinforced concrete as the key to progress: comparatively cheap, strong and easy to shape. He envisioned entirely new forms for houses that would be efficient, hygienic and free of clutter. Modern homes could be treated like any other industrial product, as "machines for living." His Villa Savoye at Poissy, near Paris, was the culmination of this direction. But like so much architecture at the cutting edge of the avant-garde, it proved too radical for the rest of the world.

Architects, designers and artists were developing similar thoughts at the great German school of modern design, the Bauhaus, founded in 1919, and closed by the Nazis in 1933. Guided by broadly socialist principles, the Bauhaus architects and designers pictured a world in which everyone could benefit from first-class, functional and elegant industrial design. This meant stripping away useless ornament, but it did not mean abandoning a sense of artistic judgment in designing what was left. The emphasis was now on satisfactory simplified shapes, rather than adornment.

Whereas Le Corbusier worked with reinforced concrete, the Bauhaus architects set more store by steel and glass, developing

LET THERE BE LIGHT
As early as 1921, the German architect Miës van der Rohe designed an experimental tower block of glass and steel. Such buildings would transform traditional concepts of space and mass in architecture.

curtain-wall construction techniques pioneered by the skyscraper builders. Later, in the hands of Walter Gropius and especially Ludwig Miës van der Rohe, this would evolve into the classic "glass-box" architecture of the International Style, which was first developed in the 1930s and really took off after the Second World War.

By the 1950s, most of the Bauhaus architects were working in the United States. The best of the International Style buildings, such as Miës van der Rohe's Seagram Building, built in 1958 in New York, have a stately elegance that can be ascribed to the judicious control of their proportions. Sadly, this was not reflected in many glass-box skyscrapers that then mushroomed in cities around the world. The International Style soon seemed to have run its course.

In response, a number of architects began to take a revised look at the sculptural potential of architecture, balancing technology and function with a more expressive approach to the look of a building. One of Le Corbusier's disciples, the Brazilian architect Oscar Niemeyer,

MASTER HOUSES In 1925-8 Walter Gropius designed three *Meisterhäuser* for teachers at the Bauhaus in Dessau. They exude a sense of style that soon became highly desirable among the avant-garde.

THE SEVEN WONDERS OF THE ANCIENT WORLD

SEVEN MONUMENTS WERE SELECTED BY THE ANCIENT GREEKS AS THE GREATEST IN THE KNOWN WORLD AND THE PASSAGE OF 2,000 YEARS HAS NOT DIMINISHED THEIR STATURE

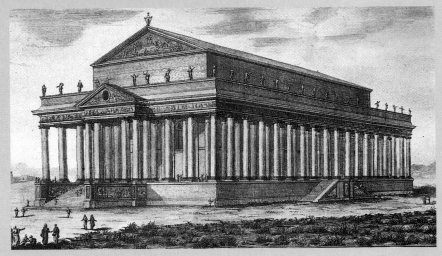

COLOSSAL SCALE The Temple of Artemis at Ephesus was the largest temple of its time. It housed a statue of the goddess that was the focus of pilgrims paying devotion to her cult.

The Seven Wonders of the Ancient World were the Pyramids of Giza, the Temple of Artemis at Ephesus, the Mausoleum at Halicarnassus, the Lighthouse of Alexandria, the Hanging Gardens of Babylon, the statue of Zeus at Olympia, and the Colossus of Rhodes. Of these, it is the most ancient that is best preserved today. The Pyramids at Giza, near Cairo, date from about 2580 to 2520 BC. The largest of the three, the Great Pyramid, was built by King Khufu, or Cheops. Standing 449 feet high, it remained the world's tallest building for about 4,000 years, until overtaken by the spires of late medieval cathedrals. It is still the largest stone building in the world: it contains 2.3 million blocks of stone weighing about 2.5 tons each, with some up to 15 tons. Given that the Great Pyramid was probably constructed during Khufu's 23 year reign, 100,000 blocks had to be put in position every year, an average of 273 a day.

The Temple of Artemis (Roman Diana), goddess of the Moon, hunting and childbirth, was a vast marble temple, built in about 350 BC at the Greek city of Ephesus (now in Turkey), the center of her cult. It was the biggest temple of its day, covering an area larger than a football field. It was destroyed by the Goths in 262 and only fragments remain.

Similarly, fragments can still be seen of the elaborate Mausoleum of Halicarnassus—some of them in the British Museum. This was the largest tomb of the ancient world, built in honor of King Mausolus of Caria at Halicarnassus, now Bodrum, Turkey, in about 350 BC. This monument is the origin of the word mausoleum. It was destroyed by an earthquake in medieval times, and in the 15th century the Knights of St. John used the stone to build a castle.

Marine archaeologists have recently discovered remains of the lighthouse that marked the entrance to one of the greatest Mediterranean ports, Alexandria in Egypt. It stood on an island called Pharos—the origin of the French word for a lighthouse, *phare*. Built in about 270 BC, it was made of white marble and apparently rose to 380 feet. Shipping was guided by a fire

reflected by bronze mirrors, and by its plume of smoke. The Pharos lighthouse was destroyed by an earthquake in 1375.

Nothing remains of the Hanging (or terraced) Gardens of Babylon. Legend has it that King Nebuchadnezzar II (605-562 BC) built the gardens to comfort a wife who pined for the greenery of her homeland. During excavations at another Mesopotamian city, Ur, drainage pipes were found on the terraces of the ziggurat, which suggest they might have been used for earth beds supporting trees and shrubs; Babylon may have had a similar arrangement. In any case, the gardens faded away as Babylon declined after the Persian invasion of 538 BC, and was a ruin by about 100 BC.

The Olympian Zeus was a huge statue by the sculptor Phidias dating from the 5th century BC. It stood in a temple at Olympia in Greece, the center of the cult of Zeus, in whose honor the games were held. Covered in gold and ivory, it was some 43 feet tall. The most famous statue of the classical world, it was probably destroyed by fire during the late Roman era.

The Colossus of Rhodes was a huge bronze sculpture, perhaps 98 feet high, of Helios the Sun god, created by the sculptor Chares. It was erected at the harbor entrance of the island's capital in about 280 BC to celebrate the successful defense of the city 20 years earlier. The idea that it stood astride the harbor mouth is a later invention. The statue was toppled by an earthquake in 226 BC, and lay where it fell until pillaged for its bronze in the 7th century AD.

ENDURING WONDER The Pyramids are the only one of the Seven Wonders that has survived more or less as the ancient Greeks might have witnessed it. Originally, they were clad in polished stone.

demonstrated the sculptural potential of reinforced concrete when he undertook the creation of an entirely new capital city, Brasília. Meanwhile, the Finnish-American architect Eero Saarinen showed the extraordinary dynamic potential of reinforced concrete with his TWA Terminal at John F. Kennedy Airport in New York. Even Le Corbusier made an uncharacteristically sculptural gesture with his chapel of Notre-Dame du Haut at Ronchamp, France. But perhaps the most famous example of an imaginative leap in concrete is the Sydney Opera House, completed in 1973.

ART NOUVEAU REVISITED Eero Saarinen's TWA Terminal at John F. Kennedy Airport reintroduced a curvaceous sensuality that had not been seen since the Art Nouveau era.

The relationship between architecture and setting was a central theme in the work of the influential American architect Frank Lloyd Wright. He believed that each project demanded a unique response to its environment through the shapes and materials used by the architect: what he called "organic modernism." Fallingwater, a private house in Pennsylvania, has a horizontal structure poised against an untamed woodland setting. His Guggenheim Museum in New York, on the other hand, applies an entirely novel solution to the requirements of an art gallery.

Technology to the fore

During the 1960s and 1970s, a younger generation of designers took a new look at the role of technology in architecture. The British architects Richard Rogers and Norman Foster were interested in exploiting state-of-the-art technology to its maximum potential, in factories, office blocks and museums. Their paramount concern is with the function of the building, and they select the most appropriate technology to match this. With the Pompidou Center in Paris, Richard Rogers and his then partner, the Italian Renzo Piano, took the architectural world by storm by putting all the building's services and ducts, normally discreetly hidden from view, on the outside.

The emphasis on high-quality engineering was seen in two buildings completed in 1986: Norman Foster's Hong Kong and Shanghai Bank in Hong Kong, and Richard Rogers' Lloyd's Building in London. In both, technology has been allowed to speak for itself, and becomes an integral, even dominant, part of

POWERFUL PREDICTIONS

In 1905, toward the end of his long life, the eminent French scientist Marcellin Berthelot, the founder of modern organic chemistry, was asked to describe his vision of the future. He believed that before many decades of the 20th century had elapsed, all food might be replicated by chemistry and produced in the form of pills in factories run on solar power or geothermal energy. He painted a Utopian image of a world freed of the drudgery of farming and mining, where all countries had equal access to power and industry. "Irregularities in the well-being of peoples due to some possessing natural advantages which others were without would thus unceasingly tend to diminish, and soon no one spot would be more favored than any other."

Berthelot's predictions demonstrate how the debate over new energy sources has run like a thread through the century. During 1905, the *Strand Magazine* of London invited comment on his ideas from some of Britain's leading scientists. The eminent physicist William Thomson, Lord Kelvin and Britain's leading zoologist Sir Ray Lankester, broadly agreed, although Lankester expressed some skepticism that chemical products would usurp farm food. The Nobel prize-winning chemist Sir William Ramsay was more dismissive: "Nature herself is, and always will be, the cheapest food factory."

Ramsay was also doubtful that geothermal power was feasible: drilling to such depths looked technically impossible, and there was no certainty that it would produce a source of steady power. Geysers,

TIME TRAVEL The world's first solar-powered car drove through the streets of London in 1960. Developed in California, it was a converted 1912 veteran car with a large solar panel on the roof. The further development of solar-powered cars has stalled over the problem of storing sufficient quantities of electricity. Below: Proving Sir William Ramsay's skepticism groundless, Iceland now supplies nearly a third of its energy needs from geothermal sources. The Nejavellir Geothermal Area uses steam emitted by a tectonic rift to produce electricity and to supply heating for houses and offices.

SOLAR EVOLUTION Under the headline "Summer, Even in Winter," a 1929 edition of a French magazine for inventors explored the effectiveness of solar panels for domestic heating. They were cumbersome solar collectors that heated water in small tubes exposed to the Sun.

after all, operate in fits and starts. But he added: "There are other forces in Nature that might be harnessed which are open to the same suggestion—the tides for instance. A tidal engine or wave machine might be constructed and serve a useful purpose . . . As to the solar engine, there is more to be said in its favor, but it would be hardly available in England. When I was in India I was approached by several of the native Princes, who contemplated the erection of solar engines."

Indeed, since the 1860s solar power had been used experimentally to drive machinery: mirrors concentrated the Sun's heat to boil water and make steam. But Ramsay also offered a tantalizing vision of the enormous energy potential of radioactive elements, as Ernest Rutherford (1871-1937) had revealed through experiments two years previously. As the *Strand Magazine* put it, Ramsay "had discovered a new substance which he believed would lead to the attainment of that for which science had been striving for so many years. Briefly, it concerns the chemical action produced by radium, and opens a wide field of speculation as to the usefulness of that wonderful substance, the scientific sensation of a new century." Behind that sensation was the distant specter of nuclear energy.

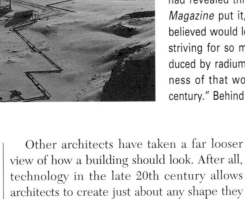

the look. Both Foster and Rogers acknowledge the value of the input from engineers, and collaborate closely with them; their buildings often seem to inhabit a grey area between the two disciplines. A similar attention to engineering detail lies behind the success of the Louvre Pyramid, built in the 1980s by the American architect I.M. Pei.

Other architects have taken a far looser view of how a building should look. After all, technology in the late 20th century allows architects to create just about any shape they choose. The American architect Cesar Pelli, for instance, chose to create a building of classical proportions when he designed London's tallest building, the Canary Wharf

Tower. But when it came to the Petronas Towers in Kuala Lumpur, Malaysia, the tallest building in the world when it was completed in 1996, Pelli produced a textured look based on an Islamic geometric pattern that was without precedent or parallel.

Just how wide open architecture has become at the end of the 20th century to

movement of the 1920s, the hallmark of its American architect, Richard Meier. There could hardly be two more contrasting buildings, yet they end the 20th century on the same resounding chord with which it began: a chord produced by the eternal tension between form and function, informed by the evolving potential of technology.

The high, mighty and lavish

Modern wonders, like the ancient ones, are not entirely confined to architecture. Some qualify for their technological achievement alone. For six years, land on either side of the narrow Strait of Dover hummed with the activity of Europe's biggest engineering project: the building of the Channel Tunnel, completed in 1994. The impressive quality of big tunnels lies in the sheer daring of their

sculptural and artistic gesture was demonstrated by one of the century's most acclaimed buildings, the new Guggenheim Museum in Bilbao by the American architect Frank O. Gehry, opened in 1997. Covered with glittering titanium, its unnamable shape sets in motion an array of poetic associations, and transmits a sense of dynamism by appearing to be on the verge of collapse. In contrast, the new J. Paul Getty Center in Los Angeles, opened the same year, evokes the cool, elegant functionalism of the Modernist

undertaking, as new machinery brings ever more ambitious projects within range. The world's longest is now the Seikan Rail Tunnel, linking the Japanese islands of Hokkaido and Honshu, completed in 1988.

Tunnels do not give much opportunity for artistic interpretation, nor do pipelines, such as the Trans-Alaska Oil Pipeline, although this does not diminish their achievement. Other grand engineering projects have a more distinct visual appeal, such as the steaming pipes of the Wairakei Geothermal Power Station, or the Thames Barrier in London. Dams, by contrast, have a spectacular beauty that derives mainly from the enormity of their scale. The Aswan High Dam in Egypt is some 2¼ miles across and 374 feet high; the Itaipú Dam, straddling the border between Brazil and Paraguay, is almost 5 miles across.

But of all the great engineering projects of this century, it is probably the bridges that

HIGH RISE New York provides the quintessential 20th-century city skyline, where the combination of new construction techniques and the high cost of land drove buildings upward. The Chrysler Building (center) and the Empire State Building (right) still rank as classics of skyscraper design.

have made the greatest aesthetic impact. Technology has allowed suspension bridges to become ever longer, but also ever more elegant as they beat each successive record. The orange-red superstructure of the Golden Gate Bridge, built in the 1930s, rising majestically over the rolling fog at the entrance to San Francisco Bay, is one of the most breathtaking sights of the entire California coast. The Humber Bridge in England, built in the 1970s, attracts numerous tourists, who come to admire its sleek and streamlined elegance as it reaches across 4,626 feet in a single span.

Like the Colossus of Rhodes, some 20th-century structures qualify on account of the extraordinary scale of their artistic ambition—such as Mount Rushmore, the statue of Christ at Rio de Janeiro, the Moscow Rocket Monument, the vast steel Gateway Arch at St. Louis, Missouri, and the monument-cum-office block of La Grande Arche at La Défense, outside Paris. Others earn our admiration for their luxurious grandeur and extraordinarily lavish decoration, testament to the ambition of the individuals who built them. Hearst Castle, dating back to the 1920s and 1930s, was a rich man's fantasy estate, a place of spectacular opulence and bountiful entertainment that took over 18

years to build. The Sultan of Brunei's Palace, built in the 1980s, is the largest palace in the world, while the Great Hassan II Mosque in Casablanca, Morocco, is probably the most sumptuous religious building created in the 20th century. The Shri Swaminarayan temple in Neasden, north London, in contrast, deserves a place not only because of its scale, but because of its intricate detail, and the extraordinary story of how it was built.

The Moscow Metro (first line completed 1935), and theme parks such as Disneyland (opened 1955) at Anaheim, California, and the Futuroscope (opened in 1987) in France, operate on a different but parallel level: they use imagination and elaborate presentation to evoke secular fantasy that will appeal to the fee-paying public.

Some projects win our wonder simply because of their ebullient eccentricity—the product of the determination of individuals to realize a dream against all the odds, and often in the face of widespread sneering and criticism. The Spanish architect Antoní Gaudí struggled obsessively with his Sagrada Familia church in Barcelona, against changing fashions and increased impoverishment. It remained only partially complete at his death, but still excites the passions of admirers from all over the world.

At the end of the 20th century, a vast basilica, Notre-Dame de la Paix, rises incongruously from the bush at Yamoussoukro, the new capital of Côte d'Ivoire in West Africa. It is said to have impoverished the nation, a charge that has also been levelled against the Columbus Lighthouse, completed in 1992, in Santo Domingo in the Dominican Republic, which projects a laser light cross into the Caribbean sky.

The same objections, no doubt, were raised over some of the Seven Wonders of the Ancient World, which in their day must have drawn criticism as an excessive drain on funds and human energies. There could hardly have been a more obvious example of this than the Great Pyramid. But without grand gestures, and the foolishness or megalomania that sometimes accompanies them, these projects would not exist to face the criticism; and no one knows at the outset whether they will attract acclaim or notoriety.

We live too close to the wonders of the 20th century to know which will stand the test of time over another 50 years, let alone 2,000 years. And who would dare to predict which of the 70 featured here would survive in a list whittled down to just seven, as the ancient world chose to do?

CROWNING ACHIEVEMENT London celebrates 2,000 years of the Christian calendar with the Millennium Dome (right). It will contain a dozen key attractions and exhibitions, including the Body Zone, a giant walk-in anatomical model of a human body, with accompanying baby.

EXTRAORDINARY DWELLINGS

LUXURY TAKES MANY FORMS. TO SOME, IT MEANS THE PRIVILEGE OF BEING AT THE VERY FOREFRONT OF AVANT-GARDE TASTE, AND EMPLOYING FASHIONABLE ARCHITECTS AT THE CUTTING EDGE OF CURRENT DESIGN THEORY AND STYLE—EVEN IF THE RESULTS ARE SHOCKINGLY SPARTAN. TO OTHERS IT MAY MEAN THE TIME-HONORED PLEASURES OF SPACE AND SUMPTUOUS SURROUNDINGS. WHATEVER THE CASE, WEALTH AND POWER APPEAR TO BE PREREQUISITES.

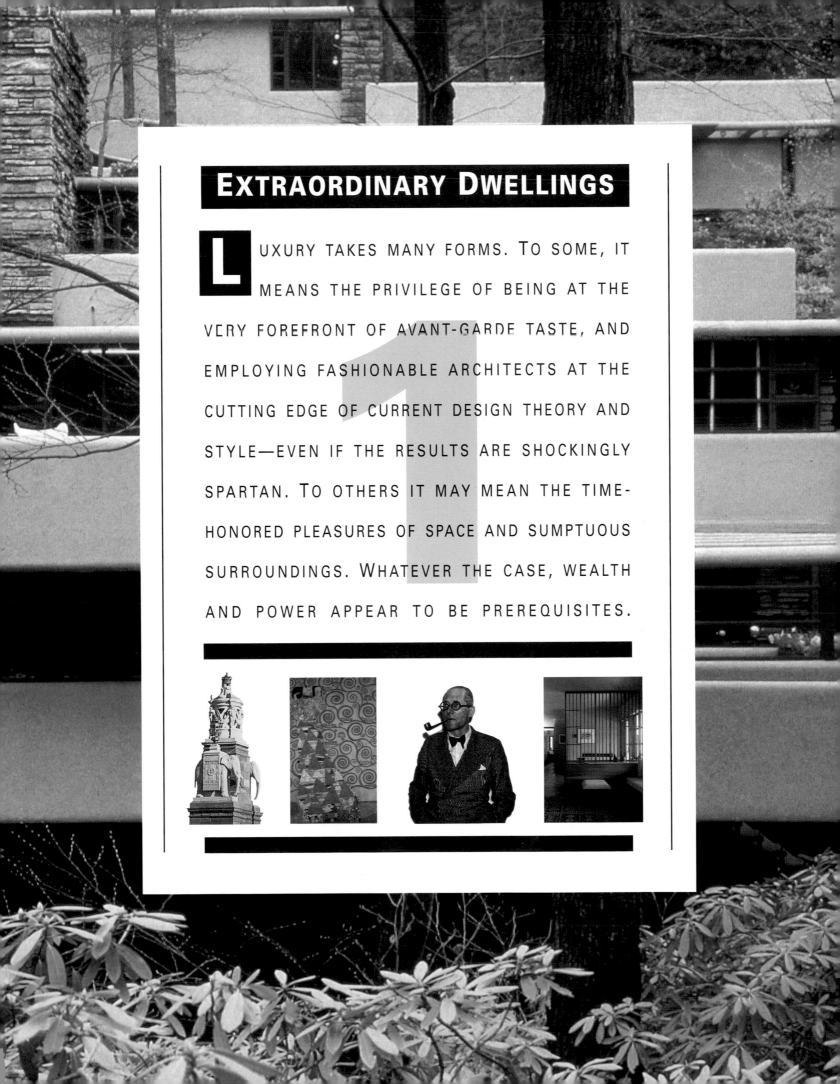

PALAIS STOCLET

WHILE ART NOUVEAU WAS THE RAGE, A PRISTINE HOME IN BRUSSELS POINTED TO THE FUTURE

Brussels, the city where in 1893 Victor Horta produced the first truly Art Nouveau house, the Hôtel Tassel, could legitimately claim to be the home of Art Nouveau. The citizens of Brussels were just beginning to take the style to heart when a strange and provocative contradiction appeared in an eastern suburb of the city. The building had been commissioned by Adolphe Stoclet (1871-1941), a wealthy industrialist and an adventurous art collector. His architect was the 35-year-old Austrian Josef Hoffmann (1870-1956), a

founder-member of the radical group of designers and artists who called themselves the Vienna "Sezession," established in 1897.

Hoffmann had effectively turned his back not just on Art Nouveau, but on the whole history of architecture. Neo-classical, neo-Gothic, Moorish, Indian, medieval, rustic—all the styles that architects of the 19th century had endlessly plundered, revised and recycled

HINT OF THINGS TO COME The Palais Stoclet prefigured the rectilinear style of avant-garde houses in the 1920s. The public face of the building on the Avenue de Tervuren (below) is the rear of the house. In later years, architects would have done away with the sculptural ornamentation (right).

THE VIENNA "SEZESSION"

Art Nouveau was barely a decade old when it took the 1900 Paris International Exhibition by storm. To many it seemed the last word in modernity—the perfect style with which to enter a new and exciting century. But there were some for whom Art Nouveau had already begun to sicken into a purely decorative froth of swirls and decadent intertwinings.

This problem was already being addressed by a number of designers, notably the Scottish architect Charles Rennie Mackintosh (1868-1928). Although associated with Art Nouveau, he gave his work a novel dynamism by minimizing curvilinear decoration in favor of bold shapes and arresting geometric arrangements. Meanwhile, the British Arts and Crafts movement stuck to the ideals established by William Morris (1834-96), emphasizing function, simplicity and craftsmanship.

Both Mackintosh and the Arts and Crafts movement had a decisive influence on two young architects in Vienna, Josef Hoffmann and Josef Maria Olbrich (1867-1908). They gathered around them a group of like-minded artists and designers, such as Gustav Klimt and the graphic artist Koloman Moser (1868-1918), and in 1897 they distanced themselves from the conservative tastes of the Viennese Academy of Arts by announcing a "Sezession." The idea was that members of the group would collaborate to produce buildings and interiors that conformed to their own radical approach to style.

In 1903, Hoffmann and Koloman Moser set up the Wiener Werkstätte to manufacture and sell the group's products. Organized along the lines of the influential Guild of Handicraft in England, the Werkstätte put the aims and ideals of the Vienna Sezession on a more practical footing.

were now unceremoniously abandoned. Instead of these, Hoffmann produced a building of uncompromising modernity: an asymmetrical compilation of rectangular blocks, underlined by exaggerated horizontals and verticals.

The no-nonsense starkness is softened only by the artistic disposition of the windows, which break through the line of the eaves, the rooftop conservatory, and the bronze sculptures of four nude males by Franz Metzner, which are mounted on the tower that rises over the stairwell. Regimented upright balustrades line the balcony, garnished with just a touch of restrained ornamentation where an Art Nouveau architect would not have been able to resist a grand and sensuous flourish.

Nothing was left to chance: early photographs of the house show that even the garden shrubs were trimmed into tight geometric shapes.

Ahead of its time

At a glance, the Palais Stoclet looks like a building of the late 1920s or early 1930s—the heyday of Art Deco. In fact, it was built between 1905 and 1911, when horse-drawn carriages were still as likely to draw up to the front gate as early automobiles.

This was the first residential project for the Wiener Werkstätte (Vienna Workshops), co-founded by Hoffmann in 1903. This center for arts and crafts aimed to pool the talents of architects, designers, painters and sculptors to produce the complete work of art—a *Gesamtkunstwerk*. Hoffmann and his colleagues designed everything, down to the door handles, light fixtures and cutlery. The interior is as spartan as the exterior, with upright, geometric furniture, an avoidance of textiles, and an abhorrence of clutter. This was a fashionably avant-garde approach, presenting a "reformed interior" where function dictates style. Bauhaus design and the International Style of the interwar years are but a step away.

The Wiener Werkstätte's products, however, were craft-based and labor intensive, and existed only by virtue of the patronage of wealthy clients. Despite the starkness of the house's interior, there are unmistakable gleams of luxury, seen in the precision of the detailing, the marble-faced columns, the parquet floor and the finely finished upholstery. Hoffmann also co-opted the talents of his fellow Sezessionist, the painter and designer Gustav Klimt (1862-1918), to create a lavish mosaic mural for the dining room. It ranks as one of Klimt's great masterpieces of decorative design. The note of luxury can also be detected in the exterior, where the walls are faced with panels of Norwegian white marble, bordered by gilded metal.

Back-to-front

The customary view of the house from the Avenue de Tervuren is not of the front of the building, but the rear. The principal façade is on the other side, with the main entrance set in a portico beneath a concave wall and between two trapezoid bays. It looks out over the fountains and formal garden to lawns and a tennis court.

This back-to-front plan gives the Palais Stoclet an unexpected note of intimacy and privacy that is not discernible from the road. Adolphe Stoclet had wanted the Avenue de Tervuren to be named after him, but when a promise of this was not forthcoming he turned his back on the street.

THE GLITTER OF WEALTH For the dining room, Gustav Klimt devised two large mosaic friezes filled with the swirling branches of the Tree of Life. This section is called *Expectation*. Klimt worked on the project over six years.

This attitude seems always to have been part and parcel of the character of the building, from its inception when it was considered deeply provocative, to today when—after incidents of pilfering—it has closed its doors to the public.

VICEROY'S HOUSE, NEW DELHI

THE LAST GRAND GESTURE OF BRITISH IMPERIALIST ARCHITECTURE LINKED STYLES OF EAST AND WEST

In 1911, during a great imperial ceremony called the Delhi Coronation Durbar, King George V announced that the capital of British India would be moved from Calcutta to Delhi. The reason given was that it made more sense to place the capital in the center of the country, but the move was also intended to allay the growing tensions between Muslim and Hindu communities in Calcutta.

Lord Hardinge of Penshurst, Viceroy of India between 1910 and 1916, played a key role in this decision, and also took an active interest in the creation of the new city. It was planned on an impressive scale, with large administration buildings and homes for the elite Civil Service, palaces for the princes and maharajahs of the "native states," and an impressive residence for the viceroy.

The British government selected one of the best-known architects of the day, Edwin Landseer Lutyens (1869-1944), to oversee the plans. Lutyens sailed to India in April 1912. In the search for a suitable site, he toured the dusty plains outside the old Mogul city of Delhi on the back of an elephant. For Lutyens, this was a dream come true, a chance to create an entire new capital city. Design of the individual buildings was shared among a team of architects. Lutyens himself took on the Viceroy's House, which was to be the climax of the whole plan—the residence of the supreme power presiding over a nation of 300 million people.

Battle of the styles

In the early 20th century, many grand public buildings were designed in a revised, pared-down neoclassical style—later adopted with fervor in Fascist Italy and Nazi Germany. To Lutyens, it represented the grandeur of the

ON GUARD Ranks of columns topped by elephants and imperial crowns at the main gate recall the spectacles of the British Raj.

classical world, combined with the intellectual rigor and humanity of the Enlightenment—perfect for imperial Britain in India. But there was strong pressure from British politicians, old India hands and Lord Hardinge himself to give New Delhi an oriental feel.

Lutyens was not convinced. He searched for inspiration, visiting sites of Indian architecture, including the Taj Mahal at Agra, the abandoned Mogul city at Fatehpur Sikri, and the Buddhist temple complex at Sanchi. With some reluctance at first, he worked a number of Indian features into his design, and eventually persuaded Hardinge to accept a moderate blend of Western classicism and oriental traditions. Such a synthesis, he suggested, was an appropriate symbol of both the permanence and the open-minded paternalism of the British Raj.

SIR EDWIN LUTYENS: BUILDING FOR A NEW AGE

There could hardly be a greater contrast between the Viceroy's House and the country houses with which Lutyens first made his name. Self-taught, he set up his own architectural practice in 1889, and shortly afterwards designed an elegant Arts and Crafts house called Munstead Wood for the garden designer Gertrude Jekyll. This was the start of a fruitful partnership: he built homes, and she designed romantic, informal gardens to integrate the houses into their landscapes.

Lutyens built up a reputation for adapting historical styles—medieval, Tudor, Queen Anne, Georgian, neo-classical—to create modern homes that had the ease and dignity of tradi-

QUINTESSENTIAL ENGLAND Lutyens' sketch of the gardener's cottage at Munstead Wood shows his natural sympathy for the traditions of rural architecture.

tional architecture. His houses were full of character and texture: he used exposed oak timbers, old bricks, large tiled roofs, balconies and loggias. Some were cottage-like; others evoked the grandeur of stately homes.

To the British, Lutyens was the best living architect, skilled at all to which he turned his attention. The man who created the moving Cenotaph war memorial in Whitehall, London (1919), also designed Queen Mary's doll's house (1924). He produced buildings with which the British felt comfortable, and the prevalence of this taste explains why few Modernist homes were built in Britain during the 1920s and 1930s. It would be wrong, though, to suggest that Lutyens was merely a reactionary recycler of old ideas. He brought an original, innovative vision to the traditions from which he borrowed, creating an architecture that bears his unique stamp.

END OF EMPIRE

The grand new buildings of New Delhi were finally inaugurated on February 10, 1931. The ceremonies unfolded against a backdrop of increasingly violent confrontation between the British authorities and Indians taking part in the campaign of civil disobedience led by Mahatma Gandhi in pursuit of independence. A report in *The Times* the following day indicates that the event was not the satisfactory demonstration of imperial power and unity that the British might have envisaged when the new capital was announced in 1911.

"Thirty-one guns thundered out a salute from the Ridge when Lord Irwin left the Viceroy's House at 11 this morning to perform what was virtually the inauguration ceremony of the Imperial Capital of the new India ...

"Then after the arrival of Lord Hardinge, to whom a particularly appropriate place of honour was given and who was referred to by all as 'the Father of New Delhi,' followed General Sir Philip Chetwode, the Commander-in-Chief, and the representatives of the Dominions, who in the part set for them of unveiling the pillars dedicated by the other nations of the British Commonwealth were really the central figures of the scene ...

"It would be idle to pretend that the ceremony had any popular support. The attendance was confined entirely to those admitted by official invitation. All the approaches to New Delhi were plastered with armed police, and little encouragement was given to anyone who desired to offer a demonstration, friendly or otherwise."

In fact, Lutyens' Viceroy's House is a triumph of synthesis. The orderliness of Greek and Roman architecture is offset by Indian forms and decorative elements in an effortless combination. Mogul-style *chattris* (small pavilions) break up the horizontal roofline, while the ranks of classical columns and the façades of red, pink and cream sandstone are shaded by the *chujja*, a projecting cornice of stone that runs round the exterior of the building. The dome is a subtle adaptation of the *stupa*, or Buddhist shrine, at Sanchi.

Imperial bombast

Progress on New Delhi was hampered by the First World War, by government hesitation, and by endless economies imposed on the architects. But after 1923, building work forged ahead, carried out by teams of 23,000 laborers and 3,000 stone-cutters. The interior of the Viceroy's House gradually took shape, with courtyards, broad ceremonial staircases, and 340 rooms, including the circular Durbar

EAST MEETS WEST The façade and columns evoke the imperial grandeur of ancient Rome, but the overhanging cornice, Mogul-style roof-top pavilions and flattened dome were inspired by Lutyens' study of Indian architecture.

Hall—the most impressive of the suite of cool, marbled state rooms—beneath the dome. The building also contained more intimate living quarters where the viceroy's family lived and entertained guests—with the assistance of several hundred servants.

At the inauguration in 1931, the Viceroy's House was hailed as a triumph. "The seventh Delhi, four-square upon an eminence," gushed the traveller and art critic Robert Byron in *Architectural Review*, "dome, tower, dome, tower, dome, red pink, cream, and white, washed gold and flashing in the morning sun. The traveller looses a breath, and with it his apprehension and preconceptions. Here is something not merely worthy, but whose like has never been seen. With a shiver of impatience, he shakes off contemporary standards, and makes ready to evoke those of Greece, the Renaissance, and the Moguls."

But history was running against Lutyens. In architecture, solid mass was being replaced by the lightness and transparency of new building materials, and the eyes of the world were turning to the skyscrapers of New York. And the writing was on the wall for the British in India. Only 16 years remained before they would have to pack their bags, turning the imperial pomp of their new capital into an empty gesture.

VILLA SAVOYE

A VILLA OUTSIDE PARIS DEMONSTRATED THE NEW VISION OF AN INFLUENTIAL ARCHITECT

Even today, nearly 70 years after its construction, the Villa Savoye looks radically experimental. When it was built, between 1929 and 1931, the citizens of Poissy—a quiet satellite of Paris nestling between the River Seine and the Forêt de Saint-Germain—felt as if an alien spaceship had landed among them. With its uncompromising geometric shapes, its ribbon-windows, flat roof and internal walkway ramps, it was so different from familiar domestic housing that it seemed not just experimental, but downright provocative.

The architect, Swiss-born Le Corbusier (Charles-Edouard Jeanneret-Gris), was no stranger to controversy. In 1925, at the famous Exposition Internationale des Arts Décoratifs et Industriels Modernes in Paris (the exhibition that launched Art Deco on the world stage), Le Corbusier's pavilion was so controversial that the organizers erected a screen to hide it from view during the opening ceremonies. The sole representative of Modernism, it was the ugly duckling of the show. While other architects were toying with

FLOATING ON AIR The Villa Savoye flouted convention on all fronts. The living quarters are on the second floor, but much of that area is devoted to an outdoor terrace. The bathroom (right) is a spartan configuration of tiled geometric shapes.

the fanciful ornament that later came to characterize Art Deco, Le Corbusier had stripped back design to the barest geometric minimum: a series of cubes and rectangles, and a circle cut in the roof to accommodate a mature tree that stood on the site.

Le Corbusier believed that, in the exciting new age of the automobile and airplane, architecture was being left behind because of a sentimental adherence to obsolete tradition. The design of houses, he contended, should be approached in the same way as the design of machines, based on a dispassionate assessment of what was required for efficient and convenient living. "The house is a machine for living in," he declared, "bathrooms, sun, hot and cold water, temperature, which can be adjusted as required, food storage, hygiene, beauty in harmonious proportions."

LE CORBUSIER

Charles-Edouard Jeanneret-Gris (1887-1965) was born in Switzerland, but in 1917 he settled in Paris and took French nationality. By 1910 he had studied under a number of pivotal European architects, including Josef Hoffmann, a leader of the Vienna Sezession; Auguste Perret, the French pioneer of reinforced concrete; and the German Peter Behrens, who also influenced the Bauhaus architects, Walter Gropius and Miës van de Rohe. While still in his twenties, he evolved a novel approach to housing with his "Domino" system. Borrowing from factory design, he created a structural unit consisting of concrete *pilotis*, or stilts, standing on a load-bearing floor and supporting another floor above. The outer walls were not structural and could therefore be made from a variety of materials, including glass, and the interior walls could be placed at will.

A MAN APART Le Corbusier's bow tie and round eyeglasses were his distinguishing trademarks.

Throughout most of the interwar years he worked in partnership with his cousin, Pierre Jeanneret, building private villas distinguished by their uncompromising Modernism—block-like and rectangular, stripped of all unnecessary ornament, with flat roofs, large plate-glass windows and spartan interiors. This approach had much in common with the work of the Dutch De Stijl group and the German Bauhaus; together they represented the sharp end of the avant-garde, but their work appealed only to a minority at the time.

From early on, Le Corbusier also developed theories about grand-scale urban planning, in which he combined high-rise residences with open public spaces and leisure facilities. He was able to realize these in the 1950s, with his "Unites d'habitation," the first of which was built in Marseilles, and in his plans for Chandigarh, the new capital of Punjab, India, designed for half a million people.

In the latter part of his career he broke away from his own theory-bound geometric buildings to produce more organic, sculptural works, notably the chapel at Notre-Dame du Haut at Ronchamp, France.

Le Corbusier, working in Paris with his cousin Pierre Jeanneret, produced a number of villas in the 1920s based on these radical ideas. The Villa Savoye is generally considered the most successful, and it incorporates many of Le Corbusier's pet themes.

Rethinking the house
The main living area is on the second floor, partly to enhance the views, and partly to hand the ground level over to cars. The D-shaped ground floor, containing the servants' quarters and a garage for three cars, occupies only part of the rectangular ground plan, leaving exposed many of the concrete stilts, or *pilotis*, that support the structure. The front door is deliberately understated. The building has no designated front or back, only a top and bottom, and all the façades are treated as equally important.

The living quarters on the second floor form a kind of bungalow in the air. Four bedrooms, two bathrooms, a kitchen, a hall and a large living room are disposed in a J-shape around an open terrace, which is accessed by sliding glass doors. The layout is relaxed and informal, and comes as a refreshing surprise after the sharp-edged severity of the external walls. These encompass even the terrace, where rectangular openings designed to frame the view continue the horizontal line of the ribbon-windows. The informality of the interior expresses the flexibility afforded by the basic structure. Because the building is supported by *pilotis*, the walls could be placed anywhere within the structure.

Over the living quarters is a flat roof-terrace, intended as a roof garden and sundeck, reflecting both the new fashion for sunbathing inspired by the French fashion designer Coco Chanel, and Le Corbusier's dislike of sacrificing valuable roof space to tiles. Linking all floors are spiral staircases and inclined ramps, an unusual feature that provides an "architectural promenade" through the building.

The Villa Savoye was so radically avant-garde that not even its owners could quite stomach it. For many years it remained abandoned and neglected. In recent years it has been carefully restored and is now open to the public—a monument to the foresight and bravura of Modernism.

FALLINGWATER

AN ELEGANT STATEMENT OF 20TH-CENTURY INNOVATION THAT HAS A TIMELESS GRACE

The most famous building by America's most celebrated architect is a country retreat perched over a series of cascades in a landscape of rocky woodlands. Fallingwater at Bear Run, Pennsylvania, is the quintessential expression of the architecture of Frank Lloyd Wright (1869-1959). It is uncompromisingly 20th century, with its terraces of steel and poured concrete and large expanses of plate glass, and is inseparable from its surroundings, rising from its rocky base as naturally as fungi growing on a fallen log.

Organic architecture

Built for a private client, Edgar J. Kaufmann, in 1935-9, Fallingwater is truly unique. Like all of Wright's buildings, it is an individually tailored response both to the client's needs

FRANK LLOYD WRIGHT

One of the major early influences on Frank Lloyd Wright was the Wisconsin countryside in which he grew up. He never abandoned his love of nature or his belief in its healing powers. In 1888 Wright joined the Chicago partnership of Adler & Sullivan as a draughtsman, and Louis H. Sullivan (1856-1924) became his mentor. Pioneer of the skyscraper, Sullivan was an early advocate of the concept that function should dictate style.

In 1889 Wright set up his own office at Oak Park, a suburb of Chicago. He became independent in 1893. That same year, the Japanese pavilion at the Columbian World Exposition in Chicago included a life-size replica of a Japanese temple. This confirmed Wright's fascination with Japanese design, which remained a major influence on his work. For the next 15 years he built his reputation with his remarkable Prairie houses, and developed his theory of organic architecture.

Wright took on a range of challenges, evolving his style as new techniques and materials became available. His buildings combined a sense of innovation with meticulous detailing,

GRAND OLD MAN Wright was 70 years old when Fallingwater was completed, and 80 when this photograph was taken.

down to the furnishings. His Larkin Office Building (1903-5) in Buffalo, New York, was one of the first to have a top-lit atrium overlooked by galleries, and steel office furniture. He designed some 800 buildings, including places of worship, a hotel and corporate headquarters. His most famous public building is the Guggenheim Museum (1956) in New York, but he is probably best remembered for his highly individualistic private houses.

LYING LOW The emphasis on horizontal lines is balanced by exaggerated verticals inside the house (above and right) as well as outside. The interior shows the influence of Japanese design on Wright's work.

and to the location. Wright was a strong believer in individuality, and detested the industrial uniformity of the International Style, which allowed preconceived, prefabricated architecture to be dropped into any environment. He advocated what he called "organic architecture." "In organic architecture," he wrote, "it is quite impossible to consider the building as one thing, its furnishings another and its setting and environment still another." It was "an architecture that develops from within outwards in harmony with the conditions of its being."

An important element in organic architecture was the use of sympathetic materials, meticulously selected, shaped and positioned. The walls of Fallingwater are made of stone, roughly dressed but artfully laid, providing a satisfying counterbalance to the concrete terraces. This rugged effect is carried into the interior, where the stone walls, open fireplaces, and a stone floor made up of irregularly shaped paving suggest the simple virtues of a woodland cabin. Some of the large rocks on the site were left undisturbed, so they protrude from the floor around the fire to provide natural supports to sit on or lean against.

Large, wood-framed windows look out in all directions, offering a variety of views and bringing the wild beauty of the untamed surroundings into the home. Some of the windows are, effectively, transparent walls. This feature, and the continuity of textures within and without, help to break down the traditional barriers between internal and external spaces. To stay at Fallingwater is to live not just surrounded by nature, but among it.

Yet, in line with all of Wright's houses, including the Prairie houses, Fallingwater is not a glass box. The building offers a strong feeling of security, satisfying a primitive need for enveloping shelter.

Contemplation and repose

The shape of Fallingwater echoes the series of stepped cascades beneath it. The terraces rise up and recede as they pass through the first-floor bedroom level to the second-story tower, which houses a gallery-bedroom. A bridge at the first-floor level leads over the driveway to the guest house that lies farther up the hill.

The stepped profile of the house is said to have been inspired by Mayan temple pyramids. But the three-dimensional qualities of the building are considerably more complex than this, presenting new and intriguing configurations from every angle. The charm is in the detail as well as the whole. Descending from the living room is a "suspended stair" leading to a small balcony set just above the stream, providing a place of quiet repose.

Each of the bedrooms and the living room has a terrace, an external space from which to contemplate the natural setting, and to listen to the hush of the woods and the patter of water tumbling over the falls. As Wright himself put it: "You listen to Fallingwater the way you listen to the quiet of the country."

NATURE IN BALANCE The highly ordered horizontal tiers are set off by the ragged stone of the vertical walls and by the surrounding woodland. The architecture suggests a deep respect for nature.

HEARST CASTLE

THE ULTIMATE AMERICAN DREAM PALACE PROVIDED A PLEASURE-DOME FOR HOLLYWOOD STARS

On Friday evenings throughout much of the 1930s, a private train travelled 200 miles up the California coast from Los Angeles to San Simeon. It carried the weekend guests of one of America's richest men, the media magnate William Randolph Hearst. Among the guests would be writers, artists, politicians and sports personalities, but most would be denizens of Hollywood—

THE BEST OF EVERYTHING From afar, San Simeon has the air of a Spanish village. The indoor Roman Pool (below) is lined with tiles made of Venetian glass and 22 carat gold.

the stars, directors, producers, up-and-coming actors and young hopefuls. At San Simeon they were met by a fleet of limousines that swept them up a winding road rising 1,600 feet in just 5 miles to La Cuesta Encantada (The Enchanted Hill), the site of Hearst's spectacular "castle."

"In Xanadu did Kubla Khan/ A stately pleasure-dome decree," wrote Samuel Taylor Coleridge in his poem *Kubla Khan*. This is what Hearst also decreed: a place where his guests could relax, pampered by all modern conveniences. The bedrooms—56 of them, distributed among the big house (La Casa Grande) and three mansion-sized cottages—were themed suites: Oriental, Venetian, Renaissance, Gothic. They were like Hollywood sets, but with one difference: they were encrusted with real antiques and treasures. There were 14 sitting rooms, two libraries and a billiard room. Outside, beside an outdoor dance floor, lay the blue-tiled Neptune Pool. There was an indoor pool beneath the tennis courts, 127 acres of landscaped gardens, and a private zoo.

The guests gathered for dinner each evening in the Assembly Room of La Casa Grande. From there, they would progress to the dining room, a huge baronial hall called the Refectory, where they sat at long tables, surrounded by wood panelling, Flemish tapestries, Sienese flags, Gothic windows and even medieval choir stalls.

Replacing the tents

Hearst's father had acquired a vast swathe of land around San Simeon in the 1870s, where family and guests would spend summers and weekends camping beneath the stars. When his mother died in 1919, Hearst inherited the estate. Shortly thereafter, he visited the San Francisco architect Julia Morgan (1872-1957), and was heard to say that he was "tired of camping out and wanted something more comfortable on the Hill."

OLD WORLD MEETS NEW
The Neptune Pool is overlooked by a genuine Greco-Roman temple transported from Europe.

CITIZEN KANE

William Randolph Hearst (1863-1951) was the only son of a mining magnate. Obliged to leave Harvard early because of a prank, he began his journalistic career working for the New York *World*, into which Joseph Pulitzer had injected a racy kind of "New Journalism." Then in 1887, at the age of 24, he took over running the San Francisco *Examiner*, a paper owned by his father.

In 1895 he bought the New York *Morning Journal* and began a circulation battle with the *World*. His main weapon was sensationalism, driving down the standards of journalism in order to create a thirst for hard-hitting, salacious and often misleading stories. He ran popular crusades, and tinkered with the truth in order to manipulate public feeling. By printing fictitious accounts of Spanish atrocities, for example, he created the outcry that launched the Spanish-American War in 1898.

Although a congressman for New York (1903-7), he was frustrated in his political career. By 1927 he owned 25 national and local newspapers and several leading magazines, including *Cosmopolitan* and *Harper's Bazaar*. He also held major interests in radio stations, film and newsreel studios. He accumulated vast wealth and spent it lavishly, indulging his acquisitive greed and his boyish sense of fun. He knew that connoisseurs laughed at his eclectic tastes as a collector, and at San Simeon's jumble of styles and its mixture of real antiques, copies and fakes.

Hearst married Millicent Willson in 1903, and she gave him five sons. But in about 1916 he met Marion Davies, a young dancer from the Ziegfeld Follies, who became his constant companion. She starred in 46 movies made by his Cosmopolitan Productions film company, and acted as hostess in his flamboyant social life.

Hearst's grip on the media and his ruthless business practices made him many enemies. In 1941, Orson Welles produced, directed and starred in *Citizen Kane*, a film excoriating a powerful newspaper magnate for corrupting the American dream. No one was in any doubt that the central character, Charles Foster Kane, represented William Randolph Hearst, or that Kane's palace, Xanadu, was Hearst Castle.

TRAVELLING COMPANIONS
Marion Davies, 34 years Hearst's junior, was his companion for the last three decades of his life.

Hearst wanted a style to suit the landscape and climate of San Simeon. It was land that had once belonged to the Spanish, and to a Franciscan mission. He therefore envisaged buildings in a Spanish style. In the end, La Casa Grande was a pastiche of the ornate Moorish-influenced *mudejár* style. The remainder of the "village," as Morgan called it, was "Mediterranean."

Morgan was a wise choice for the job. She was a disciple of the Arts and Crafts movement, and adapted traditional styles. This ability was essential as Hearst was a great traveller, with wide-ranging tastes as a collector. As the project got under way, a specially built warehouse in San Simeon began filling up with antique treasures shipped in from abroad, including whole staircases, wooden panelling, bas-relief sculptures and carved ceilings. All had to be incorporated into the designs.

In the end, Hearst Castle cost about $5 million—an astronomical sum at the time—and that excluded Hearst's own spending on antiquities. During the 1940s, Hearst's family and corporation began to put restraints on his spending, and he was obliged to cease building. He paid his last visit there in 1947, now a sick man at 83. He then moved to Marion Davies' home in Beverly Hills, where he died four years later.

SULTAN OF BRUNEI'S PALACE

THE WORLD'S LARGEST PALACE IS HOME TO THE WORLD'S WEALTHIEST MAN

The statistics are mesmerizing: 1,788 rooms; a banquet hall that can seat 4,000 guests; a multi-sports complex and five swimming pools, one of which is Olympic-size; 12 apartment suites for the royal children; underground parking for a private collection of over 150 cars; 257 bathrooms; 564 chandeliers; 51,490 light bulbs.

With building costs estimated at $900 million, it is fitting that the world's largest residence should belong to the world's richest man, the Sultan of Brunei Darussalam, His Majesty Sir Haji Hassanal Bolkiah Mu'izzaddin Waddaulah. Born in 1946, he became sultan of this tiny state on the north coast of Borneo in 1967, on the voluntary abdication of his father. The nation's huge oil and gas reserves form the basis of his wealth, augmented by worldwide investments.

Regal splendor

The sultan's palace, the Istana Nurul Iman, lies 2 miles from the center of the national capital, Bandar Seri Begawan, in grounds covering 297 acres along the Brunei River. Remarkably, it took just three years to build, and was completed in time for the ceremonies held on January 1, 1984, to mark Brunei's return to independence after nearly 100 years as a British protectorate. Designed and built by a Filipino architect and construction company, it incorporates components imported from over 30 countries. But with its sweeping, concave roofs and project-

> ### COMPARATIVE SPLENDOR
>
> On the Sultan of Brunei's first state visit to Britain in November 1992, the world's richest man met the world's richest woman. The Queen of England is said to be worth about $14 billion, if her art collection is included. The Sultan of Brunei, however, possesses an estimated $75 billion.

ing gables, and its domes glittering with 22 carat gold, it is unmistakably Southeast Asian and Islamic in character.

The interior speaks of spacious magnificence, an oasis of cool, airy tranquillity compared to the tropical humidity outside. Off the marbled halls and the courtyards filled with splashing fountains lie the great set-pieces of regal splendor, such as a throne room large enough to seat 2,000 delegates. It is illuminated by twelve huge crystal chandeliers, each weighing 2 tons.

DOMES OF SPLENDOR At night the Istana Nurul Iman looks like a magical palace, ablaze with lights that trace the outlines of its dipping roofs. The Sultan of Brunei (left) built the palace in the 1980s with oil wealth accumulated by his family since the 1920s.

COMMERCIAL VENTURES

TWO FACTORS HAVE DICTATED THE PATTERN OF COMMERCIAL BUILDING IN THE 20TH CENTURY: EFFICIENCY AND MONEY. THE HIGH COST OF PRIME SITES IN MAJOR U.S. CITIES LED TO THE DEVELOPMENT OF VERY TALL BUILDINGS—NICKNAMED SKYSCRAPERS—ON SMALL PATCHES OF LAND. THE RICH AND THE POWERFUL SOON REALIZED THAT HUGE PUBLICITY COULD BE GAINED FROM OWNING THE WORLD'S HIGHEST BUILDING, AND THE COMPETITION CONTINUES TO THIS DAY.

FLATIRON BUILDING

ONE OF THE FIRST SKYSCRAPERS OF THE CENTURY IS STILL ONE OF THE MOST UNUSUAL

When New York's Fuller Building was completed in 1903, it caused a sensation. Rising from its wedge-shaped site between Broadway, Fifth Avenue and 23rd Street, it cut an extraordinary profile that soon earned it the nickname "the Flatiron Building." Early photographs of the Flatiron Building show the streets busy with horse-drawn cabs. It is hardly surprising that the early skyscrapers seemed a wonder of the age and attracted the attention of the world's press.

The Flatiron Building was something of an oddity. It was a measure of the high value of property in Manhattan that the developers of this speculative office block

WEDGED IN A view down Broadway and Fifth Avenue shows the narrowness of the site. The structure is approaching its full height.

" A NEW PARTHENON

The celebrated American photographers Alfred Stieglitz (1864-1946) and Edward Steichen (1879-1973) were fascinated by the Flatiron Building and photographed it repeatedly in a range of weather and light conditions. Stieglitz later recalled one occasion:
"With the trees of Madison Square covered with fresh snow, the Flat Iron impressed me as never before. It appeared to be moving toward me like the bow of a monster ocean steamer—a picture of new America still in the making...The Flat Iron is to the United States what the Parthenon was to Greece."

were prepared to consider a site with enough space for only four rooms at one end and just one room at the other. The property company, led by George A. Fuller before his death in 1900, employed the Chicago architectural partnership Daniel H. Burnham & Company to come up with a solution. Daniel Burnham (1846-1912) was a force in architecture, but not himself a practicing architect; it is not known for certain who within the partnership was responsible for the ingenious design of the building.

Greek column

The basic structure consists of a steel skeleton with extra-strong bracing to contend with gusting winds, and rests on concrete footings driven into bedrock 37 feet below ground. The skeleton supports the elaborate façades, which were designed in the "tripartite system" favored at the time by architects influenced by the Ecole des Beaux Arts, Paris. The building façade was divided into lower, middle and upper sections, corresponding to the division and rough proportions of ancient Greek columns into pedestal, shaft and capital.

The five lower floors (the "pedestal") contained a row of shops at ground level, with the large display windows that steel-frame construction permitted. A projecting single-story spur was added to the sharp end of the triangle during construction in 1902, to accommodate additional shop space.

Most of the offices were contained in the 12 story "shaft" of the building above the fifth floor. The two long sides of the building

SPACE AT A PREMIUM

During the late 19th century, real estate at the centers of American cities such as New York and Chicago became scarce and costly. The solution was to build upward.

In traditional buildings, the weight of the floors and roof is carried by the walls, but the higher the building, the stronger and thicker the walls have to be at the base. Using this method, buildings can rise to a maximum of about five stories before the ground-floor walls become impracticably thick.

Two major technological breakthroughs were needed for the emergence of buildings that could break through this barrier. The first was to shift load-bearing from the walls to a rigid cage-like structure of cast iron or steel inside the building —a construction method previously applied to industrial buildings. Architects found that an iron or steel skeleton could support virtually all the weight of the walls. The walls lost their structural role and became "curtains."

The second breakthrough overcame the difficulty of access to the upper floors. In 1857, Elisha Otis, adapting technology used in warehouses, installed a steam-driven "passenger elevator" in a shop in New York. Improved versions were installed in high-rise offices, and elevators soon made the upper floors more desirable than the lower floors, reversing a time-honored tradition.

The term "skyscraper" became current during the 1890s, as the race to construct ever higher buildings got under way. The public was impressed, but also nervous: the architect of the first skyscraper in New York, the Tower Building (1889), lived on the 11th floor to demonstrate that it was safe.

The Chicago architect Louis H. Sullivan recommended a fresh approach to style. "It would be greatly for our aesthetic good," he remarked, "if we should refrain entirely from the use of ornament for a period of years in order that our thought might concentrate acutely upon the production of buildings well formed and comely in the nude." His buildings are sparely decorated, and their exteriors echo the skeletal nature of the internal structure.

But the 1893 Chicago World Exposition promoted a more elaborate "Beaux-Arts" style that borrowed from past architectural traditions, particularly the neoclassical. This style was adopted in New York, where new skyscrapers were given handsome stone façades, and ornate summits resembling Roman temples and Renaissance palaces. Some people suggested that these skyscrapers heralded an "American renaissance."

BRIEF REIGN In 1908-9 the Singer Tower in New York, part of the headquarters of the sewing-machine company, was the tallest building in the world.

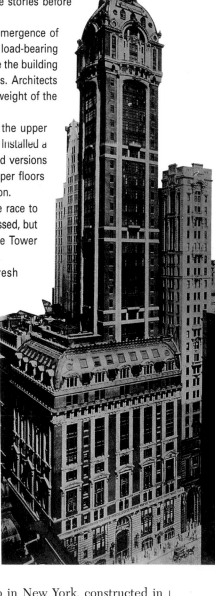

have three vertical strips of oriel windows between the 8th and 15th floors, and the terracotta surfaces are richly decorated with bands of relief ornament. They create a richly textured surface, which rises to the four-story crescendo at the top of the building (the "capital"), capped by a projecting cornice. The 21 stories reach a total height of 307 feet, but in 1903 this was still well short of the world's tallest skyscraper, the Park Row

CUTTING EDGE The converging streets emphasize the Flatiron Building's resemblance to the prow of a ship.

Building, also in New York, constructed in 1896-9 and reaching 391 feet.

The position and shape of the Flatiron Building meant that it was surrounded by space, and light could penetrate into the interior. But one characteristic was the ferocious winds that whipped through the open spaces of Madison Square and down the adjacent avenues, producing a notorious downdraught around the building. This was the cause of complaint and an early tragedy: shortly after the building's completion, a gust caught a messenger boy and pushed him into the street, where he was killed by a passing car.

WOOLWORTH BUILDING

THIS IMPRESSIVE HEADQUARTERS BUILDING WAS FOUNDED ON AN EMPIRE OF FIVE-AND-DIME STORES

In 1912, Frank Winfield Woolworth created a giant retail company by buying out his main rivals. This put him in possession of over 1,000 stores and a huge personal fortune. It was the crowning achievement of his career, matched only by his plans—already well advanced—to put his headquarters in the world's biggest skyscraper.

Rising from its prime site on Manhattan's Broadway, the Woolworth Building took just three years to construct and was completed in 1913. It was not only the biggest such building; it was widely acclaimed as the most magnificent of the fanciful and ornate "Beaux-Arts" skyscrapers that had been built since the 1890s. However, whereas many of these had taken their inspiration from classical models, the Woolworth Building was neo-Gothic.

HEIGHT OF AMBITION F.W. Woolworth requested Cass Gilbert to make the Woolworth Building taller than any other building in New York.

This was a style favored by Woolworth himself, who was deeply impressed by the British Houses of Parliament, completed in 1860. His building reaches a crescendo in a spire piled high with neo-Gothic flying buttresses, stonework tracery, arches, lanterns and gargoyles, inviting comparison with medieval cathedrals. One commentator, a cleric, dubbed the building a "Cathedral of Commerce." This oft-repeated epithet irritated the architect, Cass Gilbert (1859-1934), who insisted that he had drawn his inspiration not from cathedrals, but from northern European secular architecture, such as the town halls of the Low Countries.

Designed to impress

To many, the Woolworth Building was an unparalleled triumph of engineering and design. Just as Woolworth had wished, it broke all records. "Make it fifty feet taller than the

"FIVE AND DIMES"

By the time F.W. Woolworth was building his splendid headquarters in New York, he was a man of immense wealth, living in a 62 room mansion on Long Island, where he dined beneath a ceiling of 14 carat gold. He had come a long way since his life as an $8 a week salesman, and the day in 1879 when he set up his first "Great Five Cents Store" in Utica, New York.

Selling a broad range of domestic goods, from tools and utensils to soap and scent, his new store heralded a revolution in retailing. Not only was everything in the shop on sale for 5 cents or less, but customers were also invited to handle, inspect and select from the goods on display, instead of waiting for a sales clerk to do this for them. Woolworth soon extended the range to include items for 10 cents as well, and the nickname "five and dime" store came into being.

By 1888, Woolworth had 12 stores in as many cities in the northeastern United States; by 1910 he had 600 across the nation; by 1913 he had 2,000. In 1909 he opened his first shop abroad, in Liverpool, England, initiating a chain of "threepenny and sixpenny" stores.

F.W. Woolworth was a man of immense drive, as might be expected of someone so insistent that his headquarters in New York should be the biggest and best. The building contractor, Louis J. Horowitz, put it succinctly: "Beyond a doubt his ego was a thing of extraordinary size; whoever tried to find a reason for his tall building and did not take that fact into account would reach a false conclusion."

THE PRICE WAS RIGHT From small beginnings, Woolworth built up a commercial empire spanning the Atlantic. This store at Lancaster, Pennsylvania, photographed in 1884, was Woolworth's first "5 and 10 cent" store.

Metropolitan Tower," he had instructed Gilbert. Its 55 stories rise to a height of 792 feet, beating the Metropolitan Life Tower (1909) by a clear 92 feet. The Woolworth Building held the record for the world's tallest skyscraper for 17 years.

STILL RIDING HIGH Horizontal bands encrusted with authentic-looking neo-Gothic detail run around the building, while the vertical lines emphasize its height.

Inside, 26 new high-speed Otis elevators and 2,800 telephones served 14,000 workers. These were employees of Woolworth, of the Irving National Bank, with which Woolworth was associated, and of tenants. As Woolworth had desired, his building had the highest income of any office block in the world, and prospective tenants were enticed by the promoters' claims that this was the "highest, safest, most perfectly appointed office structure in the world, fireproof beyond question, elevators accident proof."

The cost of the building was $13.5 million. An initial problem was posed by the site: with bedrock at 115 feet below the surface and the water level at 35 feet, the foundations had to be excavated inside watertight steel structures, and onto these was grafted the most up-to-date kind of steel frame.

The main block rises to 30 stories from a U-shaped ground plan, which allows plenty of light to penetrate. This is capped by decorative carving and dormer windows beneath sloping roofs, while the tower rises another 25 stories, with three setbacks. The windows are recessed between terracotta ribs that run all the way up the sides of the building. The entrance is especially grand. With marbled walls, gilded moldings and ceilings of brilliant mosaic tiles, it recalls the jewel-like interior of a Byzantine church.

On April 24, 1913, the stage was set for the official opening. At 7:30 p.m. President Woodrow Wilson pressed a button in the White House in Washington, triggering the illumination of 80,000 electric bulbs in, on and around the building, immersing it in light.

THE BAUHAUS

A GLASS-BOX WORKSHOP EPITOMIZES THE DYNAMISM OF AN INFLUENTIAL DESIGN SCHOOL

According to Walter Gropius, the first director of the Bauhaus school: "The nature of an object is determined by what it does." He wrote that: "Before a container, a chair or a house can function properly, its nature must be studied . . . From such research into the nature of objects, forms can emerge that also take account of modern methods of production and construction and of modern materials—forms that diverge from existing models and often seem unfamiliar and surprising."

The products of the Bauhaus were certainly unfamiliar and surprising in the 1920s

BOX OF GLASS The use of stark rectangular shapes, combined with large areas of glass, showed the architects straying into new territory of building design. The school's name is announced in typically unfussy lettering.

and early 1930s, but so great did the influence of the Bauhaus become that today they seem commonplace—so commonplace that it requires a concerted leap of the imagination to see just how innovative and revolutionary they were at the time.

The Bauhaus was essentially a design think tank. It was founded in the German city of Weimar in 1919 when the architect Walter Gropius merged the Grand-Ducal Saxon School of Arts and Crafts with the Grand-Ducal Saxon Academy of Fine Art. He called the new school Das Staatliche Bauhaus (State House of Building), a deliberately downbeat title that emphasized his determination to focus on the practical aspects of building and design.

Gropius wanted a school in which architects, engineers, artists, craftworkers, filmmakers, printers, graphic designers and furniture-makers all worked together and pooled their skills and ideas. "The ultimate goal of the Bauhaus is the collective work of art," he wrote, "in which no barriers exist between the structural and decorative arts." This central concept was not new: it had

been explored by the Arts and Crafts movement in England in the late 19th century, and by the Wiener Werkstätte (Vienna Workshops) that evolved from the Vienna "Sezession" in 1903. What was new was the Bauhaus's emphasis on exploiting the potential of new materials and the industrial techniques of mass production. Gropius was aiming at effective design for the machine age, which meant stripping objects back to their essential functions. As he put it, speaking of his own field: "We want an architecture adapted to our world of machines, radios and fast motor cars, an architecture whose function is clearly recognizable in the relation of its forms."

The Bauhaus developed against a backdrop of political and economic turmoil in Germany in the wake of the country's defeat in the First World War and the abdication of the kaiser, Wilhelm II. The school incorporated a certain amount of left-wing, revolutionary zeal and utopianism, along with a strong conviction that design could transform the lot of the masses and help to bring about a better world. Gropius brought to this

DESIGN CLASS Rows of chairs designed by Marcel Breuer fill the auditorium in the Bauhaus. The partitions at the end of the room could be removed to create a larger space.

project his own experiences as a leading avant-garde architect. The Bauhaus school was also heavily influenced by the architects of the Dutch *De Stijl* group, especially Theo van Doesburg (1883-1931), who taught at the Bauhaus in 1922. *De Stijl* architects were striving to reduce architecture to elegant minimalist forms, to compositions of intersecting rectangles and planes without any ornament except strips of primary colors—rather like the geometric, abstract paintings of the *De Stijl* artist Piet Mondrian (1872-1944).

Dessau

In 1925, the Bauhaus was forced to relocate to Dessau, about 60 miles northeast of Weimar. The move gave Gropius the opportunity to put his architectural ideas into practice. Working with his partner Adolf Meyer, he set about designing a brand new complex for the school. Built mainly during 1925-6, it turned out to be one of the 20th century's most influential buildings, a herald of the International Style that would dominate international architecture for the next 50 years.

The new Bauhaus complex incorporated a series of interconnected, intersecting cuboid buildings, each with its own modifications in style to suit its specific function. By far the most impressive and eye-catching of these is the three-story workshop, which has three walls consisting almost entirely of glass, divided only by slender black glazing bars. The purpose of all this glass was entirely functional: to allow the maximum amount of natural light into the workshop spaces inside. No one had taken the concept of the glass curtain wall this far before. The building is supported by internal reinforced-concrete columns and steel beams, so the exterior walls do not need to carry any load, which makes the use of so much glass possible. There are no corner columns, so the glazing could be taken right to the corners, giving the building an unprecedented sense of lightness and transparency.

Leading off the workshop was a contrasting, low-level building containing a canteen, auditorium and theater. The partitioning between these rooms could be removed to create a single, large space. Beyond this lay a five-story residential block for students,

BAUHAUS DESIGN

In 1925 Marcel Breuer (1902-81)—a Hungarian-born pupil, then teacher, at the Bauhaus—produced his "Wassily Chair," one of the world's first tubular-steel chairs. Simple, elegant and practical, it became a symbol for the work of the school. The Bauhaus was not attempting to nurture individuality and craftsmanship. Instead, it encouraged multi-disciplinary collaboration, the use of new industrial materials, and the development of designs and techniques that could be readily translated into mass production. "Art and technology: a new unity!" was the Bauhaus slogan.

The intention was to design good, well-engineered products for everyday use that, above all, fulfilled their function. All subjects for design were considered, from housing, factories and furniture, to cutlery, door handles, textiles and photography. Bauhaus designers hoped that mass production would make good design affordable to all, so that even people on low incomes could enjoy efficient homes.

The general public, however, was not so ready to adopt the utilitarian living arrangements devised by Bauhaus designers. Many Bauhaus products never reached mass production, but were made by craftsmen for wealthy avant-garde clients. Nonetheless, they had a timeless appeal that the world eventually caught up with. The push-button bedside light, the pivoting desk lamp, the lever door handle and the flat, panel-less door have become so familiar that few would guess they were once the controversial products of one of Europe's most dynamic design schools.

FORM AND FUNCTION Despite its starkness, the broad, springy form of this tubular-steel chair by Marcel Breuer suggests comfort.

containing 28 studio apartments and a gymnasium. The balconies—rectilinear planes intersecting a trim, rectangular block—reflect the influence of the *De Stijl* architects.

This set of buildings was linked to the third main building in the complex by a bridge section, designed to span a road that was planned but never constructed. Raised on reinforced-concrete columns, the bridge contained school administration offices, as well as offices for Gropius's private architectural practice. It also served an aesthetic function, helping to lighten the overall aspect of the complex and adding another element of visual surprise.

The third main building housed the Dessau Technical College, which joined up with the Bauhaus at this new location. Again, the shape of the block is an uncompromising flat-roofed rectangle, but here the walls are broken up into horizontal strips of white concrete separated by the ribbon windows on each floor level. A dark band at the half-basement level helps to link this building visually with the rest of the complex.

CURTAINS OF LIGHT To emphasize the lightness of the structure of the main building at Dessau, the glass walls project beyond the structure at the corners so that glass meets glass.

In addition to the main buildings, Gropius designed a director's house and three semidetached masters' houses, flat-roofed, geometric blocks of white concrete pierced by generous rectangles of plate glass, creating a pleasing abstract composition. As with much Bauhaus work, the masters' houses were designed as prototypes for mass production, consisting of modular "building blocks" that could be prefabricated and assembled on site—a novel concept in domestic construction. Their occupants included many of the leading names associated with the Bauhaus, including the Russian painter Wassily Kandinsky (1866-1944), the Swiss painter Paul Klee (1879-1940), and the Hungarian artist and graphic designer Lásló Moholy-Nagy (1895-1946).

WALTER GROPIUS

Born into a family of architects, Walter Gropius (1883-1969) studied architecture in Berlin and Munich before training under Peter Behrens (1868-1940), one of the central figures in the early development of Modernist architecture. In 1910, Gropius set up a partnership with Adolf Meyer (1881-1929), and together they designed the Fagus shoe factory at Alfeld, south of Hannover, in 1910-14. With its cuboid shape and large glass-and-steel curtain walls, it was an early signal of the stylistic elegance of this uncompromisingly modern approach.

Gropius's career was interrupted by the First World War, during which he won the Iron Cross. The war also forced the Belgian designer, Henry van de Velde (1863-1957), to give up the directorship of the Grand-Ducal Saxon School of Arts and Crafts in Weimar, which he had built up into a major force in European design. On leaving, van de Velde recommended that Gropius should succeed him. From this platform, Gropius forged the Bauhaus in 1919, moving it in 1925 to the new complex at Dessau.

Inspired by Henry Ford, the pioneer of the production line, Gropius was keen to apply industrial techniques to housing, using prefabricated concrete units. He left the Bauhaus in 1928 to develop a workers' housing project at Siemensstadt, outside Berlin. After fleeing Nazi Germany in 1934, he lived in England for three years before accepting a post at Harvard University in the United States. There he developed his ideas on cooperative design, and formed The Architects' Collaborative (TAC) in 1945, which produced various ground-breaking buildings, such as the Harvard Graduate Center (1950) and the U.S. Embassy in Athens (1961).

GERMAN-AMERICAN Gropius became professor of architecture at Harvard.

Walter Gropius resigned as director of the Bauhaus in 1928 in order to devote more time to his own projects. His place was taken first by the Swiss architect Hannes Meyer, and then, in 1930, by the German Ludwig Miës van der Rohe, another leading figure of 20th-century architecture. However, Germany was now descending into the maelstrom of Fascism. The left-wing stance of the Bauhaus, as well as its unconventional, non-traditional and cosmopolitan approach to design, offended the nationalistic prejudices of the Nazi party. In September 1932, the Dessau school was closed down by the local parliament. Miës van de Rohe moved the school to Berlin where it reopened for a few months, but in April 1933, shortly after Adolf Hitler became Chancellor of Germany, the Berlin Bauhaus was forced to close. The students and teachers dispersed; many fled abroad.

Germany's loss proved to be America's gain. Walter Gropius, Miës van der Rohe, Marcel Breuer and Lásló Moholy-Nagy all took up teaching posts in the United States, making the U.S. the main center for architectural and design innovation in the postwar era. Remarkably, perhaps, the Bauhaus buildings survived the war more or less intact, and, after a desultory existence in postwar East Germany, they now contain a museum devoted to the achievements of this far-sighted design school.

CHRYSLER BUILDING

A CLASSIC EXAMPLE OF ART DECO DESIGN REMAINS A STAR IN THE NEW YORK FIRMAMENT

In late 1929 a battle was being waged high above the streets of New York City. Two architects had been commissioned by major corporations to create the tallest building in the world for their respective headquarters. In November, William van Alen announced that his Chrysler Building had reached 925 feet. Rival architect and former partner H. Craig Severance, designing the Bank of Manhattan in nearby Wall Street, sensed triumph: a few days later he announced that his building had been topped out with a 50 foot flagpole to reach 927 feet.

THE PINNACLE OF ART DECO The gargoyle-like eagles at the 61st floor level were inspired by the emblems on the hoods of Chrysler cars, while the fan-like tiers of the steel-faced crown are pure Art Deco: layered, dynamic and glamorous.

This was the moment that van Alen had been waiting for. In a carefully orchestrated publicity stunt, his construction team secretly assembled the building's prefabricated metal spire, and in just one and a half hours they fed it up through a hole in the roof and bolted it to the top of the Chrysler Building. It was a gesture to which Severance could find no answer.

At 1,046 feet, the Chrysler Building was now not just the world's tallest building, but the world's tallest structure, robbing the Eiffel Tower in Paris of the title it had held for over 40 years. At the time, it was generally accepted

ART DECO

After the First World War, many architects and designers searched for a new look to match their hopes for a bright future. Extrapolating ideas from radical prewar movements, such as the Vienna "Sezession," Cubism and Futurism, and adopting a positive attitude toward the machine age, they came up with clean, geometric and angular shapes with rounded corners, using silver, chrome and stainless steel. To this were added various exotic influences, such as Aztec design, the vivid colors of the Ballets Russes costumes, and, in particular, motifs adapted from the Ancient Egyptians, following the sensational discovery of Tutankhamun's tomb in 1922. The result was a sleek and exciting style that was considered entirely modern.

To begin with, this so-called *style moderne* was seen mainly in luxury goods by designers such as the French furniture-maker Emile-Jacques Ruhlmann, or the jewelry firm Cartier. But in 1925, the Exposition Internationale des Arts Décoratifs et Industriels Modernes in Paris demonstrated how the *style moderne* could be adapted to architecture. In the 1960s, when this style began to be appreciated again after a period in the wilderness, the term Art Deco was coined from the title of the 1925 Paris Exposition.

The Wall Street crash of 1929 set Art Deco on a new course. During the 1930s it borrowed imagery from the industrial world, such as lightning bolts and the streamlined look of locomotives and cars. Although it still retained its glamour, it was also applied to mass-produced industrial goods, such as mirrors, hairbrushes, radios and light fixtures. Its popularity waned after the 1940s.

ARCHITECTURAL FANCY The 1925 Paris Exposition contained a number of inflated extravagances, such as the "Primavera" pavilion of the Printemps department store.

BEAU OF THE BALL The Chrysler Building stood out when William van Alen and his wife attended a "Beaux-Arts Ball" at the Hotel Astor in New York in 1931.

that any geographical feature over 1,000 feet was a mountain, and it was reported in the press that van Alen had cheekily asked the National Geographic Society of America if his building might also qualify.

Automotive style

But the Chrysler Building is not celebrated for its height alone. What sets it apart from both contemporary and later skyscrapers is its extraordinary seven-story summit, a tiered pyramid sparkling with sunbursts and finished in stainless steel. One of the classic manifestations of Art Deco, it heralded a new era for the style as designers began to turn their attention toward industrial products and high-speed transport—a trend that later became known as "streamlining." Art Deco touches can also be seen in the interplay between exaggerated horizontals and

verticals in the arrangement of the windows, reminiscent of the *nemes*, or ritual striped headdress, of the Egyptian pharaohs.

Inside, the theme was echoed in the extravagant entrance lobby, with its African marble walls and chrome clock. The elevators were stylishly appointed with Deco-patterned wood inlay, while the staircases were faced in luxurious black and chocolate-brown marble set off by angular, stainless-steel handrails.

The building was also customized for the automobile industry. Van Alen based his designs for the top of the building on automobile motifs used by Chrysler. The projecting metal gargoyles are enlarged versions of chrome ornaments found on engine hoods. Elsewhere, hubcaps were used as decorations, bas-relief sculptures take the form of cars, and ceiling murals featuring cars adorn the lobby, where new Chrysler models were to be displayed on a revolving stand.

Art Deco had always played along the fine line between glamour and kitsch, but van Alen's designs fit the bill. Walter Percy

CLEAN NEW WORLD

Chrysler understood the value of architecture as publicity. The Hoover Company borrowed a leaf from the same book when it built its new factory outside London in 1931-5. The Hoover factory at Perivale, Ealing, remains one of the most striking monuments to Art Deco design in Britain.

Built on Western Avenue, the A40 out of London, it competed with other new factories to catch the eye of motorists—a new and increasingly important breed of consumers. Designed by Wallis, Gilbert & Partners, it broke the unwritten rule that factories should reflect their function as places of manufacture. The Hoover factory, by contrast, looks like a palace. Modern and gleaming white, it suggested the hygiene and efficiency that could be afforded by Hoover's state-of-the-art domestic appliances, which were manufactured on this site until 1982.

The front is essentially a façade fixed to a functional, steel-skeleton factory building. It is neatly framed by a comb-like surround of concrete relief, while strips of blue, red and turquoise ceramic tiles run the breadth of the building and line the large, metal-framed windows, picked out in pastel green. At either end of the building, the recessed staircase towers contribute a note of individuality with their quarter-circle corner windows and strident vertical windows running almost to full height. The separate canteen block was added in 1938.

DINING FIRST CLASS The Hoover factory canteen shows the clear influence of cruise-ship design on Art Deco.

Chrysler wanted a provocative building that sang out his success. Having started out as a machinist's apprentice, he had risen to become vice-president of General Motors at the age of 41, and founded his own Chrysler Corporation in 1925. In the four years prior to commissioning this huge headquarters, his company had risen rapidly to take its place among America's major car manufacturers.

Most beautiful skyscraper

The 77 floor, steel-and-concrete structure of the building is conventional. Van Alen does not rank among the great structural innovators—although the Chrysler Building was the first skyscraper to be decorated in exposed stainless steel. The stepped profile of the building corresponded to a recent development in skyscraper architecture. It was not so much a stylistic statement as a response to building regulations introduced in 1916 to prevent new skyscrapers from rising sheer from their site and blocking out the light of their neighbors. Under the zoning laws, the tower of a skyscraper could occupy only 25 percent of the total ground plan.

This stepped look soon became a theme in Art Deco style. Similarly, the merits of the Chrysler Building rest in its style—which it broadcasts with an upbeat swagger that is part and parcel of the city itself. But it may not have seemed quite like this when the building was inaugurated. Chrysler had signed the contract before the Wall Street crash of October 1929. By completion the following year, the economic outlook was grim. Then, within months, the Empire State Building rose to snatch the prize as the world's tallest building. But Walter P. Chrysler could take comfort. If there was a beauty contest among the skyscrapers, the Chrysler Building would have won it then and at the end of the century as well.

CROWNING GLORY The summit of the Chrysler Building stands out from the crowd high above the streets of Manhattan.

EMPIRE STATE BUILDING

THE RECORD-BREAKING SKYSCRAPER THAT CAPTURED THE PUBLIC'S IMAGINATION

The palatial, three-story, marble-lined lobby of the Empire State Building is decorated with eight large paintings. They depict the Seven Wonders of the Ancient World and the newly proclaimed Eighth Wonder—the Empire State Building itself.

Modesty was never part of the agenda of this record-breaking building. It was intended by its developers to be the most handsome and impressive skyscraper ever built, as well as the tallest. Designed by Shreve, Lamb & Harmon, it was to be a marvel of architectural engineering and construction, and from the very start it aroused great public attention. Crowds of spectators lined the sidewalks below to watch its steel skeleton grow at the staggering speed of four and a half stories a week. The construction workers rose to the occasion: showmen of hair-raising daring, they strode nonchalantly along the exposed steel beams hundreds of feet above the city streets, without safety harnesses or protective helmets, casually tossing red-hot rivets to one another, grappling with vibrating compressed-air hammers, and dangling their feet over oblivion as they sat on the girders for a meal break.

Conscious of the public interest, the developers commissioned the photographer Lewis Hine to record the construction. Often exposing himself to the same risks as the workers, and sometimes dangling in a mesh basket suspended from a winch in order to obtain a more dramatic angle, Hine thrilled the world with his superb pictures, inducing vertigo in magazine readers with their feet firmly on the ground. But the dangers were real enough: 14 construction workers lost their lives.

Breaking records

The Empire State Building went up in record time. Excavation of this prime site on Fifth Avenue, in midtown Manhattan, commenced in January 1930. Construction

BUILT TO LAST The receding tiers have a restrained elegance, set off by touches of Art Deco ornament at the top of the columns and around the mast.

began two months later when more than 200 steel-and-concrete piles were driven 35 feet into the ground, down to the granite bedrock on which New York City rests. The masonry of all 102 floors was finished before the year was out, and in just 14 months the building was complete.

Rising to 1,250 feet it was the tallest building in the world, 200 feet higher than

MIDAIR COLLISION

On July 28, 1945, pedestrians were alarmed to hear the roar of an unusually low airplane. It was a U.S. Air Force B-25 bomber, lost and way off course, and flying at a speed of 250 mph. Suddenly it crashed into the Empire State Building, plunging into the 78th and 79th floors. A fuel tank exploded and set six floors ablaze; an engine cannonballed through the service shafts, sending an elevator plummeting to the ground floor; and the sidewalks below were showered with debris. Fourteen people were killed, including the pilot and his two passengers, but this figure would have been higher had the crash occurred during the work week, when some 25,000 people worked in the building. It is a tribute to the structural strength of the Empire State Building that it was able to survive such a collision without greater destruction.

DAMAGE LIMITATION Lost in low cloud, a B-25 bomber ploughed into the Empire State Building and burst into flames. The damage was estimated at $1 million.

the Chrysler Building, which had held the crown for only a few months. The Empire State Building trumpeted this height loud and clear: the exterior, with its receding clusters of tall, slim tiers and the lines of narrow, vertical bands formed by the 6,500 windows and glinting stainless-steel panels, was deliberately designed to emphasize the structure's verticality.

The speed of construction was achieved by a logistics exercise of military precision. Because there was very little storage space on site, components were delivered only as they were needed. Each day, trucks arrived bearing steel beams and girders, prefabricated curtain-wall panels, thousands of bricks for the interior wall linings, service components and machinery. All these items had to be hoisted immediately into the building for installation by a workforce numbering 3,400 at peak times. It has been calculated that if all the components had been delivered at the same time, they would have filled a freight train 56 miles long.

Despite the speed of construction, the building was completed to a very high standard of strength and safety—considerably higher than would be deemed necessary today. The steel frame, the exterior walls faced with Indian limestone and granite, the brick wall linings, and the poured concrete floors combine to make it unusually robust and sturdy, even in the high winds that habitually gust around the building.

LIGHT SHOW On clear nights, the Empire State Building shines like a beacon over New York City. The colored lights on the mast are changed to indicate holidays and special days: red and white signal St. Valentine's Day.

The Empire State Building was officially opened on May 1, 1931, when President Herbert Hoover pressed a button in Washington DC and turned on the lights on its summit. By this time, the United States was firmly in the grip of the Depression, which had begun with the Wall Street crash of October 1929—just months after this ambitious new building project had been initiated. The black cloud of depression did, however, have its silver lining for the developers: they were able to keep the construction costs down to $25 million—half the original estimate.

Unlike many previous record-breaking skyscrapers, such as the Woolworth Building and the Chrysler Building, the Empire State Building was conceived not as a corporate headquarters, but as an office block for multiple tenancy. Its name was an allusion to a nickname for New York City in a boisterous, prosperous and all-conquering mood: the "Empire City," in the "Empire State" of New York. But in 1931, tenants in search of new and prestigious office space were hard to find, and for several years New Yorkers wryly referred to the structure as the "Empty State Building." The public, however, showed a great thirst for visiting the world's tallest building, and income from ticket sales kept the developers solvent through the deepest gloom of the Depression.

On top of the world

Visitors were whisked up to the 86th floor observatory platform in one of the 73 elevators in the service core of the building. From there they could continue to the 102nd floor, 200 feet higher still, where there was a smaller observatory—a round button with viewing windows and an exposed deck—just beneath the mast. From these observation platforms, weather conditions permitting, they had an unprecedented view out over the rooftops and spires of New York.

At this mind-boggling height, peculiar weather phenomena were part and parcel of the experience. There are days when the summit is engulfed in low, swirling cloud and fog, others when rain and snow appear to "fall" upward. In the fierce electrical storms that occasionally crackle around New York's bristling skyline, fingers poked through the metal fence of the observatory platform can induce the unearthly phenomenon of static electricity known as St. Elmo's Fire. On one occasion, in November 1958, guards on the summit of the building were able to make snowballs while rain was falling in the streets below—a measure of the building's height.

The original mast was intended as a mooring site for dirigible airships. This was the era when airships, such as the huge German Zeppelins, seemed to many to represent the bright new future of long-distance travel, a notion that finally evaporated with the *Hindenburg* disaster of 1937. However, the idea of mooring an airship in the notoriously gusty heights at the top of the world's tallest building proved totally impractical: only one airship succeeded in doing so, but had to cast off after three minutes. In 1951 a new television mast took the place of the mooring mast, raising the total height of the building to 1,472 feet.

Although now eclipsed by several taller buildings, the Empire State Building has retained a special place in the world's collective imagination. This is partly the legacy of its 42 year reign as the world's tallest building—until the twin towers of the World Trade Center in New York were completed in 1973. But it is also because, with its streamlined look and thrusting height, it remains in many people's minds the quintessential skyscraper.

GOING UP A worker takes a ride on a crane hook in October 1930, as the Empire State Building raced toward completion, captured by photographer Lewis Hine, who was commissioned to record construction work.

THE ULTIMATE FILM SET

MONSTERS OF FILM AND ARCHITECTURE A poster shows King Kong towering over the city skyline, victim in hand.

At the climax of the classic film *King Kong*, the giant gorilla grabs the sensual, hysterical heroine, played by Fay Wray, in his vast, hairy hand and storms through the center of New York, crushing cars underfoot and sending the terrified citizens scattering for their lives. Desperately seeking refuge, King Kong climbs the Empire State Building, where fighter planes swarm around him like flies. At last he falls to his death, maddened and uncomprehending, and Fay Wray is rescued by the valiant Bruce Cabot, who clasps her in his arms on a ledge high above the traumatized city.

King Kong was made in 1933, just two years after the Empire State Building had been completed. The building was still hailed as an unrivalled and daring marvel, the biggest and latest of a series of skyscrapers that—to some at least—seemed to challenge the laws of nature. It was a fitting setting, therefore, for this cataclysmic denouement in which a symbol of the brute force of nature clings to a symbol of the material aspirations of "civilized" humankind. However, the film was also a triumph of special effects, shot entirely in Hollywood. *King Kong*, which appears as a 50 foot monster in the film, was actually an animated model just 18 inches high, and the set for the summit of the Empire State Building was a replica that stood just 10 feet off the ground.

Nonetheless, the Empire State Building bathed in the reflected glory of this hugely successful film, and will always be associated with it. In 1983, to celebrate the 50th anniversary of the film, an 84 foot-high inflatable King Kong was erected on the outside of the building—but suffered a similarly premature fate to that of the film character. A gust of wind caught it and punctured it, and it had to be hastily dismantled and brought down to earth.

THE PENTAGON

THE WORLD'S MOST POWERFUL MILITARY MACHINE OCCUPIES THE WORLD'S LARGEST OFFICE BUILDING

In 1941, with clouds of war billowing over the Pacific and Europe, the United States decided to consolidate its War Department under one roof. At the time, the five branches of the U.S. Armed Forces—the Army, Navy, Air Force, Marines and Coast Guard—were housed in 17 separate buildings in Washington DC, posing huge and costly logistical and communications problems.

Work began in September 1941, just two months before the Japanese bombed Pearl Harbor and catapulted the U.S. into war. The site chosen was close to the heart of the city, to the west of the Potomac River and at the southern end of the Arlington National Cemetery. It was an area of swampy wasteland and over 41,000 concrete piles had to be driven into the unstable ground to secure the foundations. The building was completed in January 1943.

The unusual, five-sided shape of the building gave it the name that has become synonymous with the U.S. military leadership: the Pentagon. It is a massive complex, but also a model of military orderliness. Its limestone façades, which echo the neoclassical style of Washington's great public buildings, rise up from manicured lawns.

NUMBER ONE TARGET

During the Cold War, the Soviets had two missiles targeted on the building in the middle of the Pentagon's center court, believing it to be the nerve center of the U.S.'s military command. In fact, it is a hot-dog stand. For this reason, it has been jokingly nicknamed Cafe Ground Zero—after the term used for the point at the center of a nuclear explosion.

Although just five stories high, including the basement, the Pentagon has a staggering 6,636,360 square feet of floor space, three times more than the Empire State Building. Inside, there are five concentric pentagonal rings of buildings, separated by light wells. The open pentagonal space in the center has been set aside as a park; covering a full 5 acres, it contains trees, lawns, benches, a cafeteria and a stage where military bands perform during the summer months.

The shape of the building was chosen by its chief architect, G. Edwin Bergstrom, for its efficiency. Despite the $17\frac{1}{2}$ miles of corridors and 131 stairways, it takes no longer than seven minutes to walk from one part of the building to any other.

Some 250 light bulbs have to be changed every day in the 16,250 light fixtures. There are 4,200 clocks, 691 drinking fountains, 284 restrooms, and 100,000 miles of telephone cables handling over 200,000 calls a day. The Pentagon has its own MetroRail commuter train station and 8,770 parking spaces in garages covering 67 acres. These facilities support a staff of 23,000, divided between civilians and Armed Forces personnel. The Pentagon is, as its own officials put it, "a city in itself."

CENTER OF OPERATIONS Covering 29 acres, the Pentagon has the largest ground area of any building in the world.

SEAGRAM BUILDING

MIËS VAN DER ROHE'S TOWERING OFFICE BLOCK IS THE MODEL FOR GLASS-BOX BUILDINGS

It was not the first, and it was certainly not the last, but to many people the Seagram Building on Manhattan's Park Avenue is the perfect example of glass-box architecture, the ultimate expression of the principles of the Modernist movement and the International Style. Completed in 1958, it posed a fundamental question: where could architecture go from here? Many architects have subsequently tried to elaborate on the theme, or to replicate its success, but their general failure to make further advances only serves to underline the masterly qualities of the original model.

Two architects were involved: the German, Ludwig Miës van der Rohe, who had been director of the Bauhaus school from 1930 to 1933, and the American, Philip Johnson (b.1906). Johnson had been an enthusiast of European avant-garde architecture and in 1932, when he was director of the architecture department at the Museum of Modern Art in New York, he co-authored a book with Henry-Russell Hitchcock entitled *The International Style: Architecture since 1922.* The term "International Style" was used thereafter to describe the pared-down, rectilinear buildings that developed in the interwar years and came to full fruition after the Second World War.

When the former Bauhaus designers Walter Gropius, Marcel Breuer, Miës van der Rohe and others arrived in the United States, Johnson was quick to grasp the significance of their work and promoted their cause. He studied under Gropius and Breuer at Harvard before returning to the Museum of Modern Art in 1946. Here he mounted an exhibition on the work of Miës van der Rohe, and a close association began.

In his early years in the U.S., Miës van der Rohe designed several private houses before embarking on the first of his Lake Shore Drive apartment blocks in Chicago, completed in 1951. This pair of severely

VOLUME AND SPACE **The Seagram Building is set back 90 feet from Park Avenue, giving it space to breathe, as well as broader perspectives from which it can be viewed.**

rectilinear glass-and-steel towers paved the way for the new headquarters of the giant distillers Seagram, which he began designing in 1954.

Less is more
Three elements combined to bring the Seagram Building to world attention. The first was its bold simplicity. It is simply a rectangular glass box, rising through 42 stories to 525 feet. A curtain of grey-tinted glass and rolled bronze panelling wraps around the building, held in place by vertical steel mullions and forming neat, sharp corners. There is no ornamentation apart from the stylistic differentiation that dims the top four stories: instead, viewers are left to

ROOM WITH A VIEW The glass walls provide spectacular views over the city. As his Bauhaus background might suggest, Miës van der Rohe equated modernity with simple shapes and uncluttered spaces.

admire the fine-edged shape and felicitous proportions of the building as a whole.

Secondly, there is the detailing. Miës van der Rohe insisted on the highest standards of engineering and craftsmanship, which can be seen, for example, in the steel beams, the glistening plate glass, and the walls of polished travertine in the entrance lobby. Simple it may be, but the Seagram Building was not cheap.

Thirdly, there is the treatment of the site. This was one of the first high-rise buildings in New York where a generous portion of the site was set aside as a public plaza furnished with seating, ponds and trees. The plaza runs between exposed ground-level columns to the entrance lobby, and so is subtly integrated with the building itself.

The double-height floor-to-ceiling glass walls of the entrance lobby are set well back from the rest of the building, giving the whole edifice the illusion of remarkable lightness, like a balloon tethered to the ground. Whereas older skyscrapers, such as the Empire State Building, speak of solid mass rooted firmly to their site, the Seagram Building suggests volume, space and transparency without mass. This had been one of the key ambitions of the pioneers of the International Style, and was a major driving force behind their pursuit of modern materials.

Miës van der Rohe's motto was "*Weniger ist mehr*" (Less is more). The Seagram Building represents the ultimate expression of the ambition to strip back architecture to its base elements, a challenge that numerous architects and designers had pursued since the 1890s. Critics complained that the logical conclusion of this trend would be the "absence of architecture." Over the coming decades, the critics' fears would be confirmed by the rash of cheaper, repetitive glass boxes that sprang up in cities across the industrialized world. But the Seagram Building stands apart, an aristocrat with an impeccable ancestry and a dignified bearing sustained by the moral purity of the International Style.

LUDWIG MIËS VAN DER ROHE

Born the son of a stone-cutter in Aachen, Germany, Ludwig Miës van der Rohe (1886-1969) trained in the influential practice of Peter Behrens in Berlin, where Walter Gropius and Le Corbusier were also employed. He came to prominence in 1929 with his design for the German pavilion at the International Exhibition in Barcelona. It was a building of glass, steel, polished travertine and marble that combined radical simplicity with extraordinary grace, a prototype that now seems many years ahead of its time. He was appointed director of the Bauhaus in 1930, but it closed under Nazi pressure in 1933.

After leaving Germany in 1938, Miës van der Rohe took up the post of director of architecture at the Chicago Armour Institute, which became the Illinois Institute of Technology. He also undertook a number of commissions for private homes, such as the seminal Farnsworth House (1946-51) at Plano, Illinois. Although consisting of little more than simple rectangles of plate glass sandwiched between a concrete platform and a flat roof, these houses exhibited a sympathy with their natural setting and a masterly attention to proportion and detail.

With the Lake Shore Drive towers, and then the Seagram Building, Miës van der Rohe was at last able to apply his theories on architecture and the use of modern materials to large-scale projects. Only the United States could have provided such opportunities, and the influx of the most talented avant-garde designers from Germany, combined with postwar American prosperity, placed the U.S. at the architectural forefront for decades. Toward the end of his life Miës van der Rohe was able to bring his talent back to Germany by designing the New National Gallery in Berlin, completed in 1967.

STRUCTURAL SIMPLICITY The glass walls of Farnsworth House enhance its park-like setting. It is raised above the ground in case of seasonal flooding.

BRASÍLIA

BRAZIL'S NEW CAPITAL EMBODIES THE DYNAMISM OF A COUNTRY LOOKING TO THE FUTURE

In the 1950s, Brazil was revelling in an economic carnival. Foreign investment was pouring in, transforming industries such as car manufacture, aviation, electronics and chemicals. When Juscelino Kubitschek was elected president for a five-year term in 1956, he promised "fifty years of progress in five."

A key element in his ambitious plan was the creation of a new capital, a city to symbolize the new Brazil: modern, and entirely Brazilian, in concept, design and construction. The site chosen lay on a savannah plain in the inland state of Goiás. Gateway to the rich resources of central Brazil, Brasília was also to be a deliberate riposte to the large and crowded coastal cities, including the old capital, Rio de Janeiro, which still looked across the Atlantic to Europe and remained mired in the corrupting influences of their long histories. The new capital, Brasília, was to represent an entirely fresh start.

Kubitschek turned to Brazil's most celebrated architect, Oscar Niemeyer (b.1907), a dedicated Modernist who had worked alongside Le Corbusier in the 1930s. Niemeyer had achieved international fame with his Corbusian Ministry of Education in Rio de Janeiro (1936-43), but he was also the designer of a number of sculptural buildings constructed in concrete and glass, such as the yacht club and casino (1942) and the Church of St. Francis (1943-6) at Pampulha, to the north of Rio.

At Niemeyer's insistence, a competition was held in 1957 to choose the best plan for the capital. The winner was Lúcio Costa (1902-63), Niemeyer's architectural partner since 1935. He had devised a dynamic scheme featuring

DIVINE INSPIRATION The concrete ribs of Brasília's cathedral evoke Christian symbols such as the crown of thorns and fingers upstretched to heaven.

two intersecting axes, one straight, one curved, with the new parliament buildings and the Supreme Court at the head of the main axis. This was the first of the capital's geometric puzzles. To some, the city's ground plan looked like a bird, to others an airplane; to Niemeyer, who was asked to design the principal buildings for Costa's scheme, it was a cross symbolizing "a deliberate act of conquest, a gesture of pioneers acting in the spirit of their colonial traditions."

The site did indeed call for a pioneer spirit. The dry scrubland was so remote that roads had to be built to give access. But in the wide open spaces of this virgin territory, Niemeyer was free to create whatever shapes he chose. He opted for a mixture of classical grace, monumentality and spectacular sculptural gesture.

A city in five years

The race was on: Kubitschek wanted a capital city before his five-year term in office expired in 1961. The first building that Niemeyer tackled was the presidential

MONUMENT TO THE FOUNDER The role of President Juscelino Kubitschek in creating Brazil's new capital is acknowledged in a sculpture by Honorio Peánha.

palace, which was set close to an artificial lake and symbolically distant from the key government buildings. Completed in 1958, it was called the Alvorada Palace, the Palace of the Dawn—the dawn of a new Brazil.

The main elements of the Alvorada Palace are echoed in the Planalto Palace, the seat of the federal government, and the Supreme Court (1958-60). These are two of the key buildings of the Praça dos Tres Poderes (Plaza of the Three Powers—legislative, executive, judiciary), the roughly triangular configuration at the head of Costa's scheme. Like the Alvorada Palace, both have glass-box interiors set between two slabs supported by curving pillars that form a shaded colonnade.

Of the three main buildings in the Praça dos Tres Poderes, the National Congress building (1958-60) is the most unusual. Set low to accentuate its horizontality, its flat roof is capped by two sculptural shapes: a dome over the part of the building occupied by the Senate, and a gigantic bowl over the

Chamber of Representatives. The roof space is accessible to pedestrians via a long, gentle ramp—a feature used repeatedly by Niemeyer in Brasília in place of stairs. In contrast, the government administrative block rises behind the National Congress, a pair of monoliths linked by a three-story bridge.

A short distance from the Praça dos Tres Poderes is the most famous of Niemeyer's Brasília buildings, the Metropolitan Cathedral (1959-70). The concept is disarmingly simple: a circle of 16 concrete boomerang-shaped ribs lean in toward a circular roof slab that holds them in position.

Utopia foiled

Niemeyer and Costa intended that the cathedral, a National Theater, museums, sculptures, pools and landscaped gardens would create an ideal and fully rounded city. Rows of six-story *superquadra* apartment blocks (1958-60) form the "wings" that run at an angle to the central administrative axis. They were designed in a uniform pattern so as to promote the concept of an egalitarian, non-hierarchical society.

As it happened, the social stratification that the architects tried so hard to avoid imposed itself after Brasília was inaugurated in April 1961. Construction workers and poorly paid laborers, who had no place in the grand plan, collected in growing shanty towns around the periphery. In 1965 the *superquadra* apartment blocks were put on the open market, and less well-off civil servants were banished by price to outlying suburbs. The very concept of the key administrative buildings as palaces of marble and glass reinforced the division between the ruling elite and the armies of workers.

But Niemeyer could not be blamed for the failure of Brazilian society to match up to the utopian ideals of government as expressed by his architecture. In 1964, against a backdrop of political turmoil and economic troubles caused in part by the cost of Brasília, the government was seized in a military coup. The generals remained in power for over 20 years, during which the economic bubble burst and Brazil amassed the world's largest foreign debt. The fact that Niemeyer, a committed Communist, was not persecuted by the military government is a measure of the high esteem in which he is held by his fellow Brazilians.

NEW CAPITALS

With its population of over 1.5 million, Brasília is the largest of the 20th century's new national and regional capitals, which include Canberra in Australia, Islamabad in Pakistan, and Chandigarh in the Punjab.

Australia decided to create a new capital shortly after it united as a Commonwealth in 1901. The Canberra site was selected because it was more or less equidistant between the rival cities of Sydney and Melbourne. The design was opened up to an international competition in 1911, won by the American Walter Burley Griffin (1876-1937), who proposed an ingenious plan based on a series of intersecting circles and radiating roads. But victory in the competition was only the start of a long process: the Australian government did not move to Canberra until 1927. Only in the 1970s, half a century after inauguration, did Canberra begin to lose its reputation as an administrative backwater.

Brasília may have to wait as long to win approval. New cities can have all the facilities of an ideal urban environment, but they cannot buy the cultural complexity, textures, traditions, history and evolutionary dynamics that imbue old cities with their distinctive character. It is a long haul to maturity.

TRANSAMERICA PYRAMID

A MODERN-DAY PYRAMID CUTS THE MOST STRIKING PROFILE IN SAN FRANCISCO'S SKYLINE

The familiar image of San Francisco is one of undulating hills lined with rows of painted Victorian houses. But in the downtown financial district, an impressive cluster of high-rise buildings hugs the shore of San Francisco Bay. One in particular, a singular-looking needle known as the Transamerica Pyramid, stands out, never failing to catch the eye.

The tallest skyscraper in the city, the pyramid was built in 1969-72 as the headquarters of the Transamerica Corporation, one of America's leading financial services companies. Tapering at an angle of 5° from vertical, its shape is so unusual and striking that the name of Transamerica is readily identified with it. The company uses an image of the building as its logo, alongside the motto: "The power of the pyramid is working for you."

But the design, devised by architects William L. Pereira Associates, is not simply a gimmick: the intention was to allow plenty of light to penetrate the building and to reach the street below. To underline this environmental concern, the square base of the building occupies only a part of the site. Much of the rest is given over to a "pocket park" that is planted with redwood trees, the celebrated forest giants of the northern California coast.

Quakeproofing

San Franciscans are well aware of the dangers of earthquakes. The San Andreas fault passes through the city, and the disastrous 1906 earthquake still looms large in the collective consciousness of the inhabitants. No building is ever totally quakeproof, but the Transamerica Pyramid was built to minimize the risks. The foundations were dug to 52 feet. Then the base was filled with a mat of reinforced concrete 9 feet thick—all poured in during a single day in December 1969 by shifts of 70 ready-mix-concrete trucks.

Vertical columns rise through the three subterranean garage levels to the ground floor, and these provide the platforms for massive V-shaped steel braces that angle in to just below the fifth floor. The braces interlock to form a web of 20 mini-pyramids around the base of the building. With the additional support of four huge steel K-braces inside the building, the lower four floors should remain rigid in the event of an earthquake, while the rest of the pyramid, a standard steel-frame structure, is allowed to flex and absorb the vibrations.

The fifth floor is in fact the widest, measuring 145 × 145 feet. Below this, the floors taper back to the width of the ground-floor lobby, with windows looking out onto the open structure of the braces. Above the fifth floor the building narrows steadily to the 48th floor, which measures just 45×45 feet.

Two windowless vertical "wings" rise above the 29th floor, which appear to belong to a building behind the pyramid, thus preserving the building's distinctive profile. The east wing houses eleva-

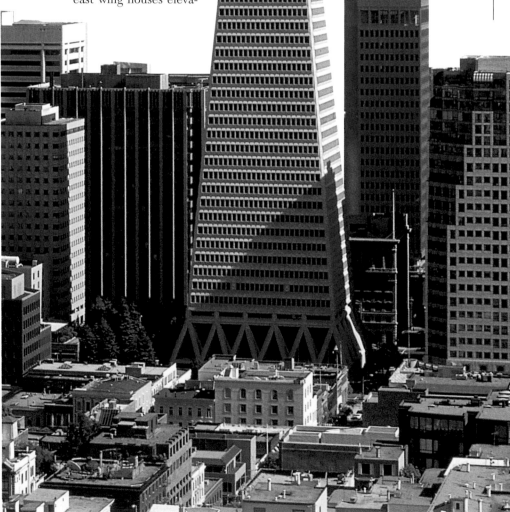

tor shafts; the west wing contains a stairwell for use in an emergency.

The main part of the building is faced in white quartz aggregate and has 3,678 windows; above the top floor, aluminum panels take over. This 212-foot spire, housing mechanical and telecommunications equipment, rises to a pinnacle that is crowned with an aircraft warning light 853 feet above the ground.

PYRAMID POWER V-shaped steel braces at the foot of the building create a set of interlocking pyramids that help support it in an earthquake. The vertical "wings" above the 29th floor contain elevators and a stairwell.

WORLD TRADE CENTER

NEW YORK'S VAST TWIN TOWERS REPRESENT THE ULTIMATE STATEMENT IN GLASS-BOX ARCHITECTURE

In 1966, the American minimalist sculptor Carl Andre produced *Equivalents VIII*, a set of 120 firebricks arranged on the floor. The Tate Gallery in London liked it enough to buy it, causing outrage among a baffled public. Meanwhile, in New York work was under way on another minimalist statement —but one on a very different scale. Two rectangular blocks of gleaming aluminum and glass were rising like the prongs of a giant tuning fork from the financial district at the southern end of Manhattan.

Designed by the American-born architect Minoru Yamasaki (1912-86) as a symbol of the role played by international trade in American life, the World Trade Center was the last word in the architectural trend for soaring glass-faced monoliths. In 1973 it stole the Empire State Building's 42 year record as the world's tallest building. Although the Sears Tower in Chicago overtook it the following year, the World Trade Center remains the tallest building in New York, and still holds the record as the world's largest rentable office space, with 12 million square feet. Eventually completed in 1976 after a decade of construction, it cost its owners, the Port Authority of New York and New Jersey, over $750 million.

The two soaring towers are the centerpiece of a building complex covering 17 acres. This includes a 47 floor office block, two 9 floor office blocks and a 22 floor hotel.

These are all built around the 5 acre Austin J. Tobin Plaza, whose large expanses of open spaces, its benches, sculpture, fountains, landscaping and shrubs are designed to offset the huge scale of the World Trade Center buildings. "The buildings went upwards to free the ground space for daily human enjoyment," Yamasaki wrote.

Beneath the plaza lie six subterranean floors containing a shopping mall and leisure center, railway and subway stations, and an underground garage for 1,800 vehicles.

High jinks

Despite its many attractions, the World Trade Center is famous for its "twin towers." Unlike most earlier skyscrapers, these towers were not built around a steel skeleton. Instead, the 110 floors are largely supported by the rigid outer grill of aluminum-faced steel, which creates a cantilever structure backed by the central elevator core. The windows, recessed between the columns, are less than 2 feet

TWIN MONOLITHS The twin towers surge upward, dominating New York Harbor. They are not lined up with one another, creating a visual conundrum.

Just after midday on February 26, 1993, a rented van converted into a huge mobile incendiary bomb exploded in the underground garage of the World Trade Center. The massive percussive force of the bomb ricocheted through the whole of the lower part of the building, blasting out a crater 100 feet deep, pulverizing 226 cars, and killing six people instantly.

Because the basement roof collapsed, fire did not spread far into the adjacent floors, and the horror of a "towering inferno" was averted. But choking smoke rose rapidly up the stairwells and elevator shafts. The building's fire control center had been knocked out by the bomb, so the task of evacuating the 150,000 people from the Center proved hazardous. Over 1,000 were injured as they made their way through the smoke, down blacked-out stairwells. The culprits were traced through the van rental agency: they were terrorists connected to a militant Islamic organization that was allegedly plotting massive destruction in New York City in protest of United States support for Israel.

wide, giving the façades a distinctive raked look. Number One Tower—the one with the radio antenna—is 1,368 feet high and has the "Windows on the World" restaurant on the top floor. Number Two Tower has an observation deck on the 107th floor and another on the roof itself, 1,362 feet above the ground.

The towers have received more than 30 million visitors since the observation decks were opened in 1975. They have also attracted their fair share of daredevils, including a man who climbed the northeast flank using suction cups. In August 1974, the French acrobat Philippe Petit crossed on a tightrope suspended between the tops of the two towers, guaranteeing that both he and the World Trade Center will have a place in the record books for many years to come.

LLOYD'S BUILDING

A CONTROVERSIAL 20TH-CENTURY HOME FOR A GREAT 17TH-CENTURY FINANCIAL INSTITUTION

The insurance association called Lloyd's of London has been operating since the 1680s, when a group of insurers, shipowners and merchants used to meet in a coffee-house in Lombard Street, London, owned by Edward Lloyd to discuss ways of sharing the risks of their ventures. Lloyd's grew to become one of the world's leading insurance markets, where syndicates of underwriters gather to set up the complex hierarchies of reinsurance needed to cover insured losses of anything from house contents to shipping fleets, nuclear power stations and earthquake damage.

Lloyd's had outgrown its offices in the City of London twice in 50 years when, in 1978, it decided to commission a new headquarters that might serve it well into the next century. The result was one of the world's most innovative office buildings, a shock of glass and stainless steel glinting among the winding lanes and neoclassical façades of London's old financial district.

The new Lloyd's Building was designed by the Richard Rogers Partnership, assisted by consulting engineers Ove Arup & Partners, who had collaborated with Rogers on his ground-breaking Pompidou Center in Paris in 1971-7. The cooperation between architect and engineer was essential to the Lloyd's Building, for this was a highly technical project, at the cutting edge of construction engineering. As with all Rogers' designs, the key criterion was to match technology to function: the look of the building followed from this.

As City wits put it: "Lloyd's started off in a coffee-house and ended up in a percolator." Gleaming metal tubes and vertical chains of glistening cylinders mount the towers, next to stacks of rectangular boxes with portholes, and cuboid "wall-climber" elevators of glass. Crowning the towers are top-heavy corrugated boxes surmounted by blue maintenance cranes. It is hard to read the meaning of this puzzle until it is understood that these are the "servant towers," thrust to the outside of the building to keep the interior clear of services. The steel-faced cylinders mask spiral staircases; the tubes are airducts; the portholed blocks are restroom "pods"; and the corrugated boxes at the top of the towers are plant-rooms housing machinery.

Six servant towers cluster around the main body of the building, which has a simple rectangular plan, dominated by a spacious atrium

SHINING IN THE NIGHT The exterior of the Lloyd's Building gives the impression of a mysterious powerhouse. Inside (right), the lower part of the atrium is surrounded by galleries where the insurance market takes place.

that rises through 13 floors to a barrel-vaulted glass roof 230 feet above the floor. The atrium, surrounded by an exterior lattice of steel bracing, is visible on the outside only from the south, away from the main entrance. The insurance syndicates operate from their tables, or "boxes," in the open underwriting hall on the ground floor and first three galleries, while the upper galleries are walled in with glass to form more conventional offices.

Richard Rogers Partnership first studied the requirements of the Lloyd's insurance market. The need for rapid circulation of up to 10,000 personnel in the underwriting hall, ready access to underwriters, modern communications, and built-in potential for future expansion, all dictated the overall concept. But the cramped site in Leadenhall Street, and the punishing construction schedule also played their part. Many elements had to be prefabricated and delivered to a precise

BOLT-ON CONVENIENCES
The prefabricated restrooms were slotted into the service towers in stacks. The more rounded shapes house spiral staircases.

timetable, to be slotted into position like a kit assembly.

Lloyd's was keen not to lose all sense of their historic roots, and various symbolic elements have been preserved. These include the leather-topped teak tables of the syndicates' boxes and the gilded neoclassical rotunda on the ground floor, in which Lloyd's famous Lutine Bell hangs. On the 11th floor is another surprise. The Adam Committee Room is an ornate, chandeliered 18th-century room that was removed from Bowood House, Wiltshire, in the 1950s and transported to London.

RICHARD ROGERS

At the close of the 20th century, two architects stood at the forefront of British architecture: Norman Foster and Richard Rogers (b.1933). They had studied together at Yale University in the U.S., and both believed that technology and high-quality engineering should be the prime criteria for creating efficient and flexible buildings, and that an appealing aesthetic could be devised based on these qualities alone. From 1963 to 1967 they and their wives formed a partnership called Team Four.

Rogers rose to stardom with his controversial Pompidou Center, designed with the Italian Renzo Piano. Richard Rogers Partnership was formed after his break with Piano in 1977.

If the Pompidou Center placed Rogers on the international stage, the Lloyd's Building confirmed his unique vision and the enduring quality of his architecture. Richard Rogers Partnership has since worked on airport terminals, television buildings, factories and commercial headquarters. It has also become involved in design solutions for public spaces and in environmentally sound architecture.

CREST OF A WAVE   Rogers was 45 in 1978, when he won the Lloyd's commission.

LA DÉFENSE

A MASSIVE HOLLOW CUBE PROVIDES A STARTLING END-POINT TO PARIS'S GREAT CENTRAL AXIS

In 1889 Paris celebrated the centenary of the French Revolution with a World Fair, and the star of the show was an engineering marvel, the Eiffel Tower. Approaching the bicentennial 100 years later, France was in search of a similarly striking monument to mark the occasion. The solution was found through an international competition held in 1982-3. The winner was La Grande Arche de la Défense, a massive, cube-shaped arch. It was the submission of a little-known but distinguished architect, Johan Otto von Spreckelsen (1929-87), whose previous work consisted mainly of a series of innovative churches in his native Denmark.

Building work began in 1985 and progressed at a furious pace to meet the deadline of the bicentennial celebrations. The shape of the building is simplicity itself: an almost perfect cube with bevelled edges leading to a hollow central area. But its scale is huge: 367 feet deep, by 361 feet high, by 354 feet wide. The upper surface of the roof section covers an area of 3 acres. Paris's great cathedral, Notre-Dame, would fit into the void in the cube's center. The two sides—effectively a pair of 35 story office blocks—were built on top of two lines of huge concrete piers. But it was the width of the roof that took engineers into unknown territory. Steel girders, specially cast on site, and high-strength concrete were needed to cover the span of 240 feet, an unprecedented width across which to support a weight of 2,500 tons.

In 1987 von Spreckelsen died, and the task of completing the project passed to his partner, Paul Andreu (b.1938), a French architect known for his work on international airports. As the deadline loomed, the finishing touches were slotted into position: the glass in the honeycomb of bevelled window-frames, and the Carrara marble covering $2^{1}/_{2}$ acres on the outside of the building.

La Grande Arche was completed for its official opening on Bastille Day, July 14, 1989, and over the following days the heads of seven of the world's leading nations, the G7, met in the roof—an area dedicated to the newly formed Foundation for the Rights of Man. It was a moment of triumph for the French president, François Mitterrand, who had been one of the project's prime movers. La Grande Arche also represented the culminating statement of La Défense, one of the most ambitious urbanization projects of the century.

Manhattan sur Seine

La Grande Arche stands at the far end of one of the principal axes of Paris. Originally conceived by the landscape architect André Le Nôtre in the 17th century, the *Grande Axe* includes the Champs Elysées and the Arc de Triomphe, then continues for 2 miles in a straight line along the Avenue de la Grande Armée and the Avenue Charles de Gaulle, to the hilltop on which La Grand Arche rises, just outside Paris's city limits.

Surrounded by a trio of neglected industrial and residential communes, Puteaux, Courbevoie and Nanterre, La Défense came

TRIUMPHAL ARCH The central void of La Grande Arche is broken up by a glass fiber "cloud" and scaffolding-like steel towers, which serve as elevator shafts to the roof.

COMMUNICATIONS HUB The provision of good road and public transportation links played a major role in persuading businesses to build their headquarters at La Défense.

under the spotlight during the 1950s when the French government wanted to create a modern, American-style business center to rival New York, Tokyo and Brussels. The first phase of building at La Défense included the Centre des Nouvelles Industries et Technologies (CNIT, 1958), an almost triangular sheet of concrete on three legs sheltering an exhibition and conference center.

This early attempt at urbanization looked doomed to stagnate until the state, under President Charles de Gaulle, took up its cause and gave full backing to the newly formed planning body, the Etablissement Public pour l'Aménagement de La Défense (EPAD). Work began in earnest in the late 1950s as thousands of dwellings and businesses were cleared from a site covering 3 square miles, and new highway and rail infrastructures were initiated. Some 25,000

local residents had to be relocated. During the 1960s and early 1970s, La Défense bristled with new high-rise buildings, including headquarters for major French companies and multinationals, such as Elf, Sony, Xerox, Fiat and Citibank. Fiat built the tallest tower, reaching 785 feet, and La Défense was soon dubbed "Manhattan sur Seine." New residential districts were created in the surrounding communes. But public distaste for soulless International Style tower blocks, and economic turmoil caused by the oil crisis, pushed EPAD close to bankruptcy.

In 1978 the scheme received new vigor as a result of renewed government intervention under President Valéry Giscard d'Estaing. La Défense finally took off, and La Grande Arche

HIGH-RISE REGRETS Tower blocks built to house displaced residents in communities such as Nanterre attracted criticism during the 1970s, when La Défense was in the doldrums.

became the centerpiece of its renaissance. Today, some 1,200 companies have offices here, and more than 110,000 people flock to them each day to work. Inventive and futuristic glass-fronted office blocks now grace the extensive pedestrian precinct called the Parvis, which is punctuated by fountains, sidewalk cafés, benches, trees, and some 70 sculptures and murals.

HONG KONG AND SHANGHAI BANK

A CLASSIC MARRIAGE OF ARCHITECTURE AND ENGINEERING AFFIRMS CONFIDENCE IN THE FUTURE

Standing in a prominent position in the crowded Central District of Hong Kong Island, overlooking Victoria Harbor and Kowloon, the headquarters building of the Hong Kong and Shanghai Banking Corporation has always courted attention. Erected between 1981 and 1986, it was said at the time to be the world's most expensive building, costing a reputed $1 billion. Its unconventional appearance is a forthright expression both of its location and of its function as a bank at the cutting edge of information and communications technology. Press reports used the terms "ultra modern," and "high tech." Its designers, Foster Associates, prefer the term "appropriate technology": it is a structure designed to fit its function like a beautifully tailored glove.

Flexible banking

The Hong Kong and Shanghai Bank wanted a headquarters building that made a firm statement about the bank, and one that also suggested confidence in Hong Kong in the uncertain times leading up to the transfer of rule from Britain to China in 1997. Furthermore, the bank wanted a building that would serve it for at least 50 years—not an easy task in the fast-changing world of international banking.

Foster Associates' answer was to provide a structure with built-in flexibility. The office floors are mainly open plan, and the thousands of cables—for power, communications and computer links—are set in floor cavities, easily accessible from removable panels made from lightweight aluminum honeycomb like that used in aircraft. Future changes in technology—such as the introduction of fiber-optic cables—can therefore be easily installed. Likewise, toilets, air-conditioning units, back-up generators and

NATURAL LIGHT The vast central atrium is dominated by giant X-shaped braces. Light is deflected from the exterior sunscoop onto the stepped mirror on the ceiling, then down through the glass floor to the plaza below.

other plant were built into interchangeable self-contained modules slotted into the sides of the building; these are the white blocks that line the corners on the exterior.

Having established these elements, Foster Associates looked for the framework that would hold them together. Their solution was a set of eight steel masts, each consisting of four columns held together by a lateral brace at each floor level. These columns and their lateral braces create the ladder-like effect that can be seen on the exterior of the building. The eight masts are held in place by sets of massive horizontal and V-shaped braces that break up the exterior façades at the 11th, 20th, 28th and 35th

SLICES OF TECHNOLOGY The main structure is supported on eight ladder-like masts. Stacks of service modules, stairs and elevator shafts form the columns at the near end.

floor levels. Most of the 47 floors inside are suspended from these horizontal braces, like the shelves of a hanging cupboard.

The interior reflects the uncompromising precision engineering of the exterior, and nowhere is this more apparent than in the seven-story atrium at the base of the building. The open-plan banking halls arranged around the atrium look out over a wide and airy space where the glass parapets, the aluminum-encased steel columns and the

SIR NORMAN FOSTER

"We maintain that architecture and interior design are indivisible and we retain control of all details of the interior of our buildings down to the fire exit signs." Such a meticulous approach to design is characteristic of Norman Foster (b.1935), one of the leading British architects of the closing decades of the century, and the founder and guiding light of Foster Associates (renamed Foster and Partners in 1992). After graduating from the University of Manchester, he won a scholarship to Yale University, and in 1963 formed Team Four with Richard Rogers.

They soon registered their desire to rethink architectural precepts and develop an approach to architecture liberated from the weight of historical precedents. The Reliance Electronics Factory (1965) in Swindon, England, demonstrated Team Four's interest in making imaginative use of new materials. In addition, they created a stylistic statement by exposing elements of the building's structure that were traditionally concealed. The flexible use of space, a built-in potential for future expansion, and prefabricated modular components were becoming key themes in Foster's approach. For his Renault Sales Headquarters (1981-3), also at Swindon, he designed tent-like steel units supported on exposed steel masts, at once both practical and visually arresting.

The Hong Kong and Shanghai Bank brought Foster world acclaim. Subsequent high-profile projects include London's third airport at Stansted, the Chek Lap Kok Airport in Hong Kong, and the new Reichstag parliament building in Berlin. Consistently innovative, the common thread in Foster's work is not so much an identifiable look, as a blend of calculated and imaginative responses to the functional requirements of a building, an unstinting attention to detail, and striking visual appeal.

IN DEMAND Norman Foster heads a partnership that is involved in numerous building projects throughout the world.

giant, three-story cross-braces create an impression of sleek efficiency.

The atrium incorporates an ingenious innovation called a "sunscoop system." In order to bring natural light to the lower floors of the building, a curved "sunscoop" has been built into the south exterior façade, running the width of the building at the 11th floor level. Mirrors on the sunscoop, programmed to track the movement of the Sun, beam light horizontally into the building, where it is reflected downward by a stepped mirror set in the ceiling of the atrium.

The reflected sunlight also passes through a curved glass floor at the base of the atrium to reach ground level, where there is a public plaza open to the air and elements. The bank's reception area is on the second floor, reached by escalators and external elevators.

Natural hazards

It is one thing to dream up innovative approaches to office architecture, but quite another to implement them in the extremely difficult and constricted conditions of Hong Kong Island. The Hong Kong and Shanghai Bank is situated on a strip of reclaimed foreshore consisting mainly of decomposed granite, and rendered more unstable by a high water table. In addition, Hong Kong has a hot, sticky climate, and is regularly hit by hurricane-force typhoons. All of these factors had to be taken into consideration.

The project engineers, Ove Arup and Partners, had to be quite certain of their

FRANKFURT'S COMMERZBANK: AN ECOLOGICAL SKYSCRAPER

SPIRAL TRIANGLE The floors of the Commerzbank rise up through the building in spiral blocks, giving it a highly distinctive profile. The walls also bulge outward slightly.

HIGH-RISE OASES In a modern equivalent of the Hanging Gardens of Babylon, a series of "winter gardens" occupy the glazed lobbies that separate the blocks of floors. The deep beds are capable of sustaining trees high above the city streets.

In recent years Sir Norman Foster, in common with other leading architects, has taken an increased interest in the environmental quality of his buildings and their ecological impact. Foster and Partners' Commerzbank Headquarters in Frankfurt, Germany, is not just Europe's tallest building, reaching up through 60 floors to 846 feet, and to 984 feet at the tip of its antenna; it is also the world's tallest "ecological skyscraper."

Constructed on a triangular ground plan sustained by three huge internal masts, it contains a soaring central atrium that rises through the full height of the building. This provides a natural ventilation chimney: unusually for a high-rise building, the windows can be opened. A staggered series of indoor winter gardens, complete with mature trees, connects the central atrium to the exterior, and these are distributed up the building as a spiral. They form a focus for four-story clusters of offices, creating an informal environment for interchange more akin to a village than a traditional office block. As Foster and Partners put it: "Our design transforms the fundamental nature of a large office building by developing new ideas for the ecology and working patterns in an office environment."

foundations. They also had to be careful not to disturb the neighbors' foundations, including those of one of Hong Kong's key historic buildings, the domed Supreme Court. The solution was to contain the basement area within massive watertight walls 3¼ feet thick. This area now contains the bank vaults and safe-deposits.

Meanwhile, the foundations of the eight masts were laid, set in concrete wells sunk 16½ feet into the bedrock. The masts themselves arrived as prefabricated units, manufactured in Scotland, and were assembled on site, like the vertebrae of a spinal column. As the masts rose, the floors were inserted, followed by the service modules—a total of 139, designed by Foster Associates down to the faucets and toilet-roll holders.

The overall design of this 590 foot high building was subjected to exhaustive tests in

BRACING ENVIRONMENT The massive structural braces counterbalance the overall effect of lightness created by the glass and the color scheme.

wind tunnels, which explored the impact of high winds from every direction, taking account of neighboring buildings, both existing and projected. This contingency explains the powerful look of the exterior. Most of the

impact of a full frontal typhoon is taken by the steel masts and transferred directly to the bedrock.

Hong Kong's climate demands good air-conditioning. Water is the usual coolant in air-conditioning systems. In Hong Kong, fresh water is scarce, so sea water is often used—up to 220 gallons a second in the case of the Hong Kong and Shanghai Bank. To provide this, a 1,140 foot tunnel was bored laterally from a position 245 feet beneath the basement level, creating a sea inlet serving the air-conditioning system and the toilets.

The Hong Kong and Shanghai Bank represented the most advanced office design of its day, but not all aspects of its construction broke with tradition. The building site was often redolent with the smell of incense wafting from the joss sticks lit by Chinese construction workers to propitiate the gods. And the bronze lions guarding the main entrance on Des Voeux Road are there to look after the bank's *feng shui*—the age-old Chinese principle of balance that ensures a building's prosperity and good fortune.

PETRONAS TWIN TOWERS

THE WORLD'S TALLEST BUILDING IS A POTENT SYMBOL OF CHANGING ECONOMIC REALITIES

In March 1996, the international press broadcast a new record. For the first time in living history, the world's tallest building intended for human occupation was no longer in the United States. The crown had passed to Malaysia, where in three years the Petronas Twin Towers had risen to dizzying heights over the nation's capital, Kuala Lumpur. On March 5 and March 11, the two towers were topped out at 1,483 feet—29 feet higher than the Sears Tower in Chicago, which had held the title for nearly 23 years. The building is a fitting symbol of Malaysia's surging economic development in the 1990s, masterminded by the country's prime minister, Dr. Mahathir Muhammad, under the catchphrase "2020 Vision."

The Petronas Twin Towers was designed by the Argentinian-born, but American-based architect Cesar Pelli (b.1926), whose

SIAMESE TWINS The two towers are linked at the 41st and 42nd floors by a "skybridge," which bonds the complex visually.

REACH FOR THE SKIES

The century's tallest inhabited buildings:

Completed	Building	Location	Height
1899	Park Row Building	New York	391 feet
1908	Singer Building	New York	612 feet
1909	Metropolitan Life Insurance Tower	New York	700 feet
1913	Woolworth Building	New York	792 feet
1930	Chrysler Building	New York	1,046 feet
1931	Empire State Building	New York	1,250 feet
1973	World Trade Center	New York	1,368 feet
1974	Sears Tower	Chicago	1,454 feet
1996	Petronas Twin Towers	Kuala Lumpur	1,483 feet

practice is in New Haven, Connecticut. In 1991 Cesar Pelli & Associates were pronounced the winners of an international competition set up by the Malaysian government for the design of the first phase of a new city center for Kuala Lumpur. The brief specified two towers that had to express the traditions and character of Malaysia.

Pelli turned for inspiration to Islam, the religion of the majority of Malaysians and a defining factor in the nation's outlook. The ground plan of each tower is based on an eight-pointed star, a typical Islamic motif, formed by two intersecting squares. Pelli incorporated a semi-circle into each corner formed by the intersecting squares, so that rounded and square facets alternate. He then inserted a very small semicircle into the new corners created between each of these facets.

The geometry of this plan becomes dazzlingly complex when thrust upward in three dimensions and cross-hatched by the repeated horizontals of the 88 floor levels. The ribbed and rippled effect of the exterior is amplified by the continuous strips of window glass and the sunshades projecting above the windows, which enhance the play of light and shadow while fending off the tropical sun.

The towers taper in a series of steps above the 60th floor; the first step is a vertical section, while the walls of the subsequent six floors are inclined toward the center at a gentle angle. The 161 foot spires give the towers their edge on the Sears Tower. Although the inspiration for the shape of the towers is Islamic, the summits are reminis-

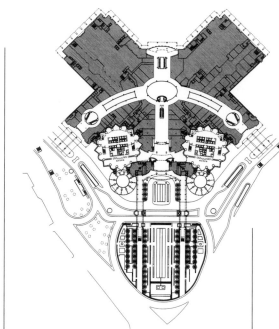

FROM THE GROUND UP The ground plan of the complex shows that the towers occupy only a comparatively small portion of the Petronas complex. They appear as the two flower-like discs at the lower end of the grey-shaded area, which represents the X-shaped main building.

WHAT A VIEW! The Skydeck observation suite atop the Sears Tower, from which 4 states can be seen, is host to 1.5 million visitors every year.

AMERICA'S TALLEST BUILDING

The Sears Tower in Chicago stands 1,454 feet tall, making it the tallest building in the United States and the second tallest in the world behind the Petronas Towers in Kuala Lumpur (1,483 feet). Designed by the architects Skidmore, Owings and Merrill, construction for the Sears Tower began in August of 1970 and ended on May 3, 1973. Starting with a hole over 100 feet deep, workers laid the foundation of 200 circular caissons into the bedrock. Premade steel in 15 x 25 foot sections called "Christmas Trees" were put into place and the Tower was built at the rate of about two floors a week. Over two million cubic feet of concrete were used in the foundation—enough to create a highway five miles long and eight lanes wide. Elevators had to be used to haul the concrete from ground level to the heights above. As the Tower rose higher, it took workers longer to get up and down from their work places. This made the creation of special kitchens part of the way up the Tower a necessity rather than a luxury. Another problem, albeit a more dangerous one, was the Windy City living up to its name—construction had to be halted at times with winds blowing so hard that workers could not stand up, much less move on the beams. However, despite these and other obstacles, the Sears Tower opened as the world's tallest building—a distinction it would hold for 23 years.

cent of Buddhist *stupas*, the domed shrines that form an integral part of Southeast Asia's religious and cultural heritage.

At the 41st and 42nd floor levels, some 560 feet above the ground, the two towers are joined by a "skybridge," which links a pair of "skylobbies" containing executive dining areas, conference suites and a *surau* (prayer room). The two main towers provide over 4 million square feet of office space, but this is not the sole function of the development. At their base is an extensive complex mostly given over to a shopping center, a concert hall, art gallery, conference center and entertainment facilities.

The dangers of creating such costly and high-profile showpieces became evident within two years of the towers' completion. A stock market and currency crisis in September 1997 had the "tiger economies" of Southeast Asia on the run after an era of boom. This may have been a temporary setback for 2020 Vision, but it demonstrated that there is a fine line between a symbol of prestige and a white elephant. However, Malaysia can take comfort from the fact that, by and large, architecture has a far longer agenda than the cycles of the world economy.

PLEASURE AND LEISURE

UNBOUNDED BY THE DEMANDS AND COM-PLEXITIES OF DOMESTIC OR WORKING LIFE, MUSEUM AND GALLERY ARCHITECTURE, AND THAT OF SPORTS STADIUMS, HAS PRODUCED SOME OF THE MOST IMAGINATIVE AND INNOVATIVE CONSTRUCTIONS OF THE CENTURY. IN THESE BUILDINGS, THE SPACE WITHIN IS ALL-IMPORTANT, INSPIRING SOME BREATHTAKING FEATS OF CONSTRUCTION, AND HIGHLY CONTROVERSIAL LIBERTIES WITH ARCHITECTURAL TRADITIONS.

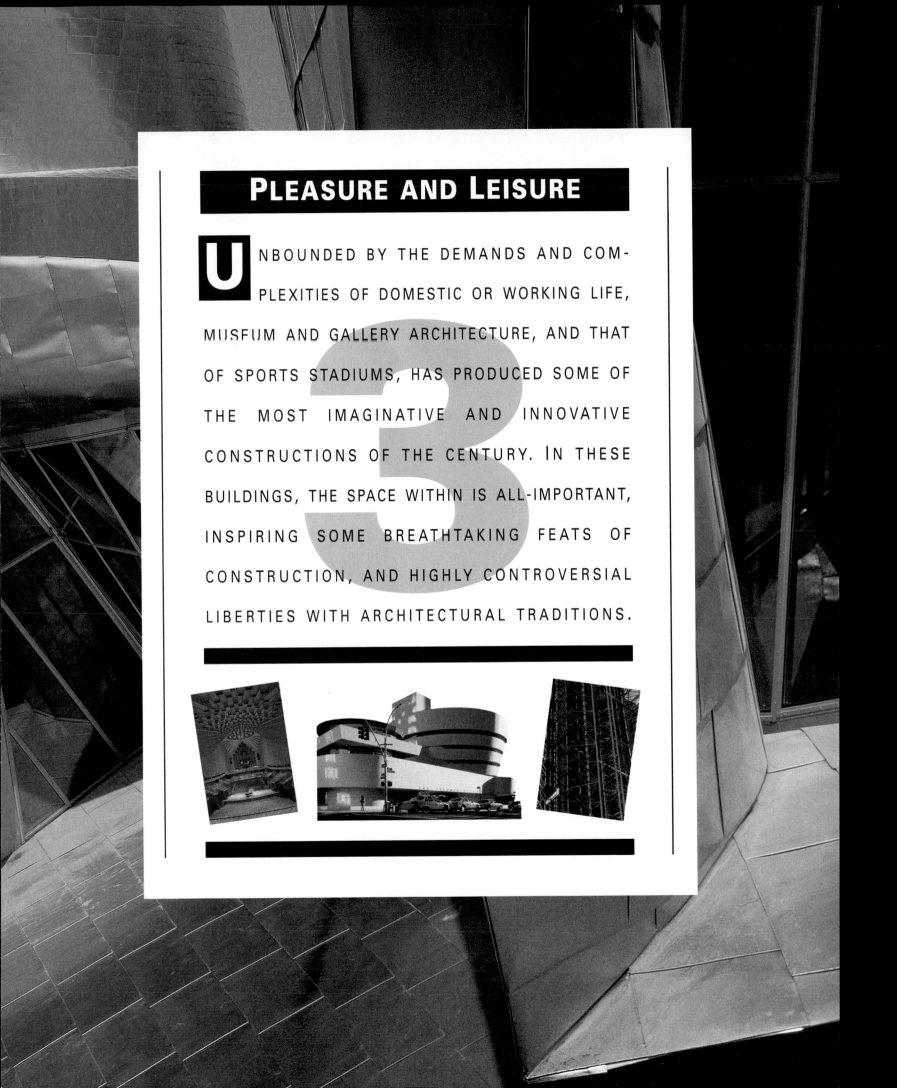

DE LA WARR PAVILION

A SOCIALIST POLITICAL PROGRAM LAY BEHIND THIS BRAVE ADVENTURE WITH MODERNISM

The 35-year-old Herbrand Sackville, 9th Earl De La Warr, was driven by a vision. In 1934, as the foundation stone was laid for the new seaside pavilion that would bear his name, he asked: "How better could we dedicate ourselves today than by gathering round this new venture of ours, a venture which is part of a great national movement virtually to found a new industry—the industry giving that relaxation, that pleasure, that culture, which hitherto the gloom and dreariness of British resorts have driven our fellow countrymen to seek in foreign lands?" Earl De La Warr was an active politician, and a minister in Ramsay MacDonald's Labor government; in 1932-4 he served as mayor of Bexhill, where he was a large landowner. Like many sympathetic to modernist architecture, he believed that design could help to precipitate social change. With this in mind, in 1933 he launched an architectural competition for the centerpiece of his plan, a multipurpose resort. It was won by the partnership of Erich Mendelsohn (1887-1953) and Serge Chermayeff (1900-96).

Mendelsohn, who had fled Nazi Germany in 1933, was a celebrated but controversial German architect, famed for his use of inventive, sculptural designs incorporating strident horizontals and clean-cut curves.

CRUISE SHIP ON LAND The pavilion echoes the streamlined shapes of liners of the 1930s, evoking associations with the leisurely pace and comfort of cruises and Atlantic crossings.

Chermayeff was of Russian origin, but had come to school in England in 1910 and then stayed on, carving out a name for himself as a leading furniture and interior designer.

Work began in 1934 and was completed two years later. With its flat roofs, large blank walls and floor-to-ceiling windows, it

CURVED ELEGANCE The curving staircase and its stainless-steel handrails bring a touch of dynamism to the entrance lobby.

was innovative and arresting. It contained all the elements deemed necessary for a modern, hygienic leisure complex, with roof decks for sunbathing and deck games, a theater, auditorium, conference hall, restaurant with dance floor, tea lounge, library, reading room and bar.

While widely praised in the national and architectural press, in some quarters of Bexhill the pavilion caused disbelief. It was a bold example of modernist architecture—a phenomenon that was rare in Britain, and even less understood. The pavilion never recovered from under-use during the Second World War, and was tampered with in ensuing decades. Since 1989, however, it has undergone a massive restoration program, and has won a new generation of admirers.

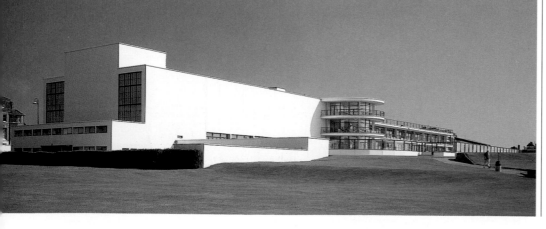

GUGGENHEIM MUSEUM, NEW YORK

AS AN OCTOGENARIAN, FRANK LLOYD WRIGHT OVERSAW ONE OF HIS MOST INVENTIVE CREATIONS

Frank Lloyd Wright believed that the highest form of art is architecture. Not surprisingly, therefore, when he turned his hand to designing an art gallery, he came up with a flamboyant tour de force that is a serious match for the art displayed within it. The Guggenheim Museum on New York's Fifth Avenue was greeted as one of the most astonishing buildings of its day when it was opened in 1959.

It was a controversial idea from the very beginning. Wright had begun to play with the concept of a spiral-based gallery in the early 1940s, a few years after completing Fallingwater, in Pennsylvania. In 1947, Solomon R. Guggenheim, the scion of a large family of wealthy industrialists, commissioned Wright to put the concept into practice. Since the 1920s, Guggenheim had been amassing a formidable collection of modern art—works by Picasso, Braque, Kandinsky, Léger, Chagall, Modigliani and many others—and needed a place to display his art in public.

THE WHITE SNAIL To many visitors, the museum's shape recalls the spiral of a snail shell, an image that conforms to the spirit of Wright's "organic modernism."

The building's history began with a long series of wrangles and delays over building codes, fire regulations, costs and policy changes by the Guggenheim Foundation. After the death of Solomon Guggenheim in 1949 the plan stalled, but was revived in 1955, by which time Wright was 86 years old. He died four years later, just five months before the museum—"my optimistic ziggurat," as he put it—was officially opened.

Ramps and spirals

The plan evolved by Wright was both logical and ingenious, combining his theories of "organic modernism" with his old interest in creating fluid and adaptable space within buildings. Visitors are whisked up to the top of the building in elevators, and they then descend along the gentle ramps that twist in a gradually tightening cantilevered spiral around the walls of the central atrium.

Temporary exhibitions are displayed on the outer walls that line the ramps, while views over the parapets lead across the great interior space. A selection of the immense permanent collection of more than 4,000 paintings, drawings and sculptures is displayed in two galleries located off the ramps at the fourth

ABSTRACT ART The cantilevered interior ramps create a tiered and corrugated effect, reaching up to the web of glass that fills the central atrium with natural light.

and second levels. After walking for a quarter of a mile down the ramps, visitors reach the exit at the base of the atrium.

The invigorating and complex interior is broadcast by the dynamic exterior. The curved tiers of poured and sprayed concrete create a vivid and otherworldly contrast to the traditional mansion blocks that surround the museum, creating an oasis of contemplation amid the street life of New York City.

DISNEYLAND

**THE FIRST OF THE WORLD'S MODERN THEME PARKS
WAS CREATED BY THE MASTER OF FILM FANTASY**

The guiding light of Walt Disney was imagination. He did not invent the animated cartoon, but he turned it into a mainstream feature of popular culture, and elevated it to a genre that could make legitimate claims to art. He was the first to put sound and color into animated films, using his own voice in *Steamboat Willie* (1928), which became famous as the cartoon that introduced Mickey Mouse to the world. It was the film, also, that turned around his career—from a skilled draughtsman and struggling maker of cartoons in Hollywood to the director of a major and powerful enterprise of international renown.

Riding on his wave of success with Mickey and Minnie, Goofy, Pluto and Donald Duck, in 1937 Disney took his biggest risk yet: he created the first full-length animated feature film, *Snow White and the Seven Dwarfs*, a project that cost $1.5 million. Previously, cartoons had appeared in supporting roles, as small, if much cherished, items at the movies, shown before the main film. Hollywood and the public were skeptical that a full-length feature cartoon could possibly succeed. But *Snow White* was a runaway success, and other full-length Disney classics followed, such as *Pinocchio* (1940), *Dumbo* (1941) and *Bambi* (1942).

In the postwar era, Disney enlarged the scope of his filmmaking to include nature films, and conventional films of such children's classics as *Treasure Island* (1950). His deep belief in the power of imagination and storytelling to create a world of enchantment—a world that would appeal to adults and children alike—prompted him to attempt to translate this world into a real, three-dimensional experience, sowing the seed of the first modern "theme park."

Black Sunday

Disneyland opened on Sunday, July 17, 1955, in an 85 acre landscaped park in Anaheim, 27 miles southeast of Los Angeles and Hollywood. Costing $17 million to construct, it had 18 principal attractions, the most famous of them all being Sleeping Beauty Castle. A fantasy in concrete and steel, it was modelled loosely on Neuschwanstein, the fairy-tale neo-Gothic castle built by King Ludwig II of Bavaria in the 1870s.

Visitors entered the park through "Main Street, U.S.A.," an idealized vision of a main street in small-town America in 1900, complete with shops and horse-drawn carriages. There were rides, such as the spinning teacups of the Mad Tea Party, and Peter Pan boats, and trips on a stern-wheeler paddle-steamer, evoking the lazy Mississippi days of Tom Sawyer. There were parades of the Disneyland Marching Band, summer firework displays, and the world's first 360° movie theater, in which the audience was surrounded by images projected by a set of 11 (later 9) synchronized projectors. Above

FANTASYLAND One of the original features of the park, Sleeping Beauty Castle is the gateway to Fantasyland, where characters from the Disney classics are brought to life in a collection of attractions.

SPLASH MOUNTAIN An artificial mountain was created to provide a spectacular setting for one of Disneyland's most popular rides.

all, children could see and shake hands with Disney's much-loved animated characters, such as Mickey Mouse and Snow White.

Flush with the spending power of America's postwar boom, families flocked to Disneyland in the thousands. In fact, the opening day attracted so many people— invited and uninvited—that it was some thing of a disaster. A 17 mile traffic jam built up on the Santa Ana freeway, several of the new rides broke down, and many of the refreshment stalls ran out of food and drink. Walt Disney spent the day travelling around the park with the ABC television personality Ronald Reagan, whose show was broadcast to 90 million television viewers.

(Seven years later Reagan would launch a political career that would take him all the way to the presidency.) When Disney learned how badly the day had gone for many of his public, he labelled it "Black Sunday." But just seven weeks later, Disneyland received its millionth visitor; over 400 million people have visited since it opened.

The Disney theme park empire has continued to grow. Its complex of parks at Orlando, Florida, first opened in 1971, and was followed by new parks in Tokyo (1983) and Paris (1992). Meanwhile, the original Disneyland has continued to grow and develop. It now employs a workforce of 12,000 at peak times, operating more than 60 attractions in eight themed "lands"; these include such favorites as the Haunted Mansion, Splash Mountain and the Indiana Jones Experience. New space-oriented rides were created for Tomorrowland's relaunch in 1998. As Walt Disney himself put it: "Disneyland will never be completed—as long as there is imagination in the world."

ARCHITECTURE OF FANTASY

When it was first built, Disneyland was so completely at odds with contemporary architecture that it was not considered in terms of architecture at all. During the 1950s, avant-garde architects were grappling with the lessons of the Bauhaus, and developing the first highly refined, glass-box office buildings, such as Lever House and the Seagram Building. At the time, it would have been heretical to suggest that "serious"architecture could digress from the stricture that form must reflect function.

Since then, there has been a radical reassessment of what architecture can and should do. "Postmodernism," which evolved in the 1970s, brought a new playfulness to buildings, permitting bold and inventive shapes that had little or nothing to do with the building's function.

New technology and new materials now give architects a free hand to create virtually whatever shapes they want; and nowhere are they given a freer hand than in Las Vegas, Nevada, where promoters of casinos and entertainment vie with each other to produce the most fantastical themed environments. A black glass pyramid and sphinx-shaped parking garage dominate the Luxor Hotel. Acrobats and trapeze artists perform nonstop in the big-top casino-hotel called Circus Circus. There are classical statues and Pompeiian murals in Caesar's Palace, where staff are dressed as Roman centurions; buccaneers stage live sea battles at Treasure Island; and there are prowling white tigers and simulated volcanic eruptions every two hours at the Mirage.

Rather than being restricted to a single theme, the New York, New York hotel brings an idealized evocation of a whole city under one roof, with the full ethnic range of New York's restaurants, streets with outdoor cafés, fake fire hydrants, graffiti, litter and manhole covers emitting steam—even a one-fifth scale reconstruction of the Brooklyn Bridge. For those who miss that edge of excitement of the real city, a rollercoaster ride leaves from the casino and shoots up to 203 feet high around the cluster of scaled-down skyscrapers that house the hotel's 2,034 rooms.

THE LITTLE APPLE "The Greatest City in Las Vegas" is how the hotel and casino complex New York, New York is promoted. Behind the half-size Statue of Liberty are replicas of New York landmarks, such as Grand Central Station and some of the most famous skyscrapers.

SYDNEY OPERA HOUSE

A VISIONARY CHOICE IN 1957 PROVIDED SYDNEY WITH A BUILDING OF WORLD STATURE

A small handful of buildings and monuments in the world rank as international icons: the Parthenon, the Taj Mahal, the Eiffel Tower, Big Ben, the Statue of Liberty and their peers. They are the elite few, readily understood as symbols of their city or nation. The Sydney Opera House ranks among them, one of the few 20th-century monuments to achieve this status. Its setting is spectacular. Sydney Opera House sits on a promontory on the south side of the bay, close to the Sydney Harbor Bridge, and in front of the shaded parks of Government House and the Royal Botanic Gardens.

In the 1950s, an international competition was launched to find the best design for a new performing arts center. Among the 233 entries from 32 countries one stood out. Sketches showed a cluster of curvaceous shells—simple but strikingly innovative. This

LEND ME YOUR EARS   The cluster of shells creates a unique sculptural profile that is suggestive of fine acoustics.

entry, by the Dane Jørn Utzon (b.1918), was proclaimed the winner in January 1957. Utzon won the prize of $10,000 and the contract to see through the construction of the building—projected at the time to cost

WORK IN PROGRESS An early model, demonstrated by Utzon in 1958, has an angular roof structure. His drawing of 1960 shows a move to more rounded shapes.

SETTING THE SCENE The Concert Hall is lined with Australian woods: white birch plywood for the wall panels and darker brush box for the stage and raised seating areas.

THE ENGINEER BEHIND THE SCENES

The engineering of the Sydney Opera House was handled by the British company, Ove Arup & Partners. The engineer Professor Derek Walker remembers Ove Arup giving a talk about the Sydney Opera House in the days before Utzon's resignation in 1966.

"The memory I retain of Ove in crisis is the clipped, no nonsense, slightly weary delivery as he turned around and around in his hand the wooden sphere illustrating the geometric order of the designs for the shells. Ove knew instinctively that the intuitive grasp of architectural and engineering fusion sat easily in his hands—the quality was going to be fine because the old man said so! It was quite anachronistic, a re-enactment of the old virtues, the same logical, precise, professional, dispassionate concern for a good product.

"Knowledge is still the engineer's solace in crisis, and fortunately Ove was able to tweak the invention and research needed to achieve solutions. The legacy of Stephenson, Paxton and Brunel [leading British engineers of the 19th century] surfaced instantly, and Arups did what they normally do when confronted with complexity and a seemingly endless series of problems—they solved them."

about $7 million. Unfortunately, his original design posed enormous practical difficulties: all solutions for turning his sketches into reality ran into insurmountable engineering problems, unacceptable compromises to the function of the building, or prohibitive costs.

Construction work went ahead in March 1959 and 580 concrete piers were sunk more than 60 feet into the soft ground of the littoral to provide foundations. Over the next four years the foundation and the base, or "podium," started to take shape, but arguments over the construction of the shells continued. The plans had to be modified; the costs rose.

In the end the political, financial and engineering bickering proved too much for Utzon, and he resigned from the project in 1966. The architecture was subsequently handled by the Australian partnership Hall, Littlemore and Todd, but it was the engineering consultant Ove Arup who found the key to the solution: the shell clusters had to be made of sections of the same sphere. Then their segments and panels could be precast to uniform specifications, greatly reducing the costs, which by 1973 had spiraled to $48 million. All the while, work was continuing. Precast concrete sections, each weighing up to 15½ tons, were strung together with tensioned steel cables to form the frames of the roof shells. By the end of 1967, the shells were complete.

The first performance took place on September 28, 1973, and the building was officially opened by Queen Elizabeth II on October 20, 1973. There are four auditoriums in all, in two rows of shells that converge at the landward side. The largest is the 2,690 seat Concert Hall (beneath the tallest shell, which rises to 220 feet above sea level). The Opera Theater seats 1,547 people, the Drama Theater seats 544 and the Playhouse seats 398.

ROOF TILES The shells were constructed on concrete sections based on a spherical module and clad in 1 million ceramic tiles.

THE CLIMATRON

**THE GEODESIC DOME WAS ADOPTED TO CREATE
A CELEBRATED CONSERVATORY**

Founded in the mid 19th century, the Missouri Botanical Garden in St. Louis is among the oldest botanical gardens in the United States. But it is also famous for its remarkable conservatory, one of the largest and most successful applications of the geodesic dome, a structure that caught the imagination of designers and the general public in the 1950s and 1960s.

Geodesic refers to the geometry of curved surfaces. In the case of geodesic domes, the curvature is created by bolting together prefabricated polygonal units. The Missouri Botanical Garden's geodesic dome was built in 1960, at a time when the concept was still comparatively new. Designed by a local St. Louis architectural partnership, and composed of 2,425 panes of Plexiglas set in an aluminum frame, it was the first geodesic dome to be used as a conservatory. The shape and structure suits the task well: it encompasses a large interior space free of columns or other supports; it provides optimum light; and the climate within can be precisely controlled. For this reason, the Missouri Botanical Garden's dome has been named the Climatron—from "climate control technology."

Microclimate technology

Reaching up to 70 feet in the center, and 175 feet in diameter, the Climatron has 24,000 square feet of floor space, the equivalent of more than eight tennis courts. Growing within this area are more than 1,200 species of plants, which include orchids, bromeliads, coconut palms and bananas, coffee and cacao trees, all placed in a landscaped setting with rocky cliffs, waterfalls, pools and walkways, and bridges leading through the tree canopy. The high humidity and temperature—averaging about 70°F—are maintained by a computerized climate-control system. To retain more daytime solar heat overnight, the original Plexiglas panes were replaced by a heat-strengthened sandwich of glass and plastic during a major renovation in 1988-90, the only interruption in nearly 40 years of constant use.

OUTSIDE IN In contrast to the Ancient World's Hanging Gardens of Babylon, the Climatron encloses an interior world of tropical plants, nurtured in a bubble of warmth.

NATIONAL MUSEUM OF ANTHROPOLOGY, MEXICO CITY

A NEW MUSEUM WAS BUILT FOR THE WORLD'S GREATEST COLLECTION OF PRE-COLUMBIAN ART

Hérnan Cortés conquered the Aztec capital, Tenochtitlán, in 1519, and within five years was master of all Mexico. By that time, the conquerors had begun the systematic destruction of the Aztec civilization, and those of the Aztecs' predecessors across 2,000 years of history: the Olmecs, the Maya, Teotihuacan, the Toltecs, the Zapotecs and the Mixtecs. The ruins of Tenochtitlán soon provided the foundations for the new capital, Mexico City.

It was only in the late 18th century that the extraordinary riches of the indigenous civilizations—the pyramid temples, stone sculptures, pottery, mosaics, jewelry and masks—began

LIGHT AND SHADE Vasquez made the most of contrasts of light with the textures of the façades and in the two zones of the central patio, one shaded and the other open.

to be unveiled. In 1825, a National Museum was established in Mexico City to house a growing collection of artifacts.

By the early 1960s, this had become the world's greatest collection of Mesoamerican treasures, and the need to rehouse them became urgent. But the plan was not simply to create a museum of the archaeological past. It was to be an anthropological museum that would tie pre-Conquest Mexico to the enduring traditions of the indigenous people. Mexico's leading architect, Pedro Ramírez Vasquez (b.1919), was appointed to oversee the design. His solution placed the new "Museo Nacional de Antropología" among the foremost museums in the world.

The patio umbrella

Space is a key characteristic of the museum. Set in Chapultepec Park, once a garden retreat for the Spanish viceroys, its central feature is a 600 foot long inner patio. Part of this is open to the sky. The remainder is shaded by a vast "umbrella" sheathed in aluminum and resting on a single pillar—the largest such structure in the world.

The collections, divided by regions and cultures—Toltec, Maya and so forth—are housed in pavilions surrounding the patio.

On the ground floor are the archaeological collections; above are the ethnological collections relating to subsequent and modern cultures. The culmination is the Sala Mexica (Aztec Hall) at the far end of the patio. This contains treasures of world renown, including alarming relics of Aztec sacrifice, and the huge round "Sun Stone" recording Aztec cosmology, which was found in 1790 in the main square of old Tenochtitlán.

The patio provides visitors with a place to relax on their progression around the 3 miles of galleries, although they can follow an interior circuit through the halls. Ramírez Vasquez says that the courtyard concept was inspired by Mayan architecture, and the blend of modernity and tradition can be seen throughout the building. The firmly delineated rectangles and the polished glass and stone surfaces of the interior are offset by textured ceiling and wall panels of pierced copper and carved woods, enlivened by specially commissioned mosaics, murals and tapestries.

Despite its size and the immense task of shipping in and displaying the exhibits—some of them weighing over 100 tons—the National Museum of Anthropology took just 19 months to build. It was inaugurated on Mexican Independence Day, September 17, 1964.

LOUISIANA SUPERDOME

A STADIUM WITH THE WORLD'S LARGEST DOME BECAME THE FOCUS OF URBAN RENEWAL

It was the vision of one man, New Orleans businessman Dave Dixon, that brought the vast Louisiana Superdome in to land like a flying saucer among a set of neglected freightyards and industrial warehouses close to the center of his city. Dixon had campaigned hard during the 1960s to upgrade the city's facilities for mounting professional football, a dream that was eventually realized when the Louisiana Superdome first opened its doors on August 3, 1975.

New Orleans now had a world-class multipurpose stadium capable of seating 76,791 spectators for football games, and rising to 97,365 for conventions. The superlatives began to roll in: the Superdome has hosted more Super Bowl championships for professional football than any other stadium; it has achieved record attendances for basketball games; 80,000 children came to Pope John Paul II's youth rally in September 1987; the Rolling Stones concert in 1981 attracted an audience of 87,500, still a record for any indoor concert. With a diameter of 680 feet, the Louisiana Superdome is also in the record books as it is the largest dome in the world.

Raising the roof

Built over four years, beginning in August 1971, the construction of the Superdome involved a number of technological innovations that pushed building experience to new limits. The vast internal space covering a total area of 13 acres—an unprecedented span for a steel building—is unobstructed by any columns or posts.

The design, conceived by architect Buster Curtis, is based on an outer tension ring supported by 96 columns, which rest on piles driven deep into the swampland ground beneath the foundations. This tension ring supports the domed roof as well as the curved steel walls, which incline outward toward the base to correspond to the direction of the downward thrust. Internal braces and K-braces around the perimeter of the roof give the structure extra support and resistance against high winds.

The roof, which rises to 273 feet at the center, is made of overlapping triangles of steel covered with layers of polyurethane and synthetic waterproofing. When it was being built, the roof was supported by scaffolding and jacks. These were finally removed on June 12, 1973, to allow the dome to stand free for the first time—an anxious moment for all concerned. But the architects and construction engineers had calculated correctly: the building worked.

The climatic impact on a 10 acre roof had to be carefully accommodated in the design. To prevent it from ballooning upward as a result of air pressure within, the roof is counterbalanced by a 75 ton gondola that hangs from the center, which also houses sound and lighting equipment. So large is the quantity of rainwater collected over the roof's surface area that it has to be gathered into 345,000 gallon gutter tubs around the perimeter of the roof and then fed slowly away so that it does not overwhelm the drainage system. To take account of the

BUTTONED UP The blank exterior of the Superdome gives little hint of its vast interior space, nor of the structure that supports it.

expansion and contraction of the roof area due to heating and cooling, the tension ring is mounted on rocker bearings, allowing movement of up to 3 inches from the center.

Mardi Gras

The stadium is used for football (it is the home field of the New Orleans Saints), basketball, boxing and many other sports, as well as rock concerts, ice-skating spectaculars, truck-pulling contests, political conventions, trade shows and exhibitions, and the annual Extravaganza Mardi Gras Parade. The concrete surface of the arena has to be dressed accordingly for each occasion—with ice, wooden floors, earth, stages, and the artificial turf that has been nicknamed "Mardi grass."

Likewise, the seating has to be arranged to suit each event. The seats in the immediate proximity of the arena are electronically operated, and can be moved into an appropriate position at the flick of a switch. The remainder of the seating is set out permanently in an elliptical shape within the circle of the dome, and raked up to 65 feet. This allows space beneath and around the seating for the Superdome's many other facilities, which include cocktail lounges and bars, a broadcasting studio, 52 convention rooms and four large ballrooms, which double as exhibition halls. Many of these facilities are soundproofed so that events can take place in them while the main arena is being used.

SPECTATOR SPORTS

Sports stadiums have attracted the attention of architects since the time of the ancient Greeks and Romans, but in the 20th century they have broken all records for both quantity and scale. The largest open-air stadium, the Strahov Stadium in Prague, completed in 1934, seats 240,000 spectators; the largest covered stadium, the Aztec Stadium in Mexico City (1968), can seat 107,000.

The design of covered stadiums was propelled forward by the development of reinforced concrete, notably at the hands of the Italian, Pier Luigi Nervi (1891-1979), who produced two spectacular stadiums for the 1960 Rome Olympics. But perhaps the most celebrated of all, for their daring innovation and elegance, is the pair of stadiums at Yoyogi designed by the Japanese architect Kenzo Tange (b.1913) for the 1964 Tokyo Olympics. The larger hall, seating 15,000 spectators for swimming events, has a sweeping, curvaceous roof supported on cables on the same principle as a suspension bridge. The smaller hall, seating 4,000 spectators for basketball, has a spiral suspended roof, shaped like the shell of a snail. Both are supremely engineered, and enhance sporting functions with a sculptural beauty that is unmatched elsewhere. Since the 1960s, new roofing materials, such as fiberglass and acrylic, supported by steel cables, have been used for the service of sports, while the 80,000 seat Pontiac Silverdome in Michigan has a fiber-glass roof supported by air pressure alone.

OLYMPIC GRACE Kenzo Tange's stadium for the Tokyo Olympics of 1964 represents a high point in stadium architecture. The graceful form of this concrete and steel building expresses the carefully engineered tensions within its structure.

The stadium also has 137 luxurious box suites around the central arena, which are used for corporate entertainment.

Initially the Superdome project met with intense political opposition. It was widely felt that the money would be better spent on social projects rather than on a massive sports stadium. In the end, construction cost about $165 million, but the stadium has earned its keep many times over. Although operated by a private company, the Superdome remains publicly owned, originally funded by local taxes and private subscription.

The people of New Orleans are proud to claim that the project represents the first example of urban renewal that can be directly attributable to a sports stadium. The vast number of visitors attending events at the Superdome—from all over the United States and abroad—has encouraged the growth of hotels, restaurants, shopping malls and office developments around the stadium and across the city. It has been estimated that revenue totalling more than the construction cost comes into New Orleans during one single week when the Super Bowl is held there, and that the Superdome has brought in $4.6 billion in its first 20 years of operation.

GAME FOR ANYTHING The scale of the interior accommodates a full-sized field for football. A high degree of flexibility has been built into the design to cater for a multiplicity of year-round events.

THE POMPIDOU CENTER

WITH ITS EXPOSED PIPEWORK, THIS CULTURAL CENTER BECAME AN ICON OF 1970S ARCHITECTURE

In 1914 the futurist manifesto *L'archittetura futurista* declared in its typical storming style: "The futuristic house must be like a giant machine. The lift should no longer hide itself like a tapeworm in the shaft of a stairwell; the now superfluous stairs must disappear and the lifts should rise like snakes of iron and glass."

It could have been a prediction for the building that suddenly emerged in the drab Beaubourg district of Paris between 1971 and 1977. The Centre National d'Arts et de Culture Georges Pompidou, otherwise known as the Pompidou Center or Beaubourg Center , became a cause célèbre. This multicoloured confection of steel ribs and glass was reviled by some as an atrocious affront to the traditional fabric of Paris: "Paris has its own monster, just like the one

FULL SERVICE The service elements are color-coded: the water systems in green, electric-wiring ducts in yellow, air conditioning in blue, the escalator and elevators in red, and the ventilation ducts in white.

in Loch Ness," raged the daily newspaper *Le Figaro*. But it was championed by many others as daring and uncompromisingly modern in the best French tradition, and just what the stagnating arts world of Paris required. The public voted with their feet: the Pompidou Center soon became the most visited site in Paris, outstripping the Eiffel Tower and the Louvre combined.

Driving visions

The idea for this new cultural center was hatched by President Pompidou at the start of his presidency in 1969. A great enthusiast for modern art, he envisioned a building that would bring art closer to ordinary people, a kind of "department store for culture." Access and flexibility were key elements in the brief. An international competition attracted 681 entries from 50 countries, and the winner was the youthful partnership of the British architect Richard Rogers and the Italian Renzo Piano (b.1937). The Pompidou Center represented the first major breakthrough on the international stage for both architects.

Georges Pompidou died in office in 1974, but his wife Claude took over the political reins to drive the project through. It was completed in 1977, and provided a fitting memorial to her husband.

EXTERIOR VIEW Visitors using the escalators have a strong sense of the building's location, as well as fine views over the city.

The structure is essentially a simple five-story rectangle of steel, concrete and glass, supported by crossbeams and two rows of 14 steel columns, the columns being evenly spaced 43 feet apart. In order to create a large, unencumbered interior space, the crossbeams (or horizontal floor trusses) must

THE MILLENNIUM DOME

Looking ahead to the year 2000, the Conservative government under Prime Minister John Major decided that Britain should mark the start of the new millennium with a grand public celebration to match the Great Exhibition of 1851, or the Festival of Britain of 1951. A site was chosen: 300 acres of derelict industrial land by the River Thames in Greenwich, to the east of the City of London. This area was considered appropriate because of its proximity not only to the heart of London, but also to the Greenwich Observatory, on which Greenwich Mean Time and the world's time zones are based.

Richard Rogers Partnership, with its proven ability in creating exhibition spaces, was commissioned to design a huge, covered exhibition area and auditorium. The "Millennium Dome"—the world's largest supported dome—consists of a vast Teflon-coated tent, held up by cables suspended from 12 angled steel spars.

In 1997, the new Labor government agreed to take on the project and the bill, estimated at over $1 billion. But it was a race against time: to build the dome and to organize an exhibition of suitable stature and complexity to draw the public.

The long-term future of the Millennium Dome remains uncertain, but Rogers sees it as part of a broader revitalization of the River Thames as a hitherto underexploited asset of London.

TEST-TUBE ARCHITECTURE Visitors can inspect the structure of the building as they move through transparent tubes around the exterior.

RINGING IN THE MILLENNIUM The 12 supporting spars were the first elements of the Millennium Dome to be erected. The tent-like dome rises to less than half their height, suspended on cables. The spars and cables remain exposed as an integral part of the design.

stretch unsupported for 157 feet. This demands an unusual degree of flexibility to prevent overstressing, so the crossbeams are attached to rocker beams or "gerberettes," which balance on pivots on the vertical columns, to allow for movement. These are counterbalanced by an external structure of smaller columns and diagonal braces held together by flexible pin-joints, set 20 feet out from the body of the building.

The complex engineering problems of this highly technical construction were resolved with the close cooperation of the consultants Ove Arup & Partners, but they also contribute to a deliberate statement of architectural style. For example, the external cross-bracing creates a distinctive web-like appearance on the outside, and provides a note of delicacy and structural lightness.

Rogers and Piano rejected the architectural convention by which the functional parts of the building were hidden away. They wanted the public to be able to read their building like a manual, and the service elements are thrust to the exterior of the building. The building contains no references to architectural styles of the past—only to its own state-of-the-art technology.

The Pompidou Center was expressly designed to be a lively and invigorating venue, easily adaptable to a variety of uses. The Musée Nationale d'Art Moderne, containing an important collection of paintings from the Fauvists on, was transferred here, but this is the only set piece. Other spaces are used for a variety of temporary exhibits; there is a music school and recording studio, a center for the integration of art, design and industry, and a movie theater. One of the most visited sections is the Bibliothèque Public d'Information, which gives public access to an open-stack library and over 2,000 periodicals.

The exterior space around the Pompidou Center adds to the building's appeal. The gently tilted Plateau Beaubourg provides an arena for street theater, performers, acrobats, jugglers, escapologists and sword swallowers, who bring their own color and animation, creating an appropriately informal open-air foyer to this busy and highly successful cultural center.

URBAN OASIS At night the Center and its surrounding buildings are unified by clever use of lighting in the Plateau Beaubourg.

LOUVRE PYRAMID

HAVING GREETED IT AS AN ATROCITY, PARISIANS WARMED TO THE GLASS PYRAMID AT THE LOUVRE

The Louvre in Paris has been a public art gallery since the revolutionary days of 1793. The buildings date back to a 12th-century royal fortress, which was subsequently much aggrandized by successive kings and emperors. The gallery itself was renovated in the 1880s, since when it remained virtually unchanged for a century.

As a result, the Louvre—housing one of the world's most celebrated collections and visited by 6 million people a year—had become notorious for its antiquated and inconvenient layout. It was large enough to display only a portion of its vast collections, a significant percentage of which had to be kept in storage or placed in other galleries on loan. The administration facilities were so poor that the gallery was often compared with "a theater without a backstage." The gallery required a radical renovation.

When François Mitterrand, the socialist leader, was elected president of France in 1981, he made the Louvre the first of his *"grands projets"*—the prestigious building projects by which French presidents can ensure their lasting legacy. He made enquiries in search of the architect best suited to this important task. Among the suggested candidates, one name came up repeatedly: Ieoh Ming Pei (b.1917), architect of the much

TIME TO REFLECT Although the pyramid is brazenly modern and geometric, while its surrounding courtyard is an ornate product of another era, the two coalesce in a shared notion of space and elegance.

admired East Building of the National Gallery in Washington, DC. Pei's solution for the Louvre was typically radical: to relocate the gallery's center of gravity in the Cour Napoléon, the courtyard that separates the two wings. To avoid compromising the unity of the existing buildings, he suggested going underground by placing the main entrance in the middle of the courtyard and providing access to the wings through a set of underground corridors flanked by galleries, a restaurant and other facilities. Most controversial of all, Pei suggested that the entrance should be covered by a large glass pyramid.

THE POLITICS OF ARCHITECTURE

At the planning stage of the Louvre Pyramid, I.M. Pei found himself embroiled in an unseemly political wrangle when detractors on the political right decried it as a tasteless socialist aberration. He was therefore no stranger to politics when he undertook to design a building for the Bank of China in Hong Kong that would make a strong impression on the Hong Kong skyline at a time when Britain had agreed to hand Hong Kong back to China in 1997. Pei, whose father had been a Bank of China employee and had fled Chinese Communism to support the republican Chiang Kai-shek, saw this as an opportunity to make a statement about reconciliation. Seventy stories high and faced with darkened glass and aluminum, his Bank of China tower was just the kind of striking landmark that the Bank of China desired.

Construction ran into a series of political problems. Normally in Hong Kong, architects and construction workers are careful to observe the omens and bidding of feng shui, the traditional system of ensuring the good fortune of a building. The Chinese communists declared that they would have none of this, and were in constant discord with their Hong Kong workforce. Worse was to come. In June 1989, Chinese students' demonstrations for democratic reform in Tiananmen Square, Beijing were brutally suppressed by the authorities. The construction workers in Hong Kong used the Bank of China tower as an appropriate place to display banners of protest. Pei likewise felt duty-bound to speak out, knowing that it would incur his client's displeasure. The ordeal became a bitter one and his good intentions for reconciliation were disappointed.

BANDED TOGETHER **The Bank of China tower in Hong Kong is based on an ingenious triangular division of the cube.**

As soon as the French press, the Parisian public, the arts administrators and critics heard about the project, they were up in arms. The idea of a glass pyramid deposited in the midst of one of France's most cherished national treasures seemed the final atrocity in a long assault by modern architects on the historic beauty of Paris. Furthermore, it was designed by a foreigner, brought in without fair competition or public consultation.

Eye for detail

Construction went ahead despite the criticism and by April 1986 the excavations were complete. Meanwhile Pei worked on the specifications for the pyramid. Fastidious as ever, he demanded a quality of glass that was clear and colorless to an unprecedented degree. It had to be thick and strong enough to match all safety requirements and security risks, which included terrorist bombs. Usually, the oxides in glass of this thickness give it a pale green hue. Pei would not accept this, and he persuaded the leading French glass manufacturers, Saint-Gobain, to carry out exhaustive research, which eventually produced glass of unique transparency. The glass was cut into 790 diamond shapes and 118 triangular shapes, and sent for assembly in Chartres, where it was fitted into aluminum frames.

The structure inside the pyramid was equally carefully engineered, with a delicate spiderweb of steel struts and cables to give the pyramid both flexibility and stability. To achieve the right degree of fine-tuning, Pei used a company that specialized in the bowstring tension systems used in state-of-the-art yacht rigging. The result is a lattice of great delicacy, with 3,000 steel joints or "knots" that create star-like points across the interior of the pyramid.

As a final flourish, Pei included a spiral staircase leading down into the galleries from the entrance level. Unsupported by columns, and engineered to minimum thinness, it presents a moment of pure architectural drama to crown the experience of entering the new Louvre. The devotion to quality is unmistakable. Not surprisingly, all but the most hardened opponents of the scheme warmed to the pyramid when it was officially opened on October 14, 1989.

GUGGENHEIM MUSEUM, BILBAO

AT THE END OF THE 20TH CENTURY, A NEW ART MUSEUM THRUST BILBAO ONTO THE WORLD STAGE

How do you draw the attention of the world's public to a city, and fix it in their minds with a strong, positive image? By commissioning a building of such thrilling appeal and daring that the city is immediately and forever associated with it.

In October 1997, the international press was filled with images of an extraordinary new building, its exterior glittering like a cluster of crushed cans. With crooked doors, bizarrely angled windows and curved walls, it might have been a set from an experimental Expressionist film of the 1920s. It seemed to have turned traditional architectural logic on its head, to be gambling with chaos and collapse. Challenging, enticing, exciting, bemusing, the Bilbao Guggenheim also looked fun, and was soon to be acclaimed as one of the great works of architecture of the late 20th century.

Bilbao is an industrial port in northern Spain—a city that previously had barely impinged on the consciousness of the world. It is also a comparatively wealthy and prosperous city, with long traditions in sea trade, shipbuilding and manufacture. In the last decades of the century, the city experienced the economic and social decay, linked to the

THE SHAPE OF THINGS TO COME The crumpled shapes of the museum speak of the freedom with which architects could work at the end of the century, freed from the limitations imposed by technology on earlier avant-garde design.

decline of heavy industry, that occurred along the "rust belt" of northern Spain. But it also showed a vigorous determination to buck the trend with a new metro railway designed by Norman Foster, and a new airport and pedestrian bridge by Santiago Calatrava, a gifted Spanish architect famed for his technical prowess.

Bilbao is also the largest city of the Basque region, which has been struggling for over half a century to assert its own identity. Distinguished from the rest of Spain by their own language, and treated cruelly during the Spanish Civil War of 1936-9, many Basques have pursued the quest for independence. The Basque terrorist organization ETA has a string of ugly kidnappings, assassinations and bomb outrages to its name.

It was in part to contest this reputation as a troubled region that the city authorities of Bilbao decided in the early 1990s to promote a new image. Their solution was to build an eye-catching cultural center of excellence that would place their city at the forefront of the contemporary art world. The Guggenheim Foundation of New York agreed to support the project, lending it their name, their expert advice and—most

" ART AND TERROR

A few days before the Bilbao Guggenheim was opened by the Spanish king, Juan Carlos, on October 18, 1997, a Basque policeman was killed at the museum by ETA terrorists. He had stumbled on their attempt to plant explosives. It seems that the Basque separatists intended to cause mayhem at the inauguration ceremony. Nonie Niesewand, writing in the London *Independent*, described how this incident cast a shadow over events:

"Two piles of flowers grow outside the main doors, which are currently sealed by security tapes. One is a 40 foot high sculpture of a Yorkshire terrier by the American artist Jeff Koons, with 60,000 pansies puncturing its green, fibrous frame and its own internal watering system causing puddles on the limestone piazza. The other is a mound of Cellophane-wrapped bouquets which mark the spot where on Monday a museum guard was shot dead by ETA, the Basque terrorist movement. The guard had stopped a van driven by three men, who shot him and drove away. Later the police found it abandoned, filled with gelignite … Tensions are running high, despite national pride in this project which has catapulted a little-known place into the international art world." "

ELEVATING ART The glimmering exterior (left), coated in quilt-like titanium sheeting, beckons the visitor to explore what lies within. The interior lives up to the promise: the soaring atrium (right) links the walkways in a delirium of architectural liberty.

importantly—providing on loan a selection of major works of art drawn from its vast collection. It was a brave and controversial move for the Bilbao authorities, who had to withstand criticism that they were buying a foreign cultural implant. Furthermore, the cost—paid largely out of city funds—was breathtaking: $100 million for the building alone, $20 million for the benefit of the Guggenheim Foundation's support, and $50 million set aside to build up a permanent collection for the museum. Bilbao hoped to recoup the outlay by attracting 400,000 tourists a year, thereby helping to kick-start the city's regeneration.

Sheathed in titanium

The chosen architect was the American Frank O. Gehry, well known for his unconventional approach to architectural forms, but also for his deft ability to meet the practical requirements of a building. He already had a track record of successful museums,

FRANK O. GEHRY

A Canadian-born American, Frank O. Gehry (b.1929) has been running his own architectural practice in Los Angeles since 1962, focusing mainly on private residences and institutions. All his best-known buildings share his iconoclastic inventiveness, combining unusual shapes and materials in surprising ways. By using cheap industrial materials—such as plywood, wire netting and corrugated iron—to decorative effect, he creates eye-catching forms that look unstable, temporary and improvised. In fact, his buildings are well engineered, and his use of unconventional materials is part of a deliberate artistic statement.

The term "deconstructivist" has been applied to Gehry's approach to architecture, a term that gained currency through an exhibition of like-minded work organized in 1988 by the veteran architect Philip Johnson. But no architects like their imagination and inventiveness to be saddled with labels. Like Utzon's Sydney Opera House and Gaudí's Templo Sagrada Familia, Gehry may have proved with his Guggenheim Museum that he is in a category of one.

including the California Aerospace Museum (1983-4) in Los Angeles.

It is the museum's exterior jumble of shapes, coated in 30,000 tiles of highly reflective titanium, that first captures the imagination. It sparkles like a rough-cut jewel in its grimy, lackluster industrial setting; its reflection bounces off the sluggish River Nervión against a line of shipping cranes. Gehry revelled in the challenge of the site. Early on in the project he declared: "To be at the bend of a working river intersected by a large bridge, and connecting the urban fabric of a fairly dense city to the river's edge with a place for modern art is my idea of heaven."

From the outside, this looks like an impossible place in which to display works of art, a criticism levelled at Frank Lloyd Wright's Guggenheim Museum in New York. However, although Gehry pays homage to Wright's museum in his design, its internal spaces have been judged considerably more accommodating to art.

Of the 19 galleries in the building, 10 are more or less conventional spaces of varying sizes. The other nine are vested with the surprise and ingenuity of the exterior, with curving walls, swooping ceiling trusses, soaring glass windows, overhead catwalks, and a kaleidoscope of intriguing architectural views through the building.

The main gallery is the largest in the world, 450 feet × 80 feet, well able to contain Richard Serra's vast walk-through sculpture of rusting sheet metal, entitled *Snake*. This is the virtue of the museum: it has a range of flexible spaces providing a sympathetic and stimulating backdrop to modern art, which is notorious for its breadth of format and scale. The museum's disadvantage is that the verve of the architecture can make the contents look mundane.

The Bilbao Guggenheim may be the building to cap a century of inventive architecture. By collapsing all traditional concepts of what a building should look like, it points the way forward for the imaginative use of new materials, and to the novel kinds of spaces that they can produce. It demonstrates that architecture can edge closer to sculpture without failing to match the needs of its users. By comparison, the playful gestures and pastiche of post-modernism seem trite—and perhaps Gehry's museum also implies that the pioneers of modernism and International Style, who launched the key architectural trends of the 20th century, may have taken themselves a little too seriously.

J. PAUL GETTY CENTER

THE WORLD'S MOST EXPENSIVE ART COMPLEX IS SET TO BECOME A CULTURAL HUB OF LOS ANGELES

When the American oil billionaire J. Paul Getty died in 1976 at the age of 83, he left in his will $700 million in Getty Oil Company stock to the trust of his museum in Malibu. This extravagant replica of the Roman Villa dei Papiri in Herculaneum contained a worthy collection of European paintings and classical antiquities, and was marvelled at as an eccentric indulgence.

By 1984, however, the J. Paul Getty Trust had acquired a very different profile. The value of the stock had grown to a staggering $4.3 billion, making it the richest art foundation in the world. Under the terms of the will, it has had to spend about $40 million a year in new acquisitions, giving it unchallenged buying power to enlarge its collection of pre-20th century art. The rest of its annual budget of $225 million is divided between a number of the trust's institutions, including centers for art conservation and restoration,

MULTILEVEL CONNECTIONS The interplay of light and shadow is accentuated by the bright California sun.

for studies in the history of art, and for the administration of its multimillion dollar international grant program.

Classic modernism

In 1984, the trust decided to bring all its activities together in a new building complex on a hilltop site of 716 acres in Brentwood, Los Angeles. The architect was the New York-based Richard Meier (b.1934), a leading proponent of "white architecture," which brought a modern slant to the classic 1920s Modernist approach of *De Stijl* and Le Corbusier.

It was to be a long haul. Meier spent the next 14 years on the J. Paul Getty Center, designing the complex of six buildings and working through a long and bruising series of planning wrangles with the Los Angeles authorities and local residents. The Center finally opened in December 1997, and was immediately hailed as one of the great museums of the 20th century. It was also by far the most expensive, estimated to have cost $700 million.

Arriving on the train that provides a shuttle service from the parking garage, visitors are presented with a serene utopian vision, like a modern interpretation of a medieval hilltop town. A series of leafy plazas and courtyards gleam in the bright California sun, surrounded by the multilayered shapes

of the buildings. These are not faced in Meier's trademark white, but in light tan aluminum panels and honey-colored Italian travertine, the result of lobbying by neighboring homeowners, who complained that pure white would be too dazzling.

The public galleries at the new Getty Center are contained in just one of the six buildings. Most of its 54 rooms follow the traditional pattern of the great national galleries—large, high-ceilinged and top-lit. They present an ever-growing collection of riches, including works by Titian, Rubens, Rembrandt, Goya, Turner, Monet, Cézanne and Van Gogh, to name but a few. Progress through the galleries is relieved by crosslinks and resting points. And here and there, the plate-glass windows allow the outside in, offering views out over landscaped gardens to the San Gabriel Mountains, and across the city of Los Angeles to the ocean.

HOUSING A LEGACY The spacious buildings and gardens of the new Getty Center overlooking Los Angeles house the late oil billionaire's art collection, along with centers for research and conservation.

MAKING CONNECTIONS

THE BRILLIANCE OF MAGNIFICENT FEATS OF TRANSPORT ENGINEERING OFTEN LIES CONCEALED WITHIN THE PRODUCT. NONETHELESS, NUMEROUS ACCOMPLISHMENTS IN THIS FIELD HAVE DRAWN THE PUBLIC'S ATTENTION, EITHER FOR THE SHEER SCALE OF THE ENTERPRISE, OR FOR THE AUDACITY OF THEIR DESIGN. BRIDGES ARE THE GREAT SHOWPIECES, AND MANY OF THIS CENTURY'S BEST HAVE BECOME WORLD-FAMOUS LANDMARKS OF QUITE BREATHTAKING BEAUTY.

SYDNEY BRIDGE CELEBRATIONS
MARCH 19TH 1932   BE THERE

PANAMA CANAL

TWO OCEANS WERE FINALLY JOINED BY A HEROIC ENGINEERING PROJECT

On October 10, 1913, President Woodrow Wilson pressed a button in the White House in Washington to detonate 40 tons of explosives 4,000 miles away. By this symbolic gesture, he removed the last natural barrier standing in the way of the completion of the Panama Canal. A week later, the first vessel made a trial run through the canal. After seven years of unrelenting toil, the dream of nearly four centuries was close to realization.

A CHANGE OF DIRECTION

Paradoxically, ships travelling through the canal from the Atlantic to the Pacific actually travel eastward. The Panama isthmus has a pronounced kink in it, and the neck of land across which the canal was built lies virtually parallel to the Equator. The exit point of the canal by Panama City on the Pacific side lies about 25 miles to the east of the entry point at Colón on the Caribbean coast.

Since the days of the Spanish conquistadores, the idea of building a canal across Central America had played on the minds of explorers, merchants, politicians and engineers. The narrow isthmus that separates the Atlantic from the Pacific—just 50 miles

EAST MEETS WEST The U.S. Pacific Fleet passing through the canal in 1919 showed the strategic implications of free movement between the Atlantic and the Pacific.

at its narrowest point—proved a costly obstacle to trade between the two. Ships from Europe and the east coast of North America had to travel around Cape Horn at the southern tip of South America to reach New Zealand, Australia, the Far East, and even the west coast of North America. A canal would cut journeys by up to 7,000 miles.

In the 1880s the French diplomat Ferdinand de Lesseps turned his attention to the problem, while still riding high on the success of his Suez Canal, built in 1859-69. For eight years, he worked to carve a path one-third of the way across the isthmus, before being defeated by the terrain, disease, a high death toll and, finally, bankruptcy.

Fresh initiative

The United States had always been interested in a canal to create a sea route to link its east and west coasts, and in 1902 the U.S. government set aside $40 million to purchase the canal concession from the French. At that time, Panama was a province of Colombia, which resisted American solicitations. But in the six months between November 1903 and April 1904, the U.S. won all it needed: it supported a revolt that achieved independence for Panama; it secured from the new Panamanian government the sovereign rights in perpetuity over a 10 mile wide canal zone; and it purchased the concession from France.

The preliminary work of surveying and

GATEWAY TO THE PACIFIC The Miraflores Locks on the Pacific side provide a two-step drop from Lake Miraflores down to sea level.

FALTERING PROGRESS A landslide in the Culebra Cut in December 1913 delayed progress in this difficult section of the canal.

THE HUMAN COST

Disease was the prime reason why Ferdinand de Lesseps failed to build his canal in 1881-9. Some 20,000 people died in the attempt, mainly from malaria and yellow fever—the "black vomit."

The Americans succeeded where de Lesseps failed, but not without cost: they lost a total of 5,060 workers to disease and accident. However, they had the advantage of knowing the causes of these diseases. In 1897, the British bacteriologist Ronald Ross proved that malaria was caused by a parasite carried by mosquitoes and transmitted by their bite. Then, in 1900, the U.S. Army Yellow Fever Commission conducted tests that established mosquitoes as the transmitters of yellow fever as well. Around this time, the U.S. Army doctor Colonel William C. Gorgas began preparatory work in the canal zone by draining mosquito-infested swampland and fumigating houses—moves that were ridiculed as excessive at the time, but which made a significant contribution to the success of the venture.

NATURE RESTORED The Gaillard (Culebra) Cut bears few scars from the struggle to forge it.

draining the land began in 1904. In 1907 construction started in earnest. The man in charge was U.S. Army engineer Colonel George Washington Goethals. The plan was to harness the immense River Chagres to create a huge artificial lake—Lake Gatún—and an adjoining canal straddling the country at 85 feet above sea level. The combined resources of the river and the lake would be used to replenish two flights of three locks toward each end of the canal, carrying shipping up from sea level and down again.

The most challenging task was to carve an 8 mile path—the Culebra Cut—through the continental divide at the southern end of the canal. Using steam shovels, 28,000 tons of explosives and pure brawn, 6,000 men excavated a passage 270 feet deep and 500 feet wide, overcoming a few setbacks as the walls of the cut collapsed. They worked through the seven-year building program and broke through. The Cut was renamed the Gaillard Cut after the engineer in charge. On August 15, 1914, the canal was opened to shipping.

MOSCOW METRO

BENEATH THE STREETS OF MOSCOW, PEOPLE'S PALACES TRUMPETED THE VIRTUES OF COMMUNISM

In the early 1930s, Joseph Stalin initiated a radical program for the reconstruction of Moscow that included a solution to its chronic public transportation problem. The city's population had doubled since the 1917 Revolution and Moscow needed a metropolitan underground railway system.

News of the Metro plan spread through communist political organizations and the youth league, Komsomol. Experts in all fields —architects, artists, sculptors, engineers, stonemasons, metalworkers, miners and railway workers—and 13,000 youth volunteers from all over the Soviet Union offered their services or were commandeered. Against the backdrop of the purges instigated by Stalin to eliminate opponents and dissidents, workers offered up their labor in the service of their Motherland.

Underground glory

They had every right to be proud of their achievements. The Moscow Metro is undoubtedly the most lavish and spectacular in the world. The first line, running through the center between Sokolniki and Park Kultury, with 13 stations, was completed in May 1935, just three years after construction began. The halls below ground, and their entrance lobbies above, reflected the streamlined, functional look of the International Style and Art Deco. "The Moscow subway makes the New York sub-

NO EXPENSE SPARED The sumptuousness of the interiors extends from the ticket booths to the platforms.

way look like a sewer when one returns to compare them," declared the American architect Frank Lloyd Wright in 1937. A second line was opened in 1938. Work on further stations and a third new line continued with unremitting energy throughout the Second World War. Even while Leningrad was suffering a devastating blockade by the German and Finnish armies in 1941-4, mosaics for the Metro were assembled there and airlifted into Moscow.

Postwar triumphalism fuelled the most flamboyant period of construction, notably on the Koltsevaya (Circular) line built 1950-4, which intersects all the others. The design of each station broadcast a theme—industry, popular culture, Belorussia, the Ukraine, the glories of Russian military history—elaborated in murals, bronze statues, relief carvings and mosaics contributed by the Soviet Union's leading artists.

The Metro was one of Stalin's pet plans and its expansion continued after his death in 1953. Today there are over 130 stations on nine lines, handling 8 million passengers a day—by far the most on any underground system in the world.

EVERYDAY SPLENDOR Commuters throng Komsomolskaya station (right). Its mosaic murals illustrate a speech by Stalin on warriors of the Russian past.

M IS FOR METRO The letter M has been the symbol of the Metro since 1935. Travellers on the underground system could enjoy the refined setting of stations such as Taganskaya (below).

GOLDEN GATE BRIDGE

ONE OF THE WORLD'S MOST BEAUTIFUL BRIDGES PUSHED STRUCTURAL ENGINEERING TO NEW LIMITS

When the American explorer John C. Fremont gazed down on the entrance to the magnificent natural harbor of San Francisco Bay in 1846, he was reminded of the "Golden Horn" of the Bosporus at Constantinople (now Istanbul), legendary gateway to the wealth and splendor of the East. He named the harbor entrance Chrysopylae, Greek for "Golden Gate," little suspecting that within a few years this coast and the fortunes of San Francisco would be transformed by real gold and the fever of the Gold Rush.

Half a century later, various interests and businesses were calling for a bridge to span

RECORD BREAKER

With towers reaching up to 746 feet, the Golden Gate Bridge remained the world's tallest suspension bridge for more than 40 years. The Akashi-Kaikyo Bridge in Japan, which opened in April 1998, claimed the records as the longest and tallest suspension bridge.

the Golden Gate, to link San Francisco with Marin County and the towns to the north. But a bridge would have to cross a channel 1½ miles wide, permit the passage of a constant stream of shipping serving a handful of burgeoning cities in the bay area, and contend with surging tides, high winds gusting up to 100 mph, and the ever-present threat of earthquakes.

Only a suspension bridge could accommodate all these factors. In 1921, the engineer Joseph B. Strauss came up with a feasible and affordable plan, but it took over a decade of negotiations before it could be put into action. No federal or state funds were available, but such was the support for the bridge that private citizens and businesses in the Golden Gate area voted to put their own property on the line to guarantee a $35

ORANGE BEAUTY Although so close to a major city, the bridge has a striking natural setting, spanning a rugged, tree-cloaked coastline. The bold orange-red color complements the lucid blue of the Pacific skies and the water.

HIGH SUSPENSE A photograph taken during construction in 1935 shows the catwalks spanning the towers, and the cable anchorage on the San Francisco side. The road deck was suspended from the cables on vertical hangers.

million loan. Seen against the backdrop of the Depression, this was a brave gesture.

The design, credited to engineer Charles Ellis, was also daring. The Golden Gate Bridge was supposed to carry a six-lane highway over a central span of approximately 4,200 feet—700 feet longer than the record holder of the day, the new George Washington Bridge in New York City.

Half way to hell

Work began in January 1933. The northern tower was built on rock close to the shore, but the foundations for the southern tower had to be excavated from the seabed 110 feet below the surface in a caisson, a watertight structure, built by deep-sea divers working during the brief periods of slack water as ferocious tides turned. The massive cables—each 3 feet in diameter, 7,650 feet long and spun from 27,572 strands of wire—were laid between the towers, and then the roadway deck was suspended from the cables using vertical hangers. To allow clearance for ocean-going vessels, the road deck was built 220 feet above the sea.

The contractors maintained meticulous safety precautions throughout construction. A safety net running the length of the road deck saved the lives of 19 men—who became involuntary members of the "Half-Way-to-Hell Club." Between 1933 and the beginning of 1937, the Golden Gate Bridge had lost just one man, a remarkable record in an era when, as a rule of thumb, large engineering projects normally claimed the life of one worker per million dollars spent. But on February 17, 1937, scaffolding crashed through the safety net, taking ten men to their deaths. The dizzying height of the central span has since proved a tragic lure for suicides.

The bridge was opened to traffic on May 28, 1937. It looks today very much as it did then, with one significant change: because of fears aroused by a violent storm in 1951, the slimline road deck was strengthened with additional bracing.

When the Verrazano Narrows Bridge across New York harbor was completed in 1964, it took over the record for the longest span. Only the height of its towers kept the Golden Gate Bridge in the record books until 1998—but its lasting fame rests rather in its intrinsic beauty and its spectacular setting. Illuminated by the sharp, ozone-filled sunlight of the Pacific coast, it spans a sparkling waterway between the green, wooded shores of the Golden Gate National Recreation Area, with San Francisco glimmering quietly in the distance. But it is even more memorable for the days when a great carpet of billowing white fog pours in from the ocean, obscuring the road deck from view but permitting the orange-red towers to be seen, standing proud against a brilliant blue sky.

GALLOPING GERTIE

Suspension bridges were becoming ever longer and slimmer until the destruction of the Tacoma Narrows Bridge over Puget Sound in Washington state. Its delicate deck spanned 2,800 feet, but it swayed so extravagantly in crosswinds that it earned itself the nickname "Galloping Gertie." On November 7, 1940, just four months after completion, a strong wind created violent oscillations along its length, causing it to twist and bend as if it were no more substantial than a steel tape measure. This remarkable sight was caught on film—including the dramatic moment when the deck finally snapped and collapsed. A number of suspension bridges, including the Golden Gate Bridge, were reinforced in the wake of this incident.

WAVE MOTION A ripple effect ran along the deck of the Tacoma Narrows Bridge just prior to its collapse.

SYDNEY HARBOR BRIDGE

THE WORLD'S MOST FAMOUS ARCH BRIDGE BECAME A KEY FEATURE IN THE SYDNEY CITYSCAPE

In the great tradition of Australian understatement, Sydneysiders call their bridge "the Coathanger." It is, in fact, one of the world's largest steel bridges and, more than 60 years after construction, it still holds the record as the widest long-span bridge in the world. Across its 160 feet girth run not just eight lanes of roadway, but also two train tracks, a bicycle path and a footway, providing a key thoroughfare

GRAND ENTRANCE Ocean-going ships gathering in Sydney harbor for the opening of the bridge in 1932 served to underline its massive scale and height.

between central Sydney and the suburbs on the northern side of the harbor.

Following the designs of Ralph Freeman (1880-1950), one of the world's leading engineers at that time, the English construction company Dorman Long began work in 1923 by first erecting pairs of massive stone towers on the shores on each side of the channel. Steel cables were passed over the towers and anchored to the ground. These provided temporary leverage to hold up the arching superstructure of the

bridge, which, because of the depth of the channel, could not be supported in any other way. Bit by bit, the arches were built out from both shores toward their meeting point over the channel. Cranes positioned on tracks at the front end of each arch fed the prefabricated steel beams along to workmen. The position of these cranes looked increasingly precarious as they slowly moved higher and farther out over the void. At last, when the two curves were separated by just 3 feet, work stopped. The steel cables were relaxed and the two sides of the arch locked into each other.

With the arch complete, the huge steel deck was raised in sections

PRIDE OF THE NATION Publicity for the opening ceremony reflects Australia's pride in this great engineering achievement.

SHOCK OPENING

The Sydney Harbor Bridge was officially opened on Saturday, March 19, 1932. The ceremony was covered by some 40 radio stations, which relayed to the nation a bizarre and dramatic turn of events. As the New South Wales premier, Jack Lang, stood beside the ribbon, scissors in hand, a mounted horseman wearing the uniform of the Royal Hussars emerged from the crowd brandishing a sword and slashed the ribbon first.

Captain Francis Edward De Groot was arrested at the scene, and it soon became clear that he was making a political protest. A member of the Fascist-style New Guard, he was vehemently opposed to Jack Lang's controversial reform and welfare program. In court, the case to prove De Groot insane was dismissed, and he was fined for offensive behavior. He later left Australia to live the rest of his life in Ireland, the country of his birth.

from barges below and slung at a height that provides clearance of 170 feet for ocean-going shipping. Before completion, the strength of the bridge was tested by placing 81 locomotives across it for eight days.

MIGHTY ARCH Ralph Freeman chose the arch for the Sydney Harbor Bridge, a form he had used on a smaller scale with his earlier bridge over the Tyne (below) at Newcastle, England.

The total length of the Sydney Harbor Bridge is 3,770 feet; its main span measures 1,650 feet. With its muscular profile and 39,000 tons of steel, it is the most famous bridge in the world and, complementing the delicate shells of the Opera House, contributes to one of the world's most entrancing city views.

A CITY OF BRIDGES

THE ISLAND OF MANHATTAN IS ACCESSED BY SOME OF THE WORLD'S GREATEST BRIDGES

New York City is comprised of five boroughs: the island of Manhattan in which many of the nation's corporations have their headquarters, and four surrounding areas to which New Yorkers go at the end of the working day. This geographical fact of life has made New York a showcase for bridge-building for the past century. Three times in its history, New York built what was at the time the world's longest bridge—the only city in the world that can make that boast.

The first such structure was the famed Brooklyn Bridge, a work about which painters created masterpieces and poets composed sonnets. Designed in 1867 by John A. Roebling and linking lower Manhattan and Brooklyn across the East River, the Brooklyn Bridge was the first suspension bridge to use steel wire cables. Although Roebling died in an accident while overseeing the last of the surveys in 1869, his son took the $9 million project over and supervised The New York Bridge Company's construction beginning in January of 1870. The bridge's two trademark granite towers were completed in 1875 and rise to the height of over 270 feet. When construction was completed and the bridge opened to the public on May 24, 1883, the Brooklyn Bridge was 1,595½ feet across—fifty percent longer than any other bridge then in existence. The cost of crossing this newly created behemoth? A hefty 3 cents.

Several other bridges were constructed over the following decades of roughly the same length until the technology was ready to attempt a bridging of the Hudson River. A suspension bridge with towers reaching in excess of 630 feet and a center span of 3,500 feet, the George Washington Bridge connects New York's Upper Manhattan to Fort Lee, New Jersey, across the Hudson. Designed by Othmar H. Ammann, construction on the bridge began in 1927 and was completed in 1931. At the time, the GWB was the longest suspension bridge in the world, although it would be bested six years later by San Francisco's Golden Gate Bridge. The George is currently the fourth longest suspension bridge in North America. Originally designed to carry eight lanes of traffic, a lower deck with more lanes was constructed from 1958-62. With the completion of the lower deck, the GWB became the world's first 14-lane suspension bridge.

Like the George Washington Bridge, the Verrazano-Narrows Bridge is a massive suspension bridge also built by Ammann. Spanning New York Harbor from Brooklyn to Staten Island, the bridge was constructed from 1959 to 1964 and its 4,260 foot main span was, until the completion of the Humber Bridge in England in 1981, the longest in the world. The double-decked, six-lane-wide roadway, 228 feet above the water at midpoint, is supported by four cables weighing 10,000 tons each hung from towers almost 700 feet high.

NYC's MAGNIFICENT BRIDGES   New York bridges tend to be record-breakers: from left, the Verrazano-Narrows, the Brooklyn Bridge and the George Washington Bridge.

AKASHI-KAIKYO BRIDGE

JAPAN STORMED INTO THE RECORD BOOKS WITH THE WORLD'S LONGEST SUSPENSION BRIDGE

The Inland Sea separates Honshu, the largest island of Japan, from Shikoku, the smallest of the country's four main islands. It is a busy waterway with major industrial cities, such as Hiroshima, Kobe and Osaka, concentrated around its coasts. It is notorious, however, for fogs, strong currents and hurricane-force typhoons.

In 1970, the Japanese government launched a plan to free Shikoku from its dependency on ferries and airplanes. The Honshu-Shikoku Bridge Authority was established, and proposed a trio of road links across the Inland Sea: the Nishi-Seto Expressway, which crosses a chain of six islands; the Seto-Chuo Expressway, which includes the Seto-Ohashi double-deck road-and-rail bridge, the longest of its kind in the world; and the Kobe-Naruto Expressway. The easternmost road link, the Kobe-Naruto Expressway, passes over Awajishima, the largest island in the Inland Sea. Two bridges were therefore needed to reach Shikoku: one over the Akashi Strait, between Kobe and Matsuho on the northern tip of the island, and the other between the southern end of the island and Naruto on Shikoku.

The project represented a huge undertaking, requiring great engineering prowess and massive investment. But the greatest challenge of all was the Akashi Strait. It is 2$^{1}/_{2}$ miles wide, 360 feet deep, and swept by fierce currents and high winds. To cross it, the engineers proposed to build a suspension bridge with the world's longest span: 6,529 feet— 1,903 feet longer than the record holder, the Humber Bridge in England. With two side spans of 3,150 feet each, the total length of the Akashi-Kaikyo Bridge would be 12,828 feet.

A 1:100 scale model was built and subjected to rigorous testing. Not only did the bridge have to be able to withstand high winds, it would also have to survive earthquakes. Kobe lies just to the north—the scene of a major earthquake in 1995 that claimed over 4,000 victims.

Construction began in May 1988. First, foundations for the two towers were dug 200 feet into the unstable silt, sand and gravel of the seabed. Prefabricated steel caissons were then towed to the scene to build the concrete bases of the towers. Meanwhile, the cable anchorages were constructed on shore. To support the weight that the cables would have to bear, the anchorage on the reclaimed land on the Kobe side weighs approximately 350,000 tons—the largest in the world.

The towers were completed in 1993, each reaching a height of 974 feet above mean sea level—another world record. Then a pair of pilot cables was strung across the tops of the towers by helicopter, so that the suspension cables could be fed across without impeding shipping. The main cables were prefabricated out of 290 strands, each strand consisting of bundles of 127 high-tensile galvanized-steel wires, producing a total cable diameter of 3 feet 7 inches. Together the two main cables contain about 186,100 miles of wire, enough to go around the world seven and a half times.

After the cable-laying was completed in 1994, the steel deck was laid, employing floating cranes to position the sections of the deck as they were fixed to the hanger ropes. After receiving its final coat of greenish-grey paint, chosen to harmonize with the sea and sky, the Akashi-Kaikyo Bridge was opened on schedule in April 1998, after ten years of construction.

HIDDEN STRENGTH **The bracing beneath the deck is designed to withstand the hurricane-force winds that whip through the strait.**

GENOA-LIVORNO AUTOSTRADA

FIFTY YEARS AFTER BUILDING THE WORLD'S FIRST HIGHWAY, ITALY CHALKED UP ANOTHER TRIUMPH

In 1924 Italy built the first ever highway, covering 35 miles between Milan and Varese. Forty years later, Italy was embarking on one of the most ambitious highway projects in Europe. The aim was to ease a traffic bottleneck to the south of the port-city of Genoa. Situated at the uppermost reach of the Ligurian Sea, Genoa has long been a gateway to the cities of northern Italy, notably Turin and Milan. To the south lies the port of La Spezia, which has an important naval base; and farther south still, over the border between Liguria and Tuscany, is the port of Livorno, which serves Pisa and Florence. It made sense to connect the three by a coastal highway, but the Apennine mountains crowd up to the sea, lining the shore with a succession of steep, rocky hills, especially between Genoa and La Spezia. Italy's highway builders would have to build a mountain road along the coast.

For construction purposes, the new A12 Genoa-Livorno autostrada was divided into two sections. The northern section, built by Società Autostrade, runs south for about 30 miles through the most challenging terrain, between Genoa and Sestri Levante. Here the lanes often follow separate paths, snaking through tunnels and half-exposed galleries and over bridges or viaducts consisting of stilts and decks of reinforced concrete. The total length of both lanes is 62 miles, almost half of which is tunnels, while 10 miles pass over viaducts. Much of the remaining 22 miles is supported by ledges created by cuttings. The road twists and winds, demanding concentration from drivers and strong stomachs from passengers; but passengers are compensated by intermittent glimpses of the sea that has given the road its nickname, "l'Autostrada Azzurra" (the Blue Highway).

The southern section, built by Società Autostrada Ligure Toscana (SALT), runs south from Sestri Levante over the highest point of the road, 1,175 feet, at the Bracco Pass, before descending to the coastal plain below the Carrara mountains. The whole of this section to Livorno is 96 miles long, half of which is in the hills; there are 25 tunnels, 159 viaducts and 54 overpasses. SALT was also contracted to build the route joining the A12 to the A11, which rises steeply from the coast to Lucca and then goes on to Florence.

ROAD ON STILTS A series of high, elegantly curving viaducts carry a section of the Blue Highway through the Tuscan hills.

MAIN-DANUBE CANAL

A WATERWAY LINKED THE NORTH SEA TO THE BLACK SEA, REALIZING A 1,200-YEAR-OLD DREAM

A ridge across Bavaria to the south of Nürnberg (Nuremberg) marks the continental watershed. To the south, tributaries feed the Danube as it heads for the distant Black Sea. To the north, tributaries lead into the River Main, which flows into the River Rhine on its way to the North Sea. It was Charlemagne's dream to join these two waterways, and in 793 he set an army of laborers to work, but they were defeated by perpetual flooding. Ludwig I of Bavaria built a canal linking the River Altmühl, a tributary of the Danube, to the River Pegnitz, a tributary of the Main. Opened in 1846, the canal soon ran into competition from the railways, and it became a backwater.

By that time a new company had been established to build a much more ambitious link. The Rhein-Main-Donau AG (Rhine-Main-Danube Company, or RMD) planned

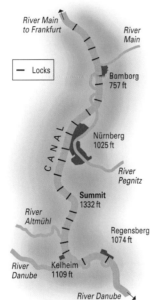

PATH OF CONTROVERSY The route of the canal (above) had to be forged through the Altmühl valley (below).

to build a canal linking Bamberg near the River Main to Kelheim on the River Danube, a distance of 106 miles. This meant widening the River Pegnitz to Nürnberg, cutting a link through to the River Altmühl, and widening the Altmühl south to the Danube. Some 50 new locks would be needed along the whole route to lift shipping to a height of 1,332 feet at the summit of the ridge, the highest point of any canal in Europe.

Ecological compromise

The plan took 71 years to bring to fruition: work was brought to a standstill by the Second World War, and in the 1960s it ran foul of the environmentalist lobby. This confrontation came to a head in the early 1980s, before receiving new impetus from German chancellor Helmut Kohl and his Bavarian minister, Franz-Josef Strauss.

By now the canal had become an environmental cause célèbre: not only was this massive canal going to alter the ecological structure of three rivers and the wildlife habitats along its path, it also threatened to destroy the tranquillity of

WORK AND PLEASURE A Euro-barge passes tourist boats docked at Berching. Per unit of energy consumed, the barges can carry 26 times more cargo than road transport.

the beautiful Altmühl valley. In the end a compromise was reached. RMD agreed to invest millions in making ecological provisions for the canal, especially in the Altmühl valley. It built levees to preserve wildlife in wetlands, created nature parks and bicycle paths, and installed a series of architect-designed bridges. These provisions were estimated to cost up to one-third of the project's entire budget of well over $4 billion.

The canal was opened on September 25, 1992. Massive Euro-barges, 600 feet long and 38 feet wide, carrying coal, sand, cement, grain, fertilizer and other heavy materials, can now travel from the North Sea to the Black Sea, a journey of 2,175 miles through ten countries.

HONG KONG AIRPORT

WITH ITS NEW AIRPORT, HONG KONG STOOD READY TO BECOME THE GATEWAY TO THE EAST

At the start of the 21st century, half the world's population lives within a five-hour flight of Hong Kong, which lies at the strategic center of the rapidly developing western Pacific Rim. In the 1980s, it seemed clear that Hong Kong was destined to become a crossroads for the region; and that its old Kai Tak Airport in Kowloon, already one of the world's busiest, would not suffice.

After just six years of construction, Hong Kong now has one of the largest airports in the world, and the most technologically advanced. Capable of handling 35 million passengers a year on opening in July 1998, it is projected to expand to a capacity of 87 million passengers a year by 2040; and cargo handling is forecast to triple to 9 million tons a year over the same period.

The airport cost $8 billion to build, and forms part of a massive infrastructure project costing some $20 billion in all. Unlike Kai Tak, which lies close to the city center, the site chosen by the Airport Authority of Hong Kong for the new airport is on an island,

Chek Lap Kok, 30 miles to the west: all connections to it had to be built from scratch. Between 1992 and 1995 Chek Lap Kok was flattened and extended by land reclamation to cover an area of nearly 5 square miles—enough room for two runways and an airport terminal nearly 1 mile long. Meanwhile, the infrastructure projects were also progressing. They included a whole new town on Lantau, a neighboring island and the largest in the Hong Kong group, and a 22 mile rail and expressway link, involving a series of bridges and tunnels, to connect Chek Lap Kok to central Hong Kong. Air passengers can reach central Hong Kong by a train ride of

QUALITY ENGINEERING The terminal interior is capped by steel-grid vaults pierced by skylights. The façade has a huge area of plate glass and distinctive gull-wing overhangs.

only 23 minutes, and by car in 40 minutes.

The most impressive segment of this new transport infrastructure is the Lantau Link, which takes the road and railway over two islands between Lantau and the mainland by means of two major bridges and a viaduct. One of these bridges is the double-deck Tsing Ma Bridge, carrying a dual three-lane road above the railway lines. With a main span of 4,518 feet, this is the world's longest road-and-rail suspension bridge. The specifications of the bridge were exacting: it has to be able to withstand the hurricane-force typhoons that frequently buffet Hong Kong. Notwithstanding, its deck hovers 203 feet above the mean water level, to allow clearance for the busy shipping lanes.

Chek Lap Kok Airport opened in July 1998, coinciding with the completion of the Lantau railway link. It was a year behind schedule, following delays caused by record rainfall in 1994, and the negotiations between China and Britain over funding for the project in the years leading up to the return of Hong Kong to China in 1997.

The airport terminal was built by the Mott Consortium, which included Foster & Partners, Hong Kong, who were responsible for the design. Based on a modular system to allow for expansion, it is built of reinforced concrete, steel and glass. The dual themes of air and light, and the clear emphasis placed on the quality of engineering, are expressed in the vast entrance façade. Road and rail services are delivered close to this entrance.

The terminal building handles both arrivals and departures, and its state-of-the-art facilities have been designed to minimize check-in times and the formalities of arrival. Passengers should need to spend no more than 30 minutes between the entrance to the terminal and the door of their plane. Their passage through the terminal is assisted by 288 computer-linked check-in desks, 12 miles of baggage conveyors capable of dealing with nearly 20,000 bags an hour, 1 1/2 miles of walking sidewalks, and the Automated People Movers (APMs)—train shuttles that operate along the Y-shaped arm of the terminal to the "airbridges" where the planes dock. The swiftness of passenger processing through the terminal allows the airport to handle 40 planes an hour—one every 90 seconds—24 hours a day, 365 days a year.

There is one other attraction awaiting passengers at Chek Lap Kok. Its island location, surrounded by water and the misty hills of Lantau and the Chinese mainland, endows it with one of the most spectacular settings of any airport in the world.

CHANNEL TUNNEL

BRITAIN WAS FINALLY LINKED TO EUROPE BY ONE OF THE CENTURY'S GREATEST ENGINEERING PROJECTS

From the moment that the Channel Tunnel was launched in 1985, it was always in the news. This was the biggest construction project in Europe. Spanning the 23¹/₂ miles that separate Britain and France, it was also the longest undersea tunnel ever attempted. It required massive, purpose-built machinery, a construction team of 15,000 working in two languages, and an unprecedented logistical operation to remove the tons of debris and deliver materials as they were needed.

For over 150 years, various plans for a tunnel under the Channel had been put forward, but each ran foul of some insurmountable problem—usually political. What had changed by the 1980s was the political will: a Channel tunnel was seen as desirable in both Britain and France. For Britain's Conservative prime minister, Margaret Thatcher, this was an opportunity to demonstrate the boundless capabilities of the private-enterprise economy. The French president, François Mitterrand, a socialist, saw it as a logical way of extending the state-owned railway system, served by its acclaimed high-speed trains, the TGVs (*train à grande vitesse*).

Work begins

Following a series of high-level negotiations to thrash out the international treaties, work began on December 1, 1987. The "Chunnel," as it was then called, in fact consists of three parallel tunnels: two rail tunnels, both linked by cross-passages to a smaller Service Tunnel—a road tunnel for maintenance and emergencies. The main rail tunnels were to be used by two separate but integrated services. A rail passenger service, called Eurostar, would operate high-speed trains to link London with Paris and Brussels. Meanwhile, a shuttle service would carry cars and busses on rail transporters between the terminals at Folkestone and Calais.

The tunnels were dug from both ends, from Shakespeare Cliff near Folkestone in England, and from Sangatte, near Calais in France. In order to install the tunnelling machinery, huge vertical shafts had to be excavated close to the coasts. From the base of the shafts, the three tunnels were dug outward under the sea, and inland toward the terminals where the trains would emerge.

The main workhorses were the tunnel boring machines, the TBMs. There were 11 altogether, operating simultaneously on both sides of the Channel. At the sharp end was a disc up to 28 feet across, armed with tungsten-carbide teeth; this churned away at the workface at a speed of three revolutions a

UNDERSEA CAVERN Track layers prepare the path for the Tunnel Boring Machine (TBM) in one of the two vast crossover caverns.

HEADING FOR FRANCE Construction workers on the British side follow in the path of the TBM, shoring up the concrete lining segments and preparing the ground for track laying.

FEARS OF INVASION

The first serious plan for a Channel tunnel was put forward by a French engineer in 1802. It was designed for stagecoaches, and an artificial island was to be built midway so they could stop to change horses. Proposed during a lull in the Napoleonic Wars, the concept was dismissed by British generals and politicians as an unacceptable breach in their island's natural defenses.

Such fears dogged all ensuing proposals for a Channel tunnel, even as the rapid developments in technology during the 19th century made the concept increasingly practicable. Various engineers suggested new schemes, and one company even began digging in 1876. Using a tunnel-boring machine, it advanced over 1 mile under the sea along the line taken by today's tunnel. But again, this venture was crushed by military objections.

Another tunnel was launched in the 1920s, and again trial borings were undertaken before the plan was scuttled by political resistance, this time inspired by fears of Bolshevik infiltration. During the 1980s, a rail tunnel was just one of a number of schemes under consideration; others included a road tunnel, a road or rail suspension bridge of unprecedented scale, and schemes combining bridges and tunnels, or tubes lying on the seabed. But the size of the Channel, its busy shipping lanes, the dangers of car fumes, and construction costs ruled these out, favoring the rail tunnel.

minute. Spoil was fed back along conveyor belts to awaiting rail wagons, then removed from the tunnels at a rate of up to 2,400 tons an hour. As the cutter-head advanced, construction workers slotted prefabricated segments of reinforced concrete into place to line the tunnel. The main rail tunnels ended up with a diameter of 24 feet 11 inches.

With its machinery, its computer-assisted control cabin, its engines and power units, pumps, dust-extraction unit and conveyor belt, a TBM and service train formed a huge, noisy caterpillar the length of two football fields. Using laser beams and computer analysis, tunnel surveyors were able to calculate the position and direction of the TBMs to within a fraction of an inch—essential if the British and French tunnels were to meet up.

Breakthrough

Working around the clock, the TBMs advanced at the rate of up to 300 feet a week. The French and British teams edged toward each other, at times digging at a depth of 245 feet beneath the seabed. In October 1990, a narrow probe was drilled from the British end of the Service Tunnel through the

MARRYING ROAD TO RAIL At the Folkestone terminal, road traffic from the highway boards the shuttle train.

remaining 325 feet of earth. It pierced the French workface to confirm that the surveyors were on target. Tunnellers worked by hand, edging their way forward through the last physical barrier separating Britain and France. On December 1, 1990, three years after digging began, they broke through. Holding their national flags, representatives from each side shook hands through a small hole.

Four years of work still lay ahead. New rail tracks were laid, and two crossover caverns were built to allow trains to swap tunnels, should any segment become blocked. Electric power lines, ventilation units, communication and signalling systems were installed. Lastly, emergency procedures had to be rehearsed. These were put to the test in December 1996, when a fire broke out on a freight train. The Channel Tunnel was opened by Queen Elizabeth II and the French president, François Mitterrand, on May 6, 1994.

SEIKAN RAIL TUNNEL

THE WORLD'S LONGEST TUNNEL CONNECTED JAPAN'S TWO LARGEST ISLANDS

The storm-prone Tsugaru Strait separates Hokkaido—the northernmost of the four main islands of Japan—from the largest island, Honshu, and the national capital, Tokyo. For decades, the Japanese had wanted to build a rail network that would link all four main islands, but the Tsugaru Strait could not be tamed. Hokkaido remained accessible only by air and ferry.

But in 1988 all this changed when the Seikan Rail Tunnel opened, linking Aomori on Honshu to Hakodate on Hokkaido. Suddenly it became possible to travel by rail all the way from Tokyo to Hokkaido's capital, Sapporo, in less than 6 hours, a journey that took the best part of two days when a ferry crossing was involved. Freight trains can now bring Hokkaido produce—potatoes, onions, butter, fish—fresh to the Tokyo markets.

FAST TRACK The main tunnel contains two rail tracks designed to take the *shinkansen*, the intercity high-speed "bullet trains" that can reach speeds of up to 136 mph.

To do this, the trains travel beneath the Tsugaru Strait in the world's longest rail tunnel—33 1/2 miles. Of this, 14 1/2 miles is under the sea, making this section the second-longest undersea tunnel in the world after the Channel Tunnel between England and France. The remainder passes underground inland to reach the portals on either side of the strait, 8 1/2 miles from the coast on the Honshu side, and 10 1/2 miles on the Hokkaido side. These elongated preludes to the undersea section are necessary to accommodate the 12° incline of the tunnel down to its full depth; for this rail tunnel is not only the longest in the world, but also the deepest, reaching down to 328 feet below the seabed, and 787 feet below sea level.

Initial work on the project began in 1946, with the first trial bores to analyze the rock strata beneath the seabed. Exploratory tunnels were dug in 1964 and excavation for the main tunnel began in 1971. The task was eventually completed in 1988, when trains began their first trial runs. Construction had taken 24 years in all, and cost the lives of 66 workers who died in construction accidents.

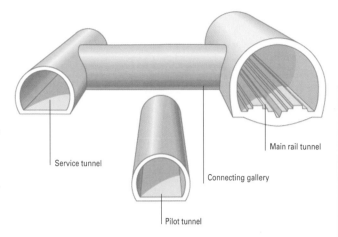

Service tunnel · Main rail tunnel · Connecting gallery · Pilot tunnel

LINKED TUNNELS The pilot tunnel was bored first to test conditions. The main tunnel is 36 1/2 feet in diameter. The service tunnel provides the principal maintenance access and ventilation.

Sets of vertical shafts on each side of the strait are equipped with air extraction fans at the surface, while machinery and personnel can reach the subterranean levels via two shafts that lead down from the surface at points close to the coast. These shafts also connect up with two underground emergency stations, called Yoshioka and Tappi, from which passengers can be evacuated should there be any problem in the tunnel—such as an earth tremor sensed on the tunnel's seismometers. Tour groups visit the stations regularly, coming to admire this great engineering feat of the 20th century.

POWER STRUCTURES

ENERGY SUSTAINS INDUSTRIAL DEVELOPMENT AND IS ESSENTIAL TO THE WORLD'S BURGEONING POPULATIONS. ONE OF THE GREAT DILEMMAS OF THE 20TH CENTURY IS HOW TO SATISFY THE EVER-INCREASING DEMAND FOR ENERGY. ENGINEERS HAVE ENDEAVORED NOT ONLY TO HARNESS NATURE'S POWER, BUT ALSO TO REIN IT IN WHEN IT THREATENS DEVASTATION. THIS HAS RESULTED IN SOME OF THE WORLD'S LARGEST AND MOST IMPRESSIVE CONSTRUCTIONS.

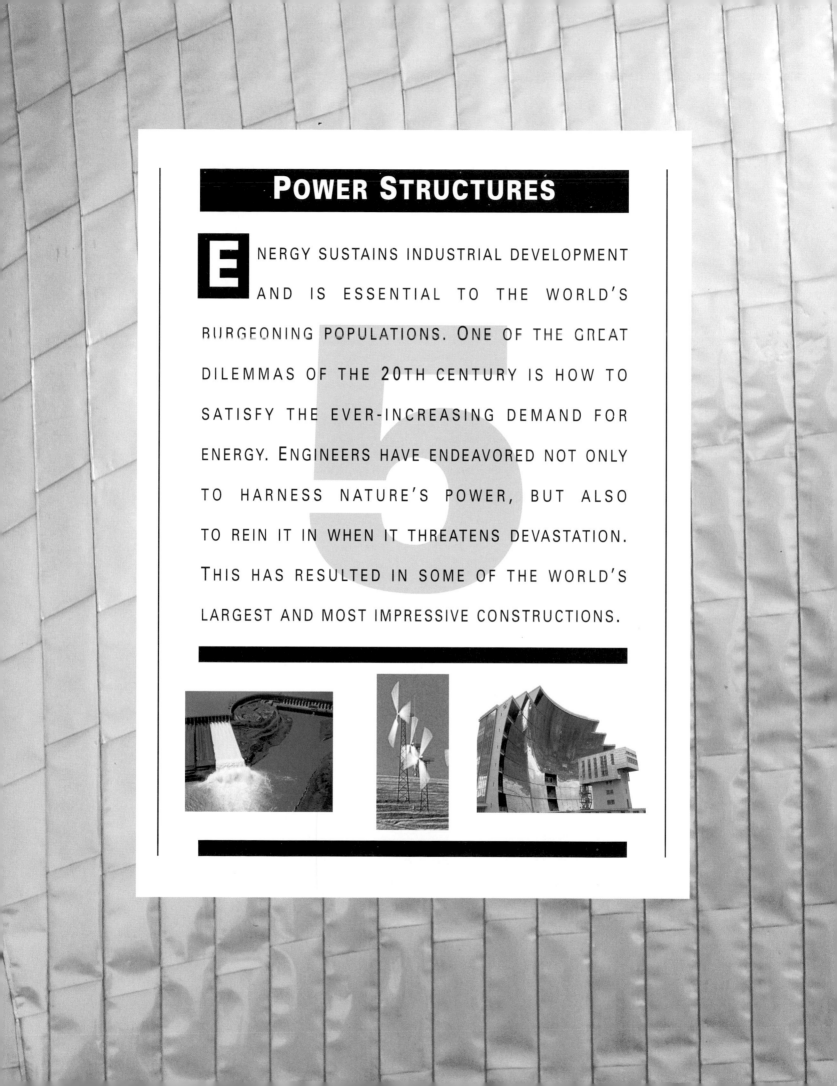

CHINON A1 NUCLEAR POWER STATION

A POWER STATION IN THE LOIRE VALLEY WAS THE LABORATORY OF FRENCH NUCLEAR POWER

In the late 1950s a futuristic apparition began to rise from the banks of the River Loire near Chinon, in a region more famous for its concentration of historic chateaux. It was a huge steel sphere 189 feet high, affectionately nicknamed "La Boule" (the ball). Inside, scientists and engineers were working at the cutting edge of a new industry: nuclear power. This was the first nuclear power station in France to produce electricity. It laid the foundation stones for a nuclear industry that now accounts for 75 percent of France's electricity needs.

During the boom that came after the Second World War, France's consumption of electricity was doubling every two years. But its coal reserves were limited and most of its hydroelectric potential had already been tapped. France needed to find a new means of generating electricity that did not depend on expensive imported fuels. The most promising source seemed to be nuclear power, but the technology was still in its infancy.

The concept of nuclear power had been developed in the late 1930s, and had come to fruition during the Second World War in the atomic bomb. By splitting an atomic nucleus (nuclear fission) with subatomic particles called neutrons, a huge amount of energy can be released. The process also produces a chain reaction of further fissions. If carried out in controlled conditions, the intense heat given off can be made to boil water and create steam; as in other types of power stations, the steam can be used to drive the turbines that generate electricity.

Radioactive elements, such as uranium, are used in nuclear power stations because they are unstable and the nuclei need only a small amount of prodding to make them split. Just $2\frac{1}{4}$ pounds of uranium can produce as much energy as 400 barrels of oil.

Small, prototype nuclear power stations were tested in the U.S. in 1951 and the Soviet Union in 1954. The first large-scale commercial nuclear power station was built at Calder Hill in England, and was operating by 1956. France was impressed. Electricité de France (EDF) assembled a team of young scientists, average age 26, to develop France's own nuclear power program. Chinon was where they put their theories to the test. Building work began in 1956 and was completed in 1963.

Inside "La Boule" was a nuclear reactor in which 1,148 cylindrical fuel elements,

PROGRESSIVE POWER The distinctive sphere of Chinon A1 once stood alone on the banks of the River Loire. Since 1965 it has been joined by the rectangular blocks of A2 and A3.

THE POWER AND THE DANGER

BLAST ZONE A month after the disaster at Chernobyl, radioactivity readings at the site left no doubts about the devastating levels of contamination emitted by the explosion.

The ultimate nuclear disaster may occur if the cooling systems in a nuclear power station fail. If this happens, the reactor core rapidly becomes overheated, releases radioactive gases, and will melt everything around it—even the concrete floor. Jokingly, critics referred to the "China Syndrome," the idea that if a complete failure and "melt-down" occurred in a U.S. power station, the reactor core would melt a hole all the way to China.

Something like this nearly happened on March 28, 1979, when a water-cooled reactor at Three Mile Island, near Harrisburg, Pennsylvania, was exposed to air and overheated. Total disaster was averted at the eleventh hour by the last line of defense, the containment building. After this, expansion of the U.S. nuclear power program was curtailed.

The full lesson of the dangers of nuclear power were not learned until April 26, 1986. Following a systems failure, and incorrect responses by staff, one of the reactors in a power station at Chernobyl, near Kiev in the Ukraine, blew up, sending a radioactive plume 3 miles into the atmosphere. The explosion killed 30 people immediately, and led to the death by contamination of around 5,000 others. Over 135,000 people had to be evacuated from nearby towns, and the health of an estimated 3.5 million people has been adversely affected. Radioactivity spread across Europe, contaminating a sheep pasture in Wales, and entering into the bloodstream of reindeer in northern Scandinavia through their diet of lichens. People are still dying as a result of Chernobyl, the memory of which has cast a long, dark shadow over the nuclear power industry.

each containing 15 rods of uranium, were lowered mechanically into a graphite core. The heat resulting from the fission was carried away by pressurized carbon-dioxide gas, the coolant, which was blown in among the fuel elements. The hot gas then entered the intestine-like tubes of the heat exchanger, which operated like a giant electric kettle, heating water to 644°F. This water, always kept separate from the reactor in a "secondary circuit," then turned to steam, which powered the turbines and generated electricity. Chinon was located next to the Loire to provide a constant supply of water. The entire process was monitored 24 hours a day from a control room equipped with paper-and-ink teleprinters and other electronic machinery, for Chinon A1 predated the age of computers.

With a generating capacity of 70 megawatts, Chinon A1 operated from 1963 to 1973, when it was decommissioned because further developments rendered it

AT ARM'S LENGTH The practice of using robotic machines to move fuel rods in and out of the reactor core was developed at Chinon A1. By the time Chinon A3 was built, the operation could be carried out by computer-assisted remote control (right). Instructions were transmitted to the robot "Isis" at the reactor core (below).

comparatively inefficient. By this time, Chinon A2 had been built next door, and this ran successfully from 1965 to 1985, with a generating capacity of 200 megawatts. Chinon A3, operating from 1966 to 1990, had a capacity of 480 megawatts, but suffered from a series of operating difficulties, and was the least successful of the trio. All three were "natural uranium gas-cooled, graphite-moderated" reactors.

In 1986, "La Boule" was opened as a museum, and has since been visited by more than 5 million people. All France's nuclear power stations can be visited by members of the public, albeit under tight security conditions. France may have run into difficulties with its costly fast-breeder Superphénix reactors, designed to "breed" an inexhaustible supply of fissionable material, but it is proud of its safety record and considers its nuclear power program to be a success story—a story in which Chinon A1 played a critical role.

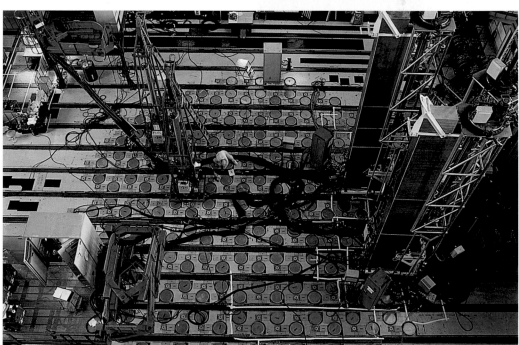

ASWAN HIGH DAM

THE WHOLE OF EGYPT DEPENDS UPON THE DAM THAT CONTROLS THE MIGHTY RIVER NILE

As the old saying goes, "Egypt is the gift of the Nile." This copious river, the longest in the world, was the foundation of ancient Egyptian civilization, providing precious water to the farmlands on its banks. Each year from July to October, the river would flood, deluging its banks and caking them with 100 million tons of silt, a natural mineral-rich fertilizer. But the River Nile was an unreliable friend. Sometimes the flood, triggered by summer rains and melting snows in the distant Ethiopian highlands, would be unusually high, causing widespread devastation. At other times it would be too meager, resulting in famine.

When President Gamal Abdul Nasser came to power following the military coup against King Farouk in 1952, Egypt faced a growing political and economic crisis. The population stood at 27 million, and was increasing at a rate of a million a year. His country could no longer afford to be prey to the whims of its great river. The Nile had to be brought under control and exploited to its maximum potential.

In fact, it was already under partial control. In 1898-1902 the British had built a dam at Aswan, in the far south of Egypt. Then the largest dam in the world, it had subsequently been raised twice, in 1912 and 1933. But the sluices of this Aswan dam served only to control the tail end of the flood, to prevent excessive inundation. Nasser conceived a far grander plan: the new Aswan High Dam would control the flow of the Nile completely. It would also provide a massive source of hydroelectricity to power Egypt's industrial development.

Nasser, however, found his path blocked. A charismatic leader, he was fast becoming the figurehead of pan-Arab socialism, and the inspiration of nationalist anti-colonial movements throughout the world. The World Bank, under pressure from the U.S. and Britain, refused to back the Aswan project, so to raise funds Nasser nationalized the Suez Canal, appropriating it from British and French control and provoking the Suez Crisis. After this, he won financial and technological backing for the Aswan High Dam from the Soviet Union, thereby assigning to the project a role in the Cold War.

The dam took 11 years to build, beginning in 1960. Slung between two granite cliffs, it forms a massive wall containing 17 times the building material used in the Great Pyramid. It is nearly 2 1/4 miles long, and 374 feet high. A four-lane highway runs across the top, which is 132 feet wide; the dam thickens toward the base to 3,215 feet wide.

Turbines were already operating by 1967, producing electricity as the construction continued. By the time the dam was completed Nasser had died, and it was his successor, President Anwar Sadat, who presided over the inauguration ceremony on January 15, 1971. It had cost an estimated $1 billion, and the lives of 451 workers. Gradually, the reservoir behind the dam, named Lake Nasser, was filling up, and eventually stretched for 310 miles, over the border with Sudan. This valley had once been inhabited by some 122,000 people, all of whom had to be moved; 69,000 Nubians and Egyptians were rehoused in new towns close to the dam, and

HOLDING BACK THE NILE The strength required to restrain the floodwaters of one of the world's greatest rivers is indicated by the breadth of the dam. The hydroelectric power station is mounted on the downriver side.

53,000 Nubians were relocated in Sudan.

The dam has helped Egypt to increase its overall area of cultivable land and its harvests, and it has enabled the country to survive the years of low rainfall in the 1980s and 1990s that caused drought and famine in Ethiopia and Sudan. Since the arrival of new American turbines in the 1980s, it has also increased its hydroelectric output, supplying more towns and villages, as well as oil refineries and iron and steel works.

But various side effects have dented the promise of the dam. The rich silt of the Nile is now piling up in Lake Nasser; in its place, Egyptian farmers use ever greater quantities of expensive chemical fertilizers. Meanwhile, the irrigated fields are suffering from increasing salinity as a result of evaporation, rendering them less fertile. Before the dam was built, these damaging mineral deposits were flushed away by the floods.

The dam also represents a colossal security risk. Both Israel and Libya have threatened to attack it in the past, and the hills around the dam bristle with military equipment. "After the dam, our land will be paradise," chanted demonstrators in Nasser's day. Since then, Egypt's population has risen from 27 million to 58 million, doubling the demand on the dam and pushing the dream of paradise further toward the horizon.

RAISING THE TEMPLE OF ABU SIMBEL

The valley flooded by Lake Nasser was at the southern limit of Egypt's power and jurisdiction. In this remote borderland, one of ancient Egypt's most powerful pharaohs built a magnificent temple to proclaim his divine authority. Ramses II was a king of the 19th dynasty. He reigned for 66 years from about 1279 to 1213 BC, during which time he extended the Egyptian Empire to its furthest limits in the Middle East, and undertook a massive building program. One of his greatest monuments was the temple of Abu Simbel, built in about 1260 BC on a site 175 miles to the south of Aswan.

This famous temple, plus a neighboring temple built by Ramses to honor his wife Nefertari, was going to be flooded by Lake Nasser. To prevent this, U.N.E.S.C.O. (the United Nations Educational, Scientific and Cultural Organization) mounted one of the most extraordinary archaeological rescues of all time. Starting in 1965, an international team of around 3,000 engineers, archaeologists and laborers worked against the clock to raise the Abu

GIANT JIGSAW
The heads of Ramses II were carefully dissected on the ground before being ferried by truck to the clifftop.

Simbel temples and set them on the hilltop 212 feet above their original positions. First a cofferdam was built to protect the site from the rising waters, and 5,000 truckloads of sand were piled up over the exterior statues to protect them as the upper part of the cliff and façade was removed. Then the temple itself was methodically dissected into 1,050 blocks of stone, using mechanical cutters and handsaws. The blocks, numbered and cataloged, were gently lowered onto sand-filled trailers and moved to the hilltop site.

Both temples had been cleared by April 1966; in September the rising lake invaded their vacated sites. Meanwhile, reconstruction had already begun. This involved not just reassembling the pieces, but creating an entire artificial hill in which to set the temples, to replicate their original backdrop. By the autumn of 1967, the temples of Abu Simbel had been saved—at a cost of $40 million.

TEMPLE REBORN Once set into the base of a cliff, the temple is now on its own artificial mound.

DELTA PROJECT

THE DUTCH RAISED THEIR DEFENSES AGAINST THE SEA WITH AN INNOVATIVE SYSTEM OF DAMS

The Netherlands is a nation at constant war—with the sea. About one-quarter of its land area is below sea level, reclaimed from the water and protected by dykes. The Dutch are accustomed to periodic flooding—usually caused by fierce winter storms and exceptionally high tides. But in February 1953, a devastating flood inundated 1,250 square miles and caused unprecedented damage: 1,835 people were killed and 72,000 had to be evacuated, 200,000 livestock were drowned and 47,000 buildings were damaged. The Dutch were determined to provide better protection for the vulnerable southwest of their country.

The result was one of the world's most ambitious coastal management projects and took nearly 30 years to complete. It was named the Delta Project because it covers a complex web of rivers, estuaries, islands and channels in the delta formed by three rivers, the Rhine, the Maas (or Meuse) and the Scheldt. Four large islands lie in the delta, and the main goal was to build a line of dams between them, facing the sea. The channels between the islands were outlets for rivers and were also busy shipping routes, so the flow of both water and traffic had to be accommodated by locks and sluice gates.

Using a scale model to test different combinations of river flow, tide, wind and currents, hydraulics engineers in Delft devised a system involving nine major dams. They needed a series of inland dams to control the flow of water within the delta, and then three major dams lining the coast. The first project, a storm flood barrier to the east of Rotterdam, on the River Issel, was completed in 1958. Then work began on the delta itself. The first dams to be completed were the inland ones, built between 1957 and 1969.

Work then focused on the seaward dams. The Haringvliet dam was the first to be completed, spanning the primary outlet for the Rhine and the Maas, a channel 2¾ miles wide. By building a ring of dykes and pumping out the water, an artificial island 1 mile long was created in the channel, and a line of 17 huge concrete piers was constructed on it to hold the sluice gates. The island was then re-flooded, and in 1971, after 14 years of construction, the dam was complete. Meanwhile, the Brouwers dam was also nearing completion. This is a similar sluice complex across a channel 4 miles wide.

The battle for the Eastern Scheldt

The last and biggest of the seaward dams spans a 5 mile wide inlet called the Oosterschelde, or Eastern Scheldt. Two artificial islands had to be created to bridge the channel. The original intention was to build a solid dam, to be completed in 1978. But there were strong environmental objections to blocking off the sea from the Eastern Scheldt and drowning the extensive tidal marshlands in a freshwater lake. After a long and bitter wrangle, the government backed down. Engineers set about designing a massive storm surge barrier, which would remain open to tidal flow but which could lower its 62 steel gates in the event of a flood warning. This is the biggest tidal barrier in the world, stretching for 5½ miles.

Because the Eastern Scheldt was now to be tidal, the adjacent Scheldt-Rhine shipping canal had to be protected by two additional inland dams. One of these, the Oester dam, is the longest in the delta: 6¾ miles.

The Eastern Scheldt dam was opened by Queen Beatrix of the Netherlands on October 4, 1986, marking the official completion of the Delta Project.

JEWEL IN THE CROWN The Eastern Scheldt, the world's largest tidal barrier, was designed to maintain the natural rhythms of the inlet.

HOOVER DAM

A NEW TECHNOLOGY OF CONSTRUCTION CREATES A DAM THAT OPENS UP THE AMERICAN SOUTHWEST

The Hoover Dam was a project born of necessity. As early as the Teddy Roosevelt administration of 1904, it was determined that the cycles of drought and flood throughout the American southwest prohibited agricultural growth in that region. It was believed that a dam that could control the flow of the Colorado River could also provide hydroelectric power, making the dam financially self-sufficient.

When the Swing-Johnson bill detailing the Hoover Dam project passed in Congress in 1927, construction companies around the country began to look over the proposals. Most agreed that the plan was a pipe dream.

The landscape was unforgiving and current technology was not advanced enough to build a dam of that size. However, despite this general pessimism, in March of 1931 five bids were made on the project—the winning bid was submitted by a conglomerate named Six Companies, Inc. They now had the daunting task of completing what many believed to be an impossible and extremely dangerous project.

Taming the Colorado

Because the dam site was so remote, the first job was to lay roads and railroad lines, and amass materials needed around the site. With access to the site secured and all the materials in place, there was still a great deal of work to be done even before the first of the concrete could be poured. The most important undertaking was the diversion of the Colorado River. Four diversion tunnels were cut over a period of a year and lined with concrete. A temporary cofferdam was constructed that pushed the river into the diversion tunnels. In the minds of many engineers, the project was now already deep into technologically uncharted territory.

Following the diversion of the river, the floor of the canyon was dredged down to bedrock. Only then could the pouring of the concrete begin. But now the builders faced their biggest obstacle: the cooling of the concrete. So large a block of concrete would crack if allowed to cool in the ambient air. Engineers calculated that the massive amount of concrete would take over one hundred years to cool and when cool, the dam could still crack.

To avoid this, the concrete was poured in rows and columns of blocks. Refrigerated water was pumped through the blocks in pipes, and the pipes were then shot full of concrete, rendering the dam a true monolith. The dam itself was completed two years ahead of schedule, in 1935. Power generation began in 1936 and turbines continued to be added to the station until 1961, when the last one went on line.

TAMING THE COLORADO Below, an aerial view of Hoover Dam shows how the design uses the natural rock formation of the canyon to buttress the dam, and contain Lake Mead. At left, Hoover Dam at night.

TRANS-ALASKA PIPELINE

A SILVER RIBBON STRADDLING THE ARCTIC CIRCLE CARRIES 1 MILLION BARRELS OF CRUDE OIL A DAY

In 1969, one of the greatest airlifts in history took place across one of the world's most remote and inhospitable landscapes. Wave after wave of airplanes and helicopters made 1,000 take-offs and landings a day, bringing personnel, prefabricated accommodation, and thousands of tons of equipment and supplies to the settlement of Prudhoe Bay on the north coast of Alaska.

In March 1968, oil had been discovered in vast quantities—upward of 12 billion barrels—beneath Alaska's North Slope, the coastal strip to the north of the Brooks Range. A consortium of oil companies planned to extract the oil and pump it 800 miles southward in a pipeline to Valdez, a port on Alaska's south coast. But 1969 proved a false dawn for the oil companies, who were forced by the Alaskan state legislature to postpone the pipeline pending a settlement of land rights. Under the Alaskan Native Claims Settlement Act of 1971, native Alaskan groups were given four years to make territorial claims to the oilfields and to lands along the proposed pipeline route.

Hot property

In 1974, the airlifts began anew, and during the following summer work crews of 20,000 men and women forged ahead with the pipeline. They were working in exceptional conditions, on the cold, wet and ecologically fragile tundra. Because the crude oil is pumped hot from the wells and then kept warm by friction to maintain the flow, the pipeline had to be raised above the ground to prevent the permafrost from melting. This permanently frozen layer of soil turns into an unstable ooze if melted, incapable of supporting the pipeline. So for much of the first 400 miles south of Prudhoe Bay, the pipeline is supported by over 78,000 H-shaped concrete-and-steel stands.

The pipeline bridges large rivers, such as the Yukon, but runs underground beneath smaller streams and in areas crossed by migrating caribou herds. In the south, most of the pipeline runs beneath the ground.

The Trans-Alaska Oil Pipeline was completed in 1977, after a long series of tussles with the authorities over compliance with stipulated safety and environmental standards, and at a cost of some $7.7 billion. Soon 600,000 barrels a day were being pumped southward from Prudhoe Bay to Valdez. Two decades later, with 13 oilfields on stream, the pipeline was carrying 1.45 million barrels a day, and accounting for about one-quarter of the U.S. domestic oil supply. Production has since tailed off, and arguments have begun about whether oil exploration should be allowed in neighboring territories so as to keep the pipeline fully operational. But neighboring land includes the protected Arctic National Wildlife Refuge, triggering an ever fiercer debate that pits the preservation of one of the world's unique wilderness environments against Alaska's need to maintain its revenues.

ZIGZAGGING INTO THE SUNSET The raised pipeline has the flexibility to expand and contract with the great variations in temperature, and provides some protection against earthquakes.

ODEILLO SOLAR OVEN

THE WORLD'S LARGEST SOLAR OVEN PRODUCES THOUSANDS OF DEGREES OF HEAT

As every schoolchild knows, it is possible to create a fire by concentrating the Sun's rays through a magnifying glass. At Odeillo, set high in the mountains at the eastern end of the French Pyrenees, the intense power of the Sun is magnified thousands of times to create a solar oven capable of producing 1,000 kilowatts of energy, and attaining temperatures of up to 6,875°F—about two-thirds of the temperature of the Sun's surface.

Because it can apply these very high temperatures swiftly and in conditions free from any fuel contamination, the "Four Solaire d'Odeillo" is a key research station for the French scientific establishment. The physical and chemical effects of very high temperatures can be observed, analyzed, predicted and controlled; the practical applications of these temperatures include forging new metal alloys and testing materials for the aerospace industry.

The high temperatures are attained by applying the magnifying-glass principle. The Sun's rays are collected by an immense parabolic mirror 177 feet wide and 131 feet high, made up of 9,500 panels. This reflects the Sun's rays toward a single focus: the solar oven positioned in a tower 59 feet in front of the mirror, and 43 feet above the ground.

However, the Sun moves through the sky as the day passes. Because of the size of the parabolic mirror, it would be impractical to turn it constantly to face the Sun. Instead, a double-reflection system is used.

The initial task of capturing the Sun's rays

MIRROR IMAGES The 63 flat reflector mirrors swivel to track the path of the Sun as it moves through the sky.

is done by 63 flat reflectors, called heliostats, which are lined up in eight rows on the hillside opposite the parabolic mirror. These are each mounted on electronically controlled machinery, which turns them toward the Sun. The Sun's rays are then reflected off the heliostats and onto the parabolic mirror, which remains stationary; in fact, the mirror is mounted on an eight-story building containing workshops and laboratories. By means of its heliostats and parabolic mirror, the Odeillo Solar Oven— which first came into operation in 1969—is able to multiply the energy received naturally from the Sun at the Earth's surface by a factor of 10,000.

CONCENTRATED SUNSHINE The parabolic mirror is the centerpiece of the Odeillo complex. It reflects light into the rectangular building, which houses the solar oven.

WAIRAKEI GEOTHERMAL POWER STATION

NEW ZEALAND TAPS THE VAST HEAT OF THE EARTH'S CORE TO GENERATE ELECTRICITY

In 186 AD Mount Taupo, at the center of New Zealand's North Island, was ripped apart by the world's most violent volcanic explosion of the past 5,000 years. This active volcanic area is famous, above all, for the hot springs at Rotorua, 40 miles to the north of the town of Taupo. But the whole region is dotted with hot springs, boiling mud pools, steaming lakes and geysers, for it is directly connected to the fault line that lies to the east of North Island, where two of the Earth's tectonic plates, the Pacific Plate and the Indian-Australian Plate, collide.

The molten core of the Earth is heated to a temperature of 7,232°F. Molten rock pushes upward through the fault lines in the Earth's plates, sometimes reaching the surface as volcanic eruptions. When underground water comes into contact with this molten rock, it becomes superheated. While under pressure the water remains liquid, but if it finds its way to the Earth's surface, reduced pressure converts it into steam with explosive force, as seen in geysers.

The idea of harnessing this "geothermal" energy to produce electricity was first developed in Italy as early as 1904, and a power station at Larderello in Tuscany had developed a modest 250 kilowatt capacity by 1913. Similar experiments were conducted in Taupo in 1906, but it was not until after the Second World War, when increased energy resources were needed to meet demand, that New Zealand began to exploit its natural geothermal resources on a large scale.

After extensive drilling and research in the early 1950s, the location chosen to build New Zealand's first geothermal power station was Wairakei, a few miles to the north

STEAM POWER Released from subterranean pressure, the steam speeds down pipes toward the turbines in the power station. Meanwhile, residue hot water cools in tanks, covering the valley with clouds of vapor.

of Taupo. Wells were dug down to hot, pressurized water aquifers, the power plant was constructed, and the Wairakei Geothermal Power Station began operations in 1958.

Power from the Earth

The wells at Wairakei have been dug to an average depth of about 3,000 feet, using drill-rigs similar to those of the oil industry. When the layer of geothermally heated water is reached, the bore hole—about 8 inches wide—is capped with a wellhead that sits in a small concrete bunker. The water, at a temperature of about 480°F, surges up to the wellhead under the force of its own pressure. A "Rogue Bore" resulting from a drilling mishap in 1960 demonstrated dramatically the scale of this pressure: it blasted a crater 72 feet deep and created a plume of steam that could be seen from 75 miles away until it died back in 1973.

At the wellhead, the water is under great pressure and only about 20 percent of it is in the form of steam. As the turbines in the power station operate on "dry steam," the water has to be removed. This is done close to the wellhead by spinning the steam-water mixture around a cylindrical separator, which uses centrifugal force to throw the water to the side. The steam is piped off, and some of the separated water is reintroduced in the form of steam as its pressure is reduced.

Meanwhile, the pressurized steam is heading off overland toward the power station at a speed of 125 miles per hour. It passes along pipes for up to 4 miles, following crooked paths that allow the metal to expand and contract as the heat varies. Where the pipes cross pasture they are raised to head height. In the past, when pipes were closer to the ground, sheep would sometimes snuggle up to them for warmth and the heat discolored their wool.

About 50 wells are now feeding into the Wairakei power station, bringing about 1,400 tons of steam per hour to the turbines that generate electricity. On the other side of the turbines, the steam is cooled by water piped in from the Waikato river. This creates a vacuum that pulls more steam toward it, adding to the surge through the turbine rotors and increasing their generating capacity. The condensed steam is then cooled and the water discharged into the Waikato river. Both Wairakei and its sister station, Ohaaki, are operated by a central control room at

THE BLUE LAGOON

Geothermal power is exploited in many countries, including Iceland, the Philippines, the U.S., Mexico and Kenya. It is used not only to generate electricity, but also to power industrial equipment, to heat swimming pools and greenhouses, and to supply hot water for domestic heating systems. New Zealand's Wairakei also supplies hot water to tanks in which tropical freshwater prawns are farmed.

Iceland has a greater concentration of geothermal activity than any other country in the world, and exploits it to supply 5.8 percent of the island's electricity and 86 percent of its domestic heating. It also heats 37 acres of greenhouses and over 80 swimming pools.

The Svartsengi Power Station to the southwest of Reykjavik has a dual role of generating electricity and supplying hot water for domestic

NATURAL ENERGY At Svartsengi, the energy from Iceland's violent geology is siphoned off to provide power and domestic heating, as well as the warm waters of the Blue Lagoon.

heating. The boreholes descend to 6,560 feet, where seawater seeps into the aquifers. Because the water from the boreholes is salty, it cannot be supplied directly to heating systems. Instead, waste water is discharged at a temperature of up to 158°F into a lake beside the plant. The mineral content and algae in the lake make the water appear a brilliant blue against the white background of deposits. The "Blue Lagoon," as it is called, is effectively a huge, warm mineral bath with known medical benefits.

BLUE HEAVEN Lying just 25 miles from Iceland's capital, Reykjavik, the Blue Lagoon receives over 100,000 visitors a year, who are able to enjoy the salty, mineral-rich water in all seasons.

Wairakei. The power station at Wairakei has a generating capacity of 153 megawatts, Ohaaki 104 megawatts—a total of 257 megawatts, or about 7 percent of New Zealand's electricity needs.

All geothermal fields decline with time as the temperature of the intermediary layers cool, even if new wells are drilled. By 1963, after five years of operation, Wairakei had 13 turbines, handling steam at various pressures and with a generating capacity of 192 megawatts. Since then, the pressure in the wells has decreased by up to 5 percent a year, so the high-pressure turbines have been decommissioned, leaving just the intermediate and low pressure ones. Wairakei is likely to remain a viable source of energy at least into the second decade of the 21st century.

ALTAMONT PASS WIND FARM

THOUSANDS OF WINDMILLS HARNESS THE ENERGY OF THE BREEZE TO PRODUCE ELECTRICITY

Wind power has been used since medieval times to drive windmills, which turned millstones to grind grain. In Holland, windmills were later altered to pump water out of reclaimed land. The idea of using wind to make electricity evolved in the 1920s. To power a generator, the sails had to turn much faster than in a traditional windmill. Multibladed fans, like those used on water pumps since the late 19th century, were adapted by Marcellus Jacobs to make wind generators that could supply modest quantities of electricity to remote farm and rural communities.

It was only in the 1970s, during the oil crisis, that wind power was seriously considered as an alternative source of electricity that could be fed into national electricity supplies. The improved efficiency of modern generators and propellers, or rotors, had made the idea increasingly practical.

In principle, wind power is one of the cheapest and cleanest ways of creating electricity. Its disadvantages are that the generators cease to produce electricity when there is no wind, and they cannot operate safely in very high winds. As with all energy sources, wind power also has an environmental impact. Wind farms consist of hundreds, or even thousands, of generators and occupy large areas of land. And not everyone is happy to live near them as the rotors make a certain amount of noise and flicker constantly. As a result, wind farms are still used only as a supplementary source of energy.

The country with the most wind farms is the U.S., and most of its wind power is in

ENERGY ON THE BREEZE Ranks of three-bladed windmills line a hillside at Altamont. This image shows less than 1 percent of the total number of windmills at the farm.

California, where it accounts for over 1 percent of the state's electricity—enough to light a city of 1 million inhabitants. The largest of California's three primary wind farms, with over 5,000 windmills, is at Altamont Pass, 40 miles east of San Francisco.

Altamont Pass conducts long-term research on wind-farm technology, testing windmills from all over the world, including Germany, Belgium, Denmark, Britain and America. The more conventional-looking horizontal axis windmills have two or three blades, like aircraft propellers. Electronic sensors turn them into the wind. Vertical-axis windmills, which look like large eggbeaters, can pick up wind from any direction.

A COLOSSAL PROTOTYPE

Engineer Palmer Putnam made the first serious attempt to build a windmill that could generate electricity for the public-service network. With S. Morgan Smith Company, he created one of the biggest wind machines ever, mounted on Grandpa's Knob, a 2,000 foot peak in Vermont. Its two 8 ton blades had a combined span of 175 feet. Capable of generating 1,250 watts, the Smith-Putnam Wind Turbine came into operation in 1941, but it was abandoned in 1945 due to mechanical problems.

The size of the blade affects the amount of power produced. All things being equal, if the size of the blade is doubled, it will produce four times the power. If the wind speed is doubled, on the other hand, the power will increase eightfold. However, large fluctuations in output are not always desirable. In fact, modern windmills "feather" if the wind becomes too strong, effectively spilling the wind to maintain a constant level of power production. Wind farms tend to exist in places where the wind is reliable, moderate and steady, above Force 3 (or 12 mph), and below Force 10 (or 55 mph).

Altamont Pass has been selected because it lies among rolling hills through which wind passes seasonally in a generally steady stream at 16-28 mph between May and September, drawn in from the coast by the warm valley beyond.

ITAIPÚ DAM

TWO SOUTH AMERICAN COUNTRIES JOINED FORCES TO BUILD THE LARGEST DAM AND POWER STATION

The Paraná river is the seventh-longest in the world, and the second-longest in Brazil after the Amazon. It once flowed over the Guairá Falls, the world's largest waterfall by volume—twice the size of Niagara Falls. But no more: in 1982 the Guairá Falls were swamped by another giant, the Itaipú dam—the biggest dam in the world at the time—118 miles downstream.

Straddling the border between Brazil and Paraguay, and owned and operated by both, the Itaipú dam is vast: nearly 5 miles long and 738 feet high, it includes 18 huge turbines with a generating capacity of 13,320 megawatts of electricity—making it the world's largest power station. Power was the inspiration: Brazil in particular wanted to create a source of energy capable of supplying a burgeoning industrial base.

Diversion tactics

The site chosen lies 6 miles north of Foz do Iguaçu, the spot where the borders of Brazil, Paraguay and Argentina meet and a base for visitors to the magnificent Iguaçu Falls, which were not affected by the dam. Work began in 1974. The first challenge was to stem the flow of the Paraná river, so that the main part of the dam could be built across its course. This was achieved by diverting the river into a new channel. But first a control dam was built on dry land in the path of the diversion channel. This was a concrete gravity dam, which uses its massive weight and the downward pressure of water on its lower sections to stay in place.

Meanwhile a 300 foot deep channel was dug for the diverted river to run through, with cofferdams on either side of the control dam to keep water from the river flowing into the new channel before the control dam was built. When the control dam was

EXCESS POWER As water from the Paraná river flows through the turbines of the power station on the right, the river level is maintained by water gushing down six open gates of the spillway.

DAMMING THE YANGTZE

Over the past 2,000 years, the Yangtze (Chang Jiang), China's longest river and the third-longest in the world, has flooded some 200 times—an average of once a decade. The people of the Yangtze basin have suffered four catastrophic floods this century, in 1931, 1935, 1954 and 1975, incurring great loss of life and widespread damage to property and agricultural land. Meanwhile, between 1970 and 1990, China's energy needs tripled. Traditionally, China has generated electricity by burning fossil fuels, particularly coal, but this has become increasingly expensive and environmentally unsound.

For these reasons, in 1992 China decided to forge ahead with a $23 billion plan to dam the Yangtze, in order both to control the river and tap its power. The site chosen lies some 850 miles upriver at Sandouping, in Hubei Province, at the eastern end of a series of narrow defiles called the Three Gorges. Work began in 1994 and should last until 2009. It has followed the same construction plan as Itaipú, beginning with a diversion channel. This was completed in 1997 after the biggest earth-moving project in history.

The main dam, a concrete gravity dam, will be 1¹/₄ miles wide and 610 feet high, and its 26 turbines will have a generating capacity of 18,200 megawatts—nearly 40 percent greater than that of Itaipú. When complete, 10,000 ton ships will be able to pass through a six-part lock and, for the first time, reach Chongqing in Sichuan, China's most important inland industrial city, which lies a further 400 miles upriver.

As with dam projects elsewhere in the world, the construction of the Yangtze dam has attracted widespread criticism. Its reservoir will drown the Three Gorges, famous for their beauty and inhabited by nearly 1 million people. The government is well aware of environmental criticisms, but knows also that the alternatives—nuclear power and fossil fuels—have equally unpalatable disadvantages, and none of the benefits of controlling a troublesome river.

A MIGHTY TASK   When it is completed, the Three Gorges Dam hydroelectric power station will outstrip Itaipú's by a considerable margin.

complete, the cofferdams were blasted away by explosives and water flowed down the diversion channel through a set of 12 huge sluice gates in the dam.

This took much of the force out of the main stream of the river, which was then blocked off with cofferdams. Twenty tractors and 100 dump trucks worked 24 hours a day over ten days, tipping rock and soil into the river to beat the annual floods and create the foundations for the upstream cofferdam. The river now flowed entirely down the diversion channel, and massive cofferdams were secured north and south of the site of the main dam. Water was then drained from the old riverbed between the cofferdams, so that the main dam—a hollow gravity dam—could be built on dry land.

Meanwhile, a curving buttress dam was being built across the west bank of the river to a 1,280 foot long spillway. This spillway would eventually take over the task of the sluice gates in the control dam: acting like the overflow pipe in a bathtub, it would tip any excess water from the reservoir back into the river through its 14 open gates. An additional earthfill-

WORLD RECORD   With 18 turbines and generating units in the main section of the dam, Brazil and Paraguay share the largest hydroelectric power station in the world.

and-rockfill dam spread eastward to contain the 520 square mile reservoir—the Itaipú Lake—that would build up behind the dam complex.

Powering up

The dam began operations in 1984, when the first generator came onstream; construction work was completed in 1991 with the installation of the eighteenth generating unit. The whole task had taken 16 years, involved a workforce of 40,000, and a cost of $25 billion.

The Itaipú Lake had taken only 40 days to fill. Some 200,000 people had to move, and 30,000 animals were rescued. The dam's operators, conscious of environmental objections, planted 15 million trees around the lake and created a series of nature reserves.

Under the treaty between Paraguay and Brazil, both nations take an equal share of the electricity generated by the dam, but Paraguay sells any surplus from its share to Brazil at a knockdown price in return for Brazil's help in financing the project. By 1996, Itaipú was providing 26 percent of Brazil's electricity needs, and 88 percent of Paraguay's.

THAMES BARRIER

AN INGENIOUS MOBILE BARRIER PROTECTS
LONDON FROM THE THREAT OF FLOODING

Downstream from the center of London, a neat row of glinting domes straddles the River Thames. Serene and otherworldly, they look as though they might be part of some ancient myth—a set of magical silver sandals perhaps, left behind by giant Roman legionaries to protect their old city from supernatural forces.

For centuries London was at the mercy of the North Sea, which from time to time surged up the broad estuary of the River Thames and inundated the city. This occurrence is associated with a combination of weather patterns. Low pressure over the Atlantic brings a large amount of water into the North Sea, which swells further as it pushes toward the narrow Strait of Dover. If this coincides with one of the high "spring tides" that occurs twice every month in the Thames Estuary, London risks being submerged. In 1928 London was flooded, and in 1953 it was saved only by the collapse of sea defenses farther east, an event which itself killed 300 people.

The southeast of Britain is slowly sinking, while the sea level globally is rising: tides in London are set to become 2 feet higher with every century. Something had to be done. Rather than make its riverbank defenses ever taller, the London authorities decided to build a barrier that could be raised in self-defense whenever the Thames threatened to flood. But the Thames is a busy river: the barrier had to be open to shipping and pleasure craft whenever it was not in operation.

The solution was ingenious. A series of ten huge concrete piers would span the river at Woolwich, 8 miles downstream from Westminster and the City. Set between the piers would be huge movable gates, which could be raised from the riverbed to form a wall whenever a flood alert is signalled. Construction began in 1974. Ten years later, on May 8, 1984, the Thames Barrier was officially opened by Queen Elizabeth. However, it had already proved its worth in February 1983, when it was used to fend off a flood for the first time.

LAST LINE OF DEFENSE The massive piers that span the Thames contain hydraulic machinery, protected beneath stainless-steel shells, that raises and lowers the barrier gates between the piers.

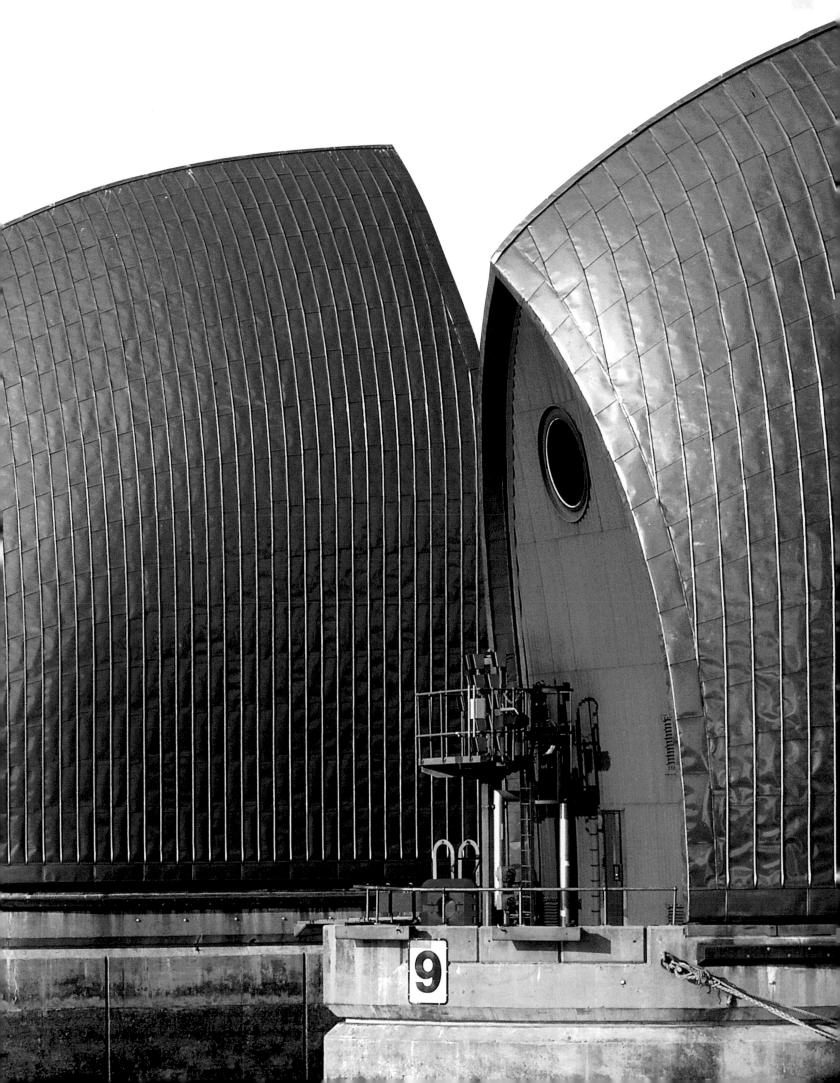

With its gleaming caps of stainless steel, the Thames Barrier looks dainty, but it is built on a massive scale. The piers are 162 feet tall, and are anchored firmly on foundations driven some 50 feet into the riverbed. The largest four gates, in the center, are 200 feet long. Made of steel, they each weigh 3,300 tons—half the weight of the Eiffel Tower. And when in operation they rise to 66 feet—the height of a five-story building. The complete barrier measures 570 yards from bank to bank.

Rising to the threat

The central gates are built like horizontal cylinders with all but one side and the ends removed—like neon strip lights without the bulb. The curved side forms the gate, and it is rotated into position like a drum spinning on the axis of the cylinder.

When at rest, the gates lie in concrete sills on the riverbed, allowing ships to pass through. In a flood alert, or during the regular rehearsals, they are raised by the action of pairs of powerful hydraulic cylinders housed in the piers. These simultaneously pull and push the yellow rocker beams to turn the gates on their axes.

Various monitoring stations on the coasts and on oil rigs at sea keep a constant eye on the weather and the sea level, and are able to warn the barrier staff well in advance if dangerously high tides look likely. These usually occur during the winter months, between October and February. But the barrier can be raised within 15 minutes if necessary, forcing back the massive weight of the incoming tidal surges.

The Thames Barrier keeps London from flooding on a regular basis, once, twice, or as many as six times every year. Costing $535 million to build, it is definitely money well spent: the cost of damage if central London is flooded is estimated at $10 billion, while the human misery would be incalculable.

AT EASE The gates are fixed to the circular hubs at the side of the piers, and as the hubs turn, the gates are raised into position. Under normal conditions, the gates lie at rest on the riverbed, allowing the free passage of shipping (below). The Docklands business district, flagged by the Canary Wharf Tower (above, left), is one of the areas that benefit from the barrier's protection.

MONUMENTS AND MEMORIALS

GREAT MONUMENTS AND PLACES OF WORSHIP OFFER AN UNMATCHED CHALLENGE TO ARCHITECTS AND DESIGNERS: AN OPPORTUNITY TO TAP THE UNIVERSAL EXPERIENCE OF SPIRITUALITY, OR TO CREATE A WORK OF SUCH SCALE OR POWER THAT IT WILL BE REMEMBERED AND ADMIRED FOR GENERATIONS TO COME. BUT EYE-CATCHING PROJECTS ALSO THREATEN THE PERILS OF FAILURE AND RIDICULE ON A GRAND SCALE.

MOUNT RUSHMORE

VAST SCULPTURES HEWN OUT OF A MOUNTAINSIDE MIRROR THE AMERICAN SENSE OF SCALE

John Gutzon Borglum, the creator of the Mount Rushmore National Memorial, demonstrated the soaring ambition of his task to create a monument to last many millennia with the ringing words: "Let us place there, carved high, as close to heaven as we can, the words of our leaders, their faces, to show posterity what manner of men they were. Then breathe a prayer that these records will endure until the wind and the rain alone shall wear them away." Only time will reveal the extent of his success, but even in Borglum's own lifetime his massive portraits of great American presidents had acquired celebrity status and world renown.

The presidents—George Washington, Thomas Jefferson, Abraham Lincoln and Theodore Roosevelt—were chosen as shining examples of America's aspirations. But the same might also be said of the story of how the sculptures were made. This was a vast, daring and almost unprecedented enterprise that took 14 years of determination and intense labor to achieve.

It all began in 1923, when a South Dakota historian named Doane Robinson dreamt up the grand plan of turning the Needles—a prominent geological feature of the Black Hills—into huge sculptures of heroes of the West such as Buffalo Bill, as a way of attracting tourists to South Dakota. He put the idea to a leading sculptor of the day, John Gutzon Borglum (1871-1941), an American of Danish descent. Borglum had trained in Paris under the great French sculptor Auguste Rodin, and had won national acclaim for his bust of Lincoln in the U.S. Capitol in Washington DC. But what made Borglum uniquely qualified for the job was his experience at the Confederate Memorial at Stone Mountain in Georgia. He was the first sculptor to tackle this vast relief carving —but in 1925 he fell out with its organizers and abandoned the project.

Borglum now turned his attention to Doane Robinson's idea, but he quickly dismissed the initial concept. For one thing, the Needles were unsuitable for sculpture. Borglum selected a new site: Mount

SCULPTING MOUNTAINS

In 1915, 50 years after the end of the Civil War, a group of Southerners decided to commemorate the defeated Confederate cause with a carving at the foot of Stone Mountain, 20 miles east of Atlanta, Georgia. They approached the sculptor Gutzon Borglum, who soon ran into conflict with the Stone Mountain Memorial Association, and stormed off in March 1925. It was left to the sculptor Augustus Lukeman to pick up the pieces. He proposed a composition featuring three key leaders of the Confederacy mounted on horseback: Confederate President Jefferson Davis, General Robert E. Lee and General "Stonewall" Jackson. Carving with pneumatic drills, his team worked for three years on the mountain face before the money ran out in 1928. The project was revived by the state of Georgia, and in 1964 work was resumed under Walter Kirtland Hancock, with Roy Faulkner as chief carver. Using thermo-jet torches their team made rapid progress, and in March 1972 the task was completed. Meanwhile, work had begun on an even larger project.

In 1939, in South Dakota, the Polish-American sculptor Korczak Ziolkowski (1908-82) was asked by a Sioux chief to create a statue of Crazy Horse, the Oglala Sioux leader who helped to wipe out General Custer's men at Little Big Horn in 1886. In 1947, work began on turning Thunderhead Mountain into a vast statue of Crazy Horse. The final statue will be 563 feet tall and 641 feet long; Crazy Horse's head alone is the size of all Mount Rushmore's heads combined. Ziolkowski died in 1982, but the work is being continued by his family, and is expected to take until the middle of the 21st century to complete.

LARGEST OF THEM ALL The triple portrait at Stone Mountain, at 90 feet high and 1¹/₃ acres, is the world's largest sculpture.

Rushmore, which offered a solid core of stable, fine-grained granite and faced the Sun for most of the day. He was also unsympathetic to Robinson's subject matter, which he felt was too trite. He proposed instead to carve busts of the greatest American presidents—vast sculptures to act as noble and dignified symbols of the virtues of the America that Borglum so much admired. He also intended to incorporate a huge inscription panel and a Hall of Records containing historic archives.

Formally commissioned in 1925, Borglum set about creating large plaster models of the presidents. Even scaled down to 1:12, each head was the size of a standing human being. Work on the mountain face began in earnest in 1927, following official dedication by President Calvin Coolidge, and now supported by federal funds as well as donations raised by the Mount Rushmore National Memorial Society. First the surface of the mountain had to be prepared. Tons of rock were removed to knock back its flanks

AT THE ROCK FACE The four presidents—from left to right Washington, Jefferson, Theodore Roosevelt and Lincoln—represent respectively the founding, political philosophy, preservation and expansion of the nation.

to a suitable core. Some 30 feet of debris had to be cut away before work could begin on the first head, that of Washington.

Instead of the usual sculptor's tools of mallet and chisel, Borglum and his team used pneumatic drills and dynamite. Winched down the cliff face in cradles like bosun's chairs, they drilled to a depth dictated by Borglum's "pointing machine," a giant enlarging tool that indicated the desired dimensions based on extrapolations from the models.

At such close quarters, it was extremely difficult for the workers to have any concept of the sculpture as a whole: they had to take directions from the pointing machine on trust. Drilling was no mean feat either, given that the drills weighed 85 pounds. To gain sufficient purchase, the drillers had to brace

INSPECTING PROGRESS   Seated in his car, President Franklin Roosevelt talks to Gutzon Borglum during a visit to Mount Rushmore in September 1936. Work is under way on the third head, that of Abraham Lincoln.

COSMETIC SURGERY   Drillers, suspended from the cliff top, pockmark the granite rock face in preparation for light blasting to shape Washington's chin and mouth.

themselves against chains fixed into the rock face and slung around their backs. The drill bits were often blunt after just 15 minutes' work, and an on-site blacksmith worked full time sharpening drill bits to maintain a supply of replacements.

Dynamite was inserted into the holes by experts largely recruited from the local mines. By this crude means, the basic shapes of the sculpture were roughed out to within a few inches of their final dimensions.

The final shaping could now begin. This was achieved by drilling the rock with countless holes of carefully regulated depth, creating a honeycomb pattern. Then the rock between the holes was knocked away with hammers and metal wedges. Lastly, the remaining rock was "bumped" with pneumatic hammers to produce a smooth finish.

The pupils in the eyes were left as a pillar of rock in a cavity—a touch that gives a surprising sparkle of animation to the faces.

Washington's head was completed in 1930. It was a moment of triumph for Borglum. The sculpture was a truly monumental achievement: some 60 feet high, it could be seen from a distance of 60 miles away. At the dedication ceremony Mount Rushmore was labelled "a Shrine of Democracy."

Heads you lose

Work then began on the next head, that of Thomas Jefferson. In the original plan, this was to appear to the left of Washington. However, further excavation showed the rock here to be unsuitable, so in 1934 Borglum was forced to resite Jefferson to the right of Washington. Jefferson was completed in 1936 and Lincoln in 1937. Work now began on the last head, that of Roosevelt, set back to a depth of 120 feet from the original flank of the mountain. A huge pile of debris was accumulating in the cleft below, a visual indicator of the many thousands of tons of rock that had been removed.

In this final phase Gutzon Borglum's son Lincoln took over the role of supervisor. Gutzon Borglum died in March 1941, seven months before his masterwork was finally completed. His achievement was overshadowed by his death and the onset of the Second World War, and the statues were not formally dedicated until July 4, 1991, when they were at last officially inaugurated and dedicated as the Mount Rushmore National Memorial.

SAGRADA FAMILIA

**AN UNFINISHED ARCHITECTURAL FANTASY HAS
PROVOKED UNENDING CONTROVERSY**

The Templo Expiatorio de la Sagrada Familia (Expiatory Temple of the Holy Family) in Barcelona is one of the world's most extraordinary and eccentric buildings, and haunts the 20th century like a half-remembered dream. Started in 1879, it remains unfinished over a century later, and no one can predict when it will be completed.

It is the most famous work of the Spanish architect Antoní Gaudí (1852-1926), who is celebrated for his highly sculptural interpretation of Art Nouveau, which gave a new range of surreal and fantastic shapes and multicolored decoration to architecture. Gaudí was 31 years old and little known in 1883 when he was commissioned to take on the Sagrada Familia following the resignation of the first architect. His client was the

WORK IN PROGRESS Only one tower of the Façade of the Nativity was complete at Gaudí's death in 1926. Capped by a colorful ceramic finial (below), it provided a pattern for the completion of the façade (right).

arch-conservative Spiritual Association for Devotion to Saint Joseph (the Josephines), a private religious foundation created in the 1860s to promote traditional family values. The Josephines in Barcelona were widely supported, and raised large sums of money to build their own center of devotion to the Holy Family.

Unique vision

Gaudí was a strange choice as architect for the Josephines, especially since they had originally decided on a conventional, neo-Gothic church. But Gaudí was fervently religious and brought a new zeal to the task. And his controversial work attracted the kind of publicity and debate that the Josephines thought beneficial.

Quite what Gaudí had planned remains unclear. His designs evolved as the years

CRIB SCENE Realistic sculptures people a traditional nativity scene above and around the main door, while the backdrop of organic shapes in draped and drizzled concrete has an whimsically unearthly quality.

passed, becoming ever more elaborate, more deeply symbolic, and more expensive to execute. He worked like a sculptor alongside the construction workers and craftsmen, constantly altering his plans as the building progressed and as new thoughts came to him. The basic plan was to create three main façades, dedicated to the Nativity, the Passion and the Resurrection. These would each be surmounted by four towers, making twelve altogether to represent the Twelve Apostles. There would be an additional tower devoted to the Virgin, and one dominant central tower, rising to 591 feet, devoted to the Savior.

When Gaudí died, in 1926, only a small portion of his grand plan had been completed: the Façade of the Nativity up to the rose window, and just one tower capped with a colorful ceramic finial. Other architects were appointed to continue the work overseeing the construction, and the Façade of the Nativity and its three other towers were completed between 1927 and 1935.

By now, money was running short as the Josephines' agenda fell from favor. In 1929, Barcelona held an International Exhibition in which Miës van de Rohe's sleek, modern, German pavilion heralded the birth of the International Style. Gaudí's architecture seemed irretrievably obsolete.

Then came the Spanish Civil War (1936-9). On the night of June 20, 1936, the Sagrada Familia, an unloved symbol of the Catholic right, was attacked by anarchists, and most of Gaudí's models and plans were destroyed. The church seemed doomed to remain an unfinished monument to Gaudí's unique vision—which is how many critics feel it should stay.

Others argued, however, that a church is traditionally the work of many generations, that Gaudí would have liked his project to be completed, and that there was enough evidence in the surviving drawings and models to show what he intended. In 1954 work resumed, the Façade of the Passion and four further towers were completed, and work has continued ever since, assisted by funding from Japanese corporations, who hold Gaudí in high regard.

A MASTER OF EXPRESSIVE FORMS

ANTONÍ GAUDÍ Gaudí's intensity and strong sense of purpose translated into obsession toward the end of his life.

It was not until the renaissance of interest in Art Nouveau in the 1960s that Gaudí's name was widely known outside Barcelona. He spent his career almost entirely in that city, the capital of Catalonia, working primarily for his great patron, the textile manufacturer Eusebi Güell. Besides the cathedral, Gaudí is best known for his two apartment blocks, the Casa Batlló and the Casa Milá (1906-10), and the Parque Güell (1900-14), an unfinished complex of residences set around a park. All demonstrate a highly personal style of undulating surfaces, zoomorphic imagery and brilliant color. These were features of the distinctly Catalan school of Art Nouveau called *modernista*, but Gaudí went further than just decoration: he was challenging traditional assumptions about architectural shape. His structural forms took contemporary materials to the edge of the possible.

The Casa Milá was Gaudí's last commission, and Eusebi Güell died in 1916. After this, Gaudí devoted himself entirely to the Sagrada Familia, and became increasingly obsessed by it. He lived like a hermit in a hut on the worksite, rarely leaving except to go knocking on doors to raise funds. Wealthy acquaintances would cross the street at his approach. Living on a meager diet, he became dishevelled and increasingly feeble as he entered his seventies, and his life came to an abrupt end when he was run over by a bus. Enthusiasm for his masterpiece may have slackened, but he remained well known in Barcelona, and was still much admired for his single-minded devotion to his work; 10,000 people accompanied his funeral procession, when he was laid to rest in the crypt of the Sagrada Familia.

NOTRE-DAME DU HAUT, RONCHAMP

ONE OF THE CENTURY'S MOST CELEBRATED CHAPELS WAS BUILT BY THE HIGH PRIEST OF FUNCTIONALISM

With its angled walls and hollow concrete roof inspired by the shell of a crab, Notre-Dame du Haut at Ronchamp, in eastern France, came as a shock when it was unveiled in 1955. Designed by Le Corbusier, one of the most vigorous proponents of functionalism, it represented an expressive and sculptural approach to architecture. In place of his box-like shapes and penetrating horizontals, here was a building with barely a straight line in it, speaking not of the hard-edged industrial future so much as of the organic shapes of nature and a rural past.

Notre-Dame du Haut is one of a series of radical new churches and chapels commissioned in France in the aftermath of the Second World War, in which leading artists and architects were given a free hand. The

PLACE OF PILGRIMAGE The architectural shapes of the chapel provide the focal point of an outdoor nave. The pulpit and altar are used during outdoor pilgrimage ceremonies, when up to 12,000 people gather for services.

chapel in Vence (1947-51) decorated by the painter Henri Matisse is another example. Le Corbusier was approached by the Archbishop of Besançon to design a replacement for a neo-Gothic hilltop pilgrimage church at Ronchamp, which had been destroyed during the war. The project appealed to Le Corbusier, partly because it lay just 41 miles from La Chaux-de-Fonds, his place of birth just over the Swiss border, and also because it was a contrast to the major projects occupying him at the time, such as the Unité d'Habitation apartment blocks and the new city of Chandigarh in India. At Ronchamp, he was able to give full expression in architecture to his own artistic talents, and to explore the sculptural potential of concrete.

Spiritual tension

Le Corbusier declared that he wished "to create a place of silence, of prayer, of peace, of spiritual joy" at Ronchamp. In fact, he did rather more than this: he created a place of finely balanced spiritual tension, poised between restlessness and meditation.

The exterior consists of a hefty cluster of bold shapes folding in on one another; the roughcast

SILENT CALM The deeply recessed windows of colored glass were mainly painted by Le Corbusier himself.

concrete walls are pierced by a haphazard configuration of windows, notably on the south wall. The main entrance is through the north wall, between the twin towers of two side chapels. The east side doubles up as an outdoor church. A relic of the Virgin Mary is visible in the window, and this provides the focus for pilgrimage ceremonies held on the grassy slopes around the chapel.

By contrast, the interior has an intense, womb-like embrace. The main body of the chapel is just 43 feet wide and 82 feet long, lit by banks of small, irregular-shaped windows. They invite the spectator to move constantly in order to view them, and with each step comes a new, changed perspective of the whole. "Good architecture 'walks' and 'moves,' inside as outside," declared Le Corbusier. "It is living architecture." And Notre-Dame du Haut is an example of his dictum.

SHRI SWAMINARAYAN MANDIR

THE LARGEST NEW HINDU TEMPLE TO BE BUILT OUTSIDE INDIA IS IN A LONDON SUBURB

Neasden is famous for its ordinariness, a north London suburb of small industrial estates, tower blocks and residential streets lined with red-brick terrace houses. It makes an incongruous setting for one of Britain's most extraordinary 20th-century buildings, the Shri Swaminarayan Mandir, a Hindu temple—"an abode of peace, love and harmony"—built to the meticulous standards of ancient religious tradition.

Its story goes back to the 1950s, when Asian followers of the Swaminarayan faith held their first organized meetings in Britain. The founder of the faith was the charismatic Shri Sahajanand Swami (1781-1830) or Swaminarayan, a Hindu saint, reformer and seer, and an advocate of nonviolence and the education of women. During his lifetime he was revered as a god and acquired a following of millions in India, notably in the state of Gujarat. The faith was also taken by emigrants to East Africa.

The population of Swaminarayan devotees in Britain swelled when Ugandan Asians were forced to flee their homeland in 1972. Many prospered in Britain, and it was against this background that the idea of a new temple took hold, inspired by His Holiness Pramukh Swami Maharaj. Money was raised through donations and fundraising, and in 1991 a large plot of land was acquired in Neasden.

The aim was to construct a temple incorporating historic Indian ideas and following Swaminarayan traditions as closely as British building regulations—and climate—would allow. As in Swaminarayan temples in India, there would be two parts to the complex: the sacred mandir, a place of devotion and prayer housing the brightly dressed holy statues, or *murti*; and, attached to the mandir, a *haveli*—a cultural center with meeting halls, a marriage hall, conference center, a vegetarian kitchen and other facilities.

Volunteer work

Working from the design concept of His Holiness, architect C.B. Sompura and his team created the mandir entirely from stone.

PROFUSION OF ORNAMENT The interior of the mandir rises through layers of ornately carved marble detailing. By contrast, the orderly and neatly delineated spaces at floor level create an atmosphere of deep, meditative calm.

It is a *shikharbaddh* or pinnacled mandir: seven tiered pinnacles topped by golden spires crowd the roofline, complemented by five ribbed domes. Inside, serpentine ribbons of stone link the columns in decorative arches, creating a sense of levitation.

All the more remarkable is the fact that this stonework was entirely carved in India. The architects searched for stone that would best stand up to the conditions of Britain. They settled on Bulgarian limestone and Sardinian granite for the exterior, and a mixture of Italian Carrara marble and Indian Ambaji marble for the interior. Nearly 5,000 tons of Bulgarian and Italian stone was shipped to India, where it was carved by a team of over 1,500 stoneworkers in 14 different sites in Gujarat and Rajasthan. A total of 26,300 carved and numbered pieces of stone were then shipped in wooden boxes to Britain, where they were assembled like the pieces of a giant jigsaw puzzle.

Building work began in August 1992. On November 24, the temple recorded the biggest-ever concrete-pour in the U.K.,

when 4,500 tons was put down in 24 hours to create a foundation mat 6 feet thick. The first stone was laid in June 1993; two years later, the building was complete.

The adjoining haveli is almost as impressive. Designed by the British architect Nigel Lane, it is essentially a functional steel-and-concrete building, and includes an assembly hall measuring 164 feet by 148 feet—big enough to accommodate 4,000 people. But again, the application of traditional models and the detailing set the building apart. Whereas stone is the medium of the mandir,

here wood—English oak and Burmese teak—has been fashioned into panels, arches and screens, all carved by craftsmen in India with a cornucopia of geometric patterns, stylized animal heads and garlands of flowers.

The Shri Swaminarayan Mandir complex represents an act of faith. Inspired by His Holiness, more than 1,000 volunteers worked on the building, and many more contributed and solicited donations, or organized sponsored walks and other activities; children raised money by collecting aluminum cans and foil for recycling.

The temple complex was completed in just 27 months, at a cost of more than $10 million, over half of which went to materials. The cost would have been far higher without the efforts of the volunteers. As a result, when the temple was opened in August 1995, a great sense of achievement was felt by all who had contributed.

DOMED SPLENDOR The mandir is the main focus of the complex. Accessed by a broad flight of stairs, it is a ceremonial center and a sanctuary for sacred images of the gods.

STATUE OF CHRIST, RIO DE JANEIRO

CHRIST THE REDEEMER TOWERS DRAMATICALLY OVER THE FORMER CAPITAL OF BRAZIL

The idea of building a large monument on the pyramid-shaped Corcovado Peak emerged when Brazil was searching for a suitable monument to celebrate the first centenary of its independence from Portugal in 1822. In 1921, a competition was organized by a popular magazine, and it was won

The gigantic statue of Christ stands over the bustling, tropical city of Rio de Janeiro as if in blessing. When spotlit at night or wreathed in low cloud, it seems to hover in an indeterminate place somewhere between Earth and Heaven.

TENDER EMBRACE The scale of the statue alone does not justify its place as one of the world's great monuments. It is the tenderness of Christ's gesture that sets it apart, and its magnificent setting: most of the city and the bay of Rio de Janeiro can be seen from its base.

by the engineer and architect Heitor da Silva Costa, who proposed a vast statue of Christ the Redeemer (*Cristo Redentor*) with outstretched arms overlooking the national capital, as Rio then was.

Across the Atlantic

Funds were raised by public donations, including a major contribution from the Vatican, and a group of engineers and sculptors met in Paris to plan the statue's construction. A French sculptor, Paul Landowski (1875-1961), took up the task of modelling the statue, working principally on the head and hands, while the engineers, including da Silva Costa, devised the best way to build the massive body. The statue had to be robust, not only to support the outstretched arms, but also to endure the high winds that scour the peak, which rises sharply to 2,329 feet above sea level.

Much of the statue, which is made from reinforced concrete and faced with soap-stone, was built in Paris and then shipped to Brazil. A 22 foot high pedestal containing a small chapel was erected on Corcovado Peak, and in 1931 the statue was raised into position on top of it. Weighing over 1,400 tons, it stands 98 feet high, while the arms span 75 feet from tip to tip.

Cristo Redentor was inaugurated on October 21, 1931, by Guglielmo Marconi, the Italian inventor of the wireless telegraph, who had designed the spotlights installed around it. Demonstrating the wonders of modern communications, he performed the inauguration by throwing a switch on his yacht in Genoa harbor, on the other side of the Atlantic.

This trick of turning on the statue's illuminations from a remote site has since been repeated twice: in 1965 Pope Paul VI inaugurated a new set of lights from the Vatican; and in 1981 Pope John Paul II again turned on the lights from the Vatican to mark the first half-centenary of the statue.

THE NEW COLOSSI

JAPANESE GIANT The bronze Buddha at Ushiku, Japan, now holds the record as the largest statue in the world.

After its completion in 1886, the Statue of Liberty in New York harbor ranked as the world's most famous giant statue, measuring 152 feet without its pedestal. But since 1990, it has been dwarfed by the vast statue representing the Motherland that has been erected outside Volgograd, Russia, to commemorate the Battle of Stalingrad (1942-3). Constructed from prestressed concrete between 1967 and 1990, it measures 270 feet from the base to the tip of the upraised sword.

The world's largest statue today, however, is a vast bronze Buddha in Japan, the centerpiece of the Jodo Teien Gardens in Ushiku, Ibaraki prefecture, to the east of Tokyo. At 394 feet, it took seven years to construct, and was completed in 1993. The statue is made from bronze panels supported on a steel frame, rather like the curtain walls of a skyscraper, while the plinth and lotus blossom at the base are made of reinforced concrete.

Erected by the Jodo Shinshu (True Pure Land), the most popular Buddhist sect in Japan, the statue represents the Amida Buddha, who presides over the Pure Land, or paradise. There is an observation platform within the statue at 279 feet, giving views over the surrounding countryside. The intention is to provide not just an external image of the Buddha for contemplation, but an internal one as well.

GATEWAY ARCH

THE WORLD'S TALLEST MONUMENT IS A SOARING ARCH OF STEEL WITH A CABLE CAR INSIDE

The city of St. Louis, Missouri, lies at about the midpoint of the great Mississippi river. Founded by the French in 1764 and named after the patron saint of King Louis XV, it lay at the heart of Louisiana, the massive French territory purchased by the United States for $15 million in 1803. As waves of new settlers pressed westward into the Great Plains beyond the Mississippi, St. Louis developed into a key center of trade and transportation, and became known as the Gateway to the West.

During the 1930s, a project was launched to build a monument in St. Louis to celebrate America's westward expansion. The Second World War intervened, and it was not until 1947 that the Jefferson National Expansion Memorial Association set up a competition to choose the most fitting design. The winner was a 37-year-old Finnish-American architect named Eero Saarinen.

Saarinen became known for his unconventional shapes, and his proposal for the Gateway monument was no exception: it was a vast steel arch, rising to 630 feet. It is the tallest sculptural monument in the world. The legs, triangular in cross-section, are spread as far apart as the arch is high. They have sides 54 feet long at the base, tapering to 17 feet at the top, giving sufficient interior space to contain a cable-car system for passengers.

Raising the arch

Although land had been cleared for a monument on the west bank of the Mississippi in 1935, building did not begin until 1963, two years after Saarinen's death. The intervening years helped to provide the technology with which to build the arch. The structure is an inverted catenary arch, its shape naturally formed by a hanging chain and one of the strongest known to engineering. Nonetheless, the vast scale of the project posed unique construction problems, which were resolved without the aid of scaffolding.

The first task was to dig foundations 60 feet deep into the bedrock. Into these were driven concrete piles and 252 steel tensioning bars for each leg, angled to take the direct thrust of the arch. Concrete piers were built at the foot of each leg; then the 12 foot prefabricated steel sections that form the arch were placed one on top of the other and welded into position. The exterior faces are covered with polished stainless steel, the interior with slightly thicker carbon steel. The last of the 142 sections was installed in February 1965, and the arch was completed on October 28 that year, 32 months after commencement.

At the summit is an observation area giving views of 30 miles or more to east and west.

MASTER OF SHAPE

Eero Saarinen (1910-61) was the son of a Finnish architect who moved with his family to the U.S. in 1923. During the 1930s, he studied at the Yale school of architecture before joining his father's firm. He later worked in association with a number of leading architects and designers, including the influential American furniture designer Charles Eames. But it was the Gateway Arch that brought Saarinen to prominence.

His success in winning the competition in 1948 was followed by a commission for the General Motors Technical Center (1949-56) in Warren, Michigan. This was a mainly rectilinear building in which he showed

mastery of the International Style, but it also included an auditorium with a steel dome. Saarinen's Trans World Airline Terminal (1956-62) at what later became John F. Kennedy Airport, New York, showed his ability to take architecture into a new dimension. The sweeping curves of the roof and interior proved the potential of reinforced concrete for aesthetically pleasing, organic design.

CONCRETE CLASSIC Saarinen's TWA Terminal at JFK Airport, New York, symbolized the exciting new world of jet-age travel.

However, as neither escalators nor elevators were suitable, an ingenious cable car system was invented by engineer Dick Bowser to take visitors up the curves of the arch. The system inside each leg consists of eight round aluminum capsules carrying five pas-sengers each. As it rises up the leg on tracks, the capsules turn on pivots to keep the seats horizontal. The journey to the top takes 6 minutes, the descent 4 minutes. Since the system became operational in July 1967, 20 million visitors have been to the top.

RAINBOW OF STEEL The arch rises majestically from its parkland setting in the middle of St. Louis. It is strong enough to bear extremes of wind: wind-tunnel trials showed that it would move only 18 inches in gusts as high as 150 mph.

VALLE DE LOS CAÍDOS

A VAST BASILICA HEWN BY FORCED LABOR OUT OF A ROCK FACE BECAME FRANCO'S MAUSOLEUM

Exactly one year after the bitter Spanish Civil War came to a close on April 1, 1939, the triumphant General Francisco Franco, "el Caudillo" (the Leader), declared that he wanted to build a great monument to honor the dead of both sides in a war that had cost the lives of over 700,000 Spaniards. Something of an architect himself, Franco drew a sketch of the monument and handed it to Pedro Muguruza, who was charged with the responsibility of bringing the design to fruition.

It was a formidable undertaking: Franco wanted to excavate a huge basilica out of the granite walls of the dramatic Guadarrama valley, to the northwest of Madrid, a region where some of the most bitter fighting of the Civil War (1936-9) had taken place.

Victory monument

The declared intention to honor both sides in the conflict was a ruse: this was to be a eulogy to Franco's victorious Nationalists, and a lasting symbol of their triumph. The decree announcing the monument, which was to be named the Valle de los Caídos (Valley of the Fallen), proposed that it should extol "the dimension of our Crusade, the heroic sacrifices involved in the victory and far-reaching significance which this epic has had for the future of Spain."

A vast cavern 860 feet long was mined and blasted out of the rock to create a massive, somber basilica, flanked by side chapels and adorned with boldly stated religious sculpture and holy images. Its mixture of ornateness and austere simplicity was calculated to echo the late medieval era of the Catholic kings, when Spain achieved a new peak of power as it completed the conquest of the Moors, began the conquest of the New World, put the Jews to flight and initiated the Inquisition. This had been a critical watershed that led into Spain's so-called "Golden Age," and Franco saw in it a parallel with his own times.

The Valle de los Caídos was inaugurated amid extravagant victory celebrations on April 1, 1959, the twentieth anniversary of the end of the war. Initially scheduled to take a year to build, in the end it had taken 20; and despite the use of forced labor, it cost some $500 million.

At the far end of the basilica, beside the plain, circular altar, a grave was made for José Antonio Primo de Rivera, one of the principal architects of Spain's Falangist (fascist) movement. Assassinated at the start of the Civil War, his body had first been interred in the royal crypt of the Escorial, the grand 16th-century royal palace nearby, but this had upset the monarchists. It soon became clear that Franco himself saw the Valle de los Caídos as his mausoleum, and that he wished to be buried in a simple soldier's tomb beside that of his mentor.

When the end came, on November 20, 1975, after years of declining health and powers, Franco's body was brought here in a long funeral cortége notable for the absence of any major head of state besides the Chilean dictator, General Augusto Pinochet. After the funeral, the Valle de los Caídos became a place of pilgrimage for Spaniards who mourned the passing of "el Caudillo" and the strong-arm rule that he represented. But with democracy restored under the rule of King Juan Carlos, Franco's appointed successor, Spain altered immeasurably over the last quarter of the century, pushing the Valle de los Caídos, and the spirit it represents, ever further into the margins.

FRANCO'S FINAL HOME The towering cross that surmounts the basilica is a blunt reminder of Franco's belief in the crusading mission of his regime.

MOSCOW ROCKET MONUMENT

A DYNAMIC MONUMENT CELEBRATES THE ERA WHEN THE U.S.S.R. LED THE WORLD INTO SPACE

In October 1957, the Soviet Union sent the first satellite into orbit around the Earth. In November 1957, the Soviet dog Laika became the first terrestrial creature to enter space, in Sputnik 2. In October 1959, a Soviet satellite orbited the Moon. Then, on April 12, 1961, a Soviet test pilot, Yuri Gagarin, became the first man in space. In June 1963, Valentina Tereshkova became the first woman in space. In October 1964, the first multicrew space mission took three Soviet cosmonauts into space in Voskhod 1. During the Voskhod 2 mission in March 1965, Alexei Leonov left his capsule to perform the first space walk.

In 1958, the Soviet authorities held a design competition for a monument to celebrate the U.S.S.R.'s achievements in space. It was won by the respected sculptor A.P. Faidysh Krandievsky (1920-67). His scheme took six years of intensive work to bring to fruition. Constructed in the Economic Achievements Park in Moscow, the monument was inaugurated on November 5, 1964.

The central feature is a rocket riding on the tip of a sweeping trail of exhaust fumes. Sheathed in the valuable stainless metal titanium, and supported by a structure of steel pipes, the monument rises to 351 feet. For Faidysh Krandievsky, however, the real artistic challenge lay in the monument's base, a triangular granite plinth designed to house a small museum of space exploration. The exterior walls are decorated with 75 foot long friezes of relief sculptures cast in bronze. These represent the history of Soviet endeavors in space, and celebrate the heroic contributions of engineers, scientists, technicians and laborers, as well as the cosmonauts.

In front of the monument is Faidysh Krandievsky's granite statue of Konstantin Tsiolkovsky, the man who in 1903 had first set out the theory of rocket propulsion, and who in 1929 devised a prototype for the multi-stage rocket—the key to space exploration.

REACH FOR THE SKIES The titanium vapor trail of the rocket is a dynamic expression of the soaring ambition of the space age.

VIETNAM MEMORIAL

CONTROVERSIAL IN ITS STARK SIMPLICITY, THIS MONUMENT MOVES MANY VISITORS TO TEARS

A dark gash lies at the heart of Washington DC, cut into the green turf of Constitution Gardens, under the shadow of the Lincoln Memorial and the Washington Monument. Two huge wedges of polished, funereal granite slice into the soil, meeting at the center to form a shallow V. And grit-blasted into the polished surface, in row upon row, are the names of the 58,183 American men and women killed or reported

WALL OF REMEMBRANCE   The monument forms a somber V-shape, cut into the soil at the heart of the capital.

missing during the Vietnam War (1954-75). There is no call for more rousing sentiments: the names, listed without rank or decorations, stand as an eloquent and heart-rending expression of America's loss and grief.

The forgotten war

The Vietnam War had ended badly for the United States, forced to withdraw by military impasse, and by the political embarrassment of vehement anti-war protests both at home and abroad. U.S. troops in Vietnam, many of them unwilling young conscripts, had lived through a kaleidoscope of vivid and nightmarish experiences. Many returned home bearing deep physical or emotional scars, only to be met by incomprehension, embarrassment, and even insults. America did not want to know. When in 1979 Jan C. Scruggs, himself wounded and decorated in Vietnam as a 19-year-old, came up with the idea of creating a memorial to the dead, it was greeted with derision, distaste and indifference by the general public.

However, there were many thousands of former servicemen, and families of the dead and missing, who craved some national recognition, and the idea of a memorial began to snowball. As donations came flooding in, politicians in Washington took up the cause. But what sort of monument should it be? The debate was thrown open to competition. There were hundreds of entries, ranging from statues of soldiers to monuments in the shape of peace symbols and helicopter gunships. One, however, stood out and haunted the judges, breathtaking in its simplicity.

A controversial decision

The winning design had been submitted by 20-year-old Maya Ying Lin, an architecture student at Yale. It was quite unlike any war memorial that preceded it. "I wanted to work with the land and not dominate it," she said. "I had an impulse to cut open the earth . . . an initial violence that in time would heal." In fact, so stark and simple was it that, to many veterans, it seemed like an offensive understatement—yet another failure of America to give due recognition to the Vietnam experience. Against mounting furor, Scruggs and fellow organizers of the Vietnam Veterans Memorial Fund gritted their teeth. They finally won government approval in March 1982.

The work began as 150 slabs of granite were cut out of a quarry in Vermont and shipped to Memphis, Tennessee, for inscription. The names had been assembled from records held by the Pentagon, and were listed in day-by-day order of death. This meant that friends and relatives would be able to find them easily, and also to recall the names of comrades-in-arms whose tour of duty coincided. To assuage critics, a lifelike statue of Vietnam soldiers was also commissioned; the war-hardened trio by sculptor Frederick Hart stands to one side of the memorial, looking in silent wonder upon the names of the dead.

All doubts about the monument were swept aside at the dedication ceremony over the weekend following Veterans Day, November 11, 1982. Tens of thousands of Vietnam veterans and their families congregated in Washington—some in wheelchairs, many in their old battle fatigues, some long-haired and ragged, many bearing medals. They came to honor their dead comrades, but they also met old friends, recalled the past and exchanged experiences, and found deep solace in being able at last to give public expression to their grief, resentment and their common cause. Among them, too, were the bereaved mothers and fathers, grandparents, brothers, sisters, and young widows with their children. All were struck by the silent power and dignity of the sea of names.

Besides flowers and wreaths, many left touching mementos: campaign medals, "dog tag" identity badges worn in combat, teddy bears, even bottles of whisky. And they discovered the strangely tactile nature of the monument: they ran their fingers over the names of comrades and loved ones, as if reaching out to touch them again.

THE SADDEST LIST   The solemn roll call of names, listed without rank or elucidation, eloquently conveys the sense of national loss.

NOTRE-DAME DE LA PAIX, YAMOUSSOUKRO

THE WORLD'S LARGEST CHURCH RISES FROM THE SCRUBLANDS OF CENTRAL CÔTE D'IVOIRE

At the end of his long life, President Félix Houphouët-Boigny (1905-93) of Côte d'Ivoire (Ivory Coast) was laid to rest in the magnificent basilica that had occupied so much of his latter years. The Basilique Notre-Dame de la Paix (Basilica of Our Lady of Peace) is the centerpiece of the president's birthplace, Yamoussoukro, which became the new capital of the nation, replacing the old port city of Abidjan 160 miles to the south.

In death as in life, Houphouët-Boigny was surrounded by controversy. His funeral was attended by the French President François Mitterrand, and his Prime Minister, Edouard Balladur. But leading figures from other nations were conspicuous by their absence.

Although Houphouët-Boigny was widely revered by his own people, who referred to him respectfully as "le Vieux" (the [wise] Old Man), and by the French, who had held faith in him since the end of their colonial rule, the rest of the world had become disenchanted. President since independence in 1960, initially he had triumphed politically and economically where other African nations failed. But the oil crisis of the 1970s spelled the collapse of Côte d'Ivoire's export economy, which was based on coffee and cocoa, and from the mid 1980s Houphouët-Boigny presided over mounting international debt.

Extravagance

It was during this period that Houphouët-Boigny decided to build what was widely considered to be the Third World's most extravagant folly: an enormous Christian basilica in the remote scrubland village of Yamoussoukro. It seemed an eccentric decision: no more than 15 percent of Côte d'Ivoire's population was Christian, and Houphouët-Boigny himself had been Christian for only 20 years. But most of all, the immense cost of the project startled a world trying to come to terms with Côte d'Ivoire's debt. The basilica was enveloped in

a cloud of notoriety. The Old Man, it seemed, had lost his sense of judgment.

No one could say precisely what Notre-Dame de la Paix cost, because Houphouët-Boigny insisted that he was paying for it from his own private means. Most estimates hover around $300 million: Houphouët-Boigny himself claimed to be one of the richest men in Africa, but of course most of his wealth derived from the country that he ruled. His private bank balance and his nation's wealth were indivisible. Meanwhile, the average annual income for Ivorians stood at $1,500.

No one could deny that Notre-Dame de la Paix is an astounding achievement.

VISIONS OF THE VATICAN The basilica is broadly based on St. Peter's, Rome, and was inaugurated by Pope John Paul II. It can accommodate a total of 18,000 people inside. The extravagant use of space is continued outside, where 300 columns at the front of the building create a piazza, and a paved area provides enough space for an additional 320,000 worshippers (below).

Covering 323,000 square feet, it is the world's largest church—larger than St. Peter's in the Vatican, on which it is modelled. In deference to the mother church of Catholicism, the dome is slightly less tall, but the cross on the top rises to 518 feet, 70 feet higher than that on St. Peter's. Its air-conditioned interior can seat 7,000 worshippers, with standing room for 11,000 more. Beneath a dome, the interior of which is covered with blue tiles, rise the massive stained-glass windows in 4,000 color shades, reaching a height equivalent to ten stories. Houphouët-

Boigny himself is portrayed kneeling at Christ's feet. The marble came from Carrara in Italy, the granite from Spain, glass from France, steel from Belgium. Some 1,500 builders and craftsmen worked on the basilica in two shifts, from 7 am to 2 am each day, with the result that it was completed in just three years, starting in 1986 and reaching completion in 1989.

Papal blessing

Meanwhile, Yamoussoukro took shape. The new city was laid out on a grid of 10 square miles, and contained the new Congress hall, two presidential palaces, an international airport, various institutes of higher education, a first-class hotel with golf course, and little else.

In 1990, President Houphouët-Boigny donated his basilica to the Catholic Church. The Vatican could hardly reject such a formidable demonstration of faith, but the gift was one that it would rather have done without. By 1990 Côte d'Ivoire had acquired a foreign debt of nearly $15 billion, and rising. Intense negotiations between the Vatican and Côte d'Ivoire ensued. In the end, in September 1990, Pope John Paul II came to Yamoussoukro to consecrate the basilica—but not before he had ensured that Côte d'Ivoire would contribute to the upkeep of the church, and would invest in youth schemes and a hospital as face-saving humanitarian gestures. The ceremony was attended by 150,000 people.

SUBLIME OR RIDICULOUS?

On completion of the basilica in 1989, journalists from the world's press searched to strike a balance between wonderment and outrage. Brian James, writing in *The Times*, illustrates this dilemma.

"The entire notion was, of course, grotesque from its genesis in the imagination of Houphouët-Boigny. Félix in Wonderland, a monument to mad pride, a *folie de grandeur*, are among the unkind things said about his plan; a grisly pastiche of medieval European architecture, 400 years out of time and 3,000 miles out of place, sum up less amiable observations as, amid clouds of red dust, the president's offering rose from the scrub.

"Yet now it is done it is hard to gaze on with curled lip and making no concession; partly because of the pure joy of those who have done this improbable thing. 'When they built St. Peter's, were there no hungry people in Rome? When England after the Great Fire built itself St. Paul's, were there no poor or homeless in London?' was the surprising remark of one Ivorian craftsman I pressed about the soaring irrelevance of his fine work...

"Already Yamoussoukro's neat and manicured boulevards are contaminated by the old Africa—free-roaming chickens, free-range children and free-strewn rubbish—like the stain of dampness widening on a silk carpet laid on a rotting floor.

"No future for Yamoussoukro can be more surreal than its present. It encourages morbid thought to stand mid-evening in the panoramic hotel-top restaurant, likely to be the only diner, and to look out on the wide roads of a nation's capital lamplit away to every horizon...and to observe not one single moving light.

"If aliens came to vacuum up all the humans from an Earth city, Yamoussoukro is what they would leave behind. And that great gleaming dome, lit up at night by 1,810 lamps of 1,000 watts each, looks uncannily like the sort of spacecraft they would arrive in."

GREAT HASSAN II MOSQUE

THE WORLD'S TALLEST RELIGIOUS BUILDING TOWERS OVER THE STREETS OF CASABLANCA

In 1980, work began on one of the most remarkable buildings of Islam. Inspired by the Koranic saying that "Allah has his throne on the water," Hassan II, King of Morocco, decreed that a splendid new mosque should be built on the coastal headland of his nation's largest city, Casablanca.

Work proceeded at a furious pace, and as the completion date approached—July 9, 1993, the king's 64th birthday—teams numbering more than 1,000 workers labored in shifts day and night. A total of 35,000 builders and craftsmen were involved.

Everything is on a colossal scale. With a main prayer hall the size of two football fields placed end to end, there is enough room for 20,000 worshippers inside the mosque, while a further 80,000 can gather in the courtyards outside. The mosque also has the world's largest minaret, 82 feet square and reaching up to 575 feet.

Chandeliers and laser

This is said to be the second-largest mosque after that of Mecca, but it is not just its scale that sets it apart. It is magnificent. Hundreds of craftsmen perched on ladders sculpted the walls and arches with intricate stucco patterning. Skilled ceramicists have supplied the ornate and colorful *zillij* tiles for the floors and wall panels, using the centuries-old traditions of geometric patterning for which Morocco is celebrated. The cedar-wood ceiling, hovering 200 feet above the prayer hall, is an intricate honey-comb of delicate carving spangled with stars, while other parts of the building are roofed with a total of 70 equally intricate wooden cupolas. And illuminating the immense prayer hall are sparkling chandeliers of Italian glass, each weighing 3,500 pounds—the only imported element in the decoration. Apart from the wall panels and the polished marble columns, there is barely an unadorned surface in the building.

Despite its close adherence to the historical traditions of Islamic design, the mosque also includes some unequivocally modern features. The wooden roof, for instance, can slide back on electronically driven motors to allow natural light to pour into the prayer hall. The top of the minaret is intended to carry a laser light pointing 20 miles eastward in the direction of Mecca. There is an underground garage for 1,000 cars and 50 busses. And the huge scale of the building has been

CENTURIES OF TRADITION The entrance demonstrates the modern craftsman's ability to transfer traditional skills to a large scale without losing their distinctive delicacy.

made possible by the application of modern reinforced-concrete technology.

The mosque cost over $1 billion to build, but it is only part of a planned cultural center, which includes a *madrassah* (Koran school), student accommodation, a library, a museum, administration offices and conference facilities. Almost all of the costs of the mosque were raised from private subscription. The vigorous campaign to raise funds through door-to-door visits and deductions from paychecks attracted criticism that the contributions were less than voluntary. But if this caused some resentment at the time, most donors are now proud to be able to claim that they have made a contribution to one of the wonders of the Islamic world.

THE VERY WEST OF AFRICA The mosque stands on a plinth overlooking the Atlantic. No mosque has surpassed it for the scale, craftsmanship and sumptuous finish of the interior (right), here seen as work was nearing completion in 1993.

COLUMBUS LIGHTHOUSE

A MONUMENT TO COLUMBUS PROJECTS AN IMAGE OF THE CROSS ONTO THE CARIBBEAN SKY

INTO THE UNKNOWN Canyon-like corridors slice through the massive structure, leading to Columbus's mausoleum.

The 500th anniversary of Christopher Columbus's arrival in the New World in 1492 was celebrated by the inauguration of a monument dedicated to his memory. It is a lighthouse, the traditional aid to mariners—but this is a lighthouse like no other. "El Faro a Colón" takes the form of a vast cross 800 feet long and 150 feet high. Housing a series of museums and a library, it rises in tiers of reinforced concrete, a looming presence over the city of Santo Domingo, capital of the Dominican Republic.

Perched over the center of the cross is a powerful light, cupped in a basket reminiscent of the simple brazier-like lighthouses of Columbus's day. But far more striking are the 149 laser lights, evenly spaced across the entire upper surface, which beam vertically into the sky to project the shape of the cross onto the Caribbean clouds.

In the heart of the cross, within a baroque tomb of marble and bronze, lie the bones of Christopher Columbus (Cristóbal Colón in Spanish)—or that is the claim. Columbus died in Spain in 1506, still under the illusion that he had discovered China and Japan. In 1540 his bones were transferred to Santo Domingo, where they were reinterred in the cathedral. In 1796, during a dispute with neighboring French-ruled Haiti, the Spanish took the bones of the now revered Columbus to Cuba. But in 1877, during renovation work in the cathedral of Santo Domingo, an urn appearing to contain Columbus's bones was found. It was claimed that the bones sent to Cuba were not those of Columbus, but this remains disputed. In 1923, an international conference decided that a monument to Columbus should be built in Santo Domingo. Work began in 1939, but the project lapsed during the Second World War. It was resumed in 1987, and a new deadline was fixed: October 1992, 500 years after Columbus's supposed first landfall on the island of San Salvador in the Bahamas on October 12, 1492.

As that day approached, Columbus's record was scrutinized and revised. His arrival in the Caribbean had heralded the conquest and demise of native peoples across the Americas. By October 1992, his reputation was no longer considered a cause for celebration. There were angry demonstrations in Santo Domingo in advance of the inauguration of the Columbus Lighthouse on October 6. The project, which had cost this impoverished nation between $70 million and $250 million, looked like a monument to oppression.

CELEBRATED IN LIGHTS When illuminated, the laser lamps mounted on the crest fill the sky with a wall of light.

FRONTIERS OF SCIENCE

IN THE 20TH CENTURY, TECHNOLOGY AND SCIENCE HAVE PROPELLED EACH OTHER FORWARD, AND THIS SYMBIOSIS HAS BEEN CELEBRATED IN A NUMBER OF MONUMENTS THAT SUCCESSFULLY COMBINE EDUCATION AND WORK WITH PLEASURE AND EXCITEMENT. MEANWHILE, SOME OF THE LARGE-SCALE ITEMS OF HARDWARE AT THE FRONTIERS OF SCIENCE, SUCH AS SOLAR TELESCOPES, HAVE THEMSELVES ACQUIRED THE STATUS OF GREAT MONUMENTS.

THE ATOMIUM

**A SURREAL MONUMENT TO SCIENCE AND INDUSTRY
HAS BECOME A SYMBOL OF THE CITY OF BRUSSELS**

Since the mid 19th century, the general public has enjoyed world fairs, and every host city has hoped to end up with an enduring monument, such as the "Crystal Palace" of London's Great Exhibition of 1851, which survived until 1936 when it was destroyed by fire, or the Eiffel Tower, built for the Paris Exposition of 1889. In 1958, Brussels achieved a similar ambition: it hosted the Exposition Universelle et Internationale and acquired a monument—the Atomium—that still serves as a key symbol of the city.

One of the main themes of the 1958 Exposition Universelle was industry, and in particular the Belgian metal industry, which was riding high on the postwar boom. For the main exhibition building, André Waterkeyn, the director of the Fédération des Entreprises des Fabrications Métalliques, hit upon the idea of a hugely enlarged model of an iron atom.

The Atomium, in fact, represents an iron atom magnified 165 billion times. It was an ambitious concept that involved suspending nine huge metal spheres on a supporting structure of tubular arms. Six of the spheres were created to be open to the public as exhibition spaces, a panoramic viewing gallery, a bar and restaurant, all reached by a high-speed elevator and escalators installed within the tubular arms.

Construction work began in March 1956, when 123 concrete piles were driven into the ground to create the foundations. Half of these were for the central mast that rises through the entrance pavilion at the base of the structure. The remainder, set at an angle of 17°, provided the foundations for the "bipod" legs, which reach up to the second-level spheres and support the whole structure, and which also double as fire escapes. The first of the spheres was then completed on top of the entrance pavilion, as the prototype that proved the feasibility of the design. It consisted of a set of 12 steel ribs covered

in 720 triangular sheets of highly polished aluminum cladding.

From here, the Atomium quickly took shape. The central sphere, connected to all the others, was constructed on the vertical mast, then the three spheres at the secondary level, supported by the bipods. Above them came the three uppermost outer spheres, which are the only spheres not open to the public. Finally came the crowning sphere, reaching a height of 335 feet.

Each of the spheres measures 95 feet in diameter. The longest tubes stretch for 115 feet, and inside them run some of Europe's longest escalators.

Brave new world

Panels around the central band of the uppermost sphere were replaced with Plexiglas windows, affording panoramic views right over Brussels. Similar windows were installed in two of the lower spheres, while the other accessible spheres have portholes. These, along with the exterior stairs in the bipods, give the impression that the Atomium represents some kind of spacecraft.

In fact, the whole of the Atomium has an otherworldly feel. Although representing one of the tiniest units of matter, seen against the open sky the giant spheres defy all notions of perspective and scale. When travelling around the interior on the escalators, it is easy to lose a sense of direction.

Completed for the opening of the 1958 Exposition, the Atomium caused a sensation, and the city of Brussels called for its preservation after the fair closed. The atom and atomic power has been one of the key themes of the century—in science, in energy resources, in military strategy and global politics. The Atomium speaks to all these issues, and is now seen not only as a curiosity, but as an enduring monument to the brave visions of the 1950s. As the century draws to a close, it is undergoing a massive renovation program, restoring its original gleaming finish to coincide with Brussels' celebrations as a European Cultural Capital in the year 2000.

THE PEACEFUL ATOM

The 1958 Exposition Universelle et Internationale in Brussels was not a trade fair: it was, rather, a fair designed to promote international understanding after the bruising experience of the Second World War. It coincided with the infancy of the nuclear power industry, and several countries—including Britain and the U.S., as well as Belgium—used their pavilions to express optimism in the peaceful use of this awesome source of energy, which the world still associated with the bombing of Hiroshima and Nagasaki.

The *Illustrated London News* ran a series of articles on the Exposition following its official opening. Its readers were left in no doubt that the Atomium was the star of the show:

"Towering above the other buildings on the huge site of the Brussels Exhibition, which was…opened by King Baudouin on April 17, is the Atomium. Like the Eiffel Tower in an earlier world display, the Atomium is the focal point and the highlight of the Exhibition. One of the aims of this great display at Brussels is to foster international understanding. The Atomium, however, aptly symbolizes the dawn of the atomic era, and the technical and scientific side of the Exhibition. A striking exhibit in itself, the Atomium also offers a series of exhibitions illustrating the peaceful uses of atomic energy in its lower spheres…

"The Exhibition is not only the first event of its kind to be held since World War II but it is the greatest in size which the world has ever known…Before lighting a 10 foot flame which will burn for the next six months, the King, speaking in French and Flemish, addressed a large audience in the Belgium Square at the Exhibition. He declared that the aim of the Exhibition, at which fifty-three countries and international organizations are represented, was 'to revive the atmosphere of collaboration and peace.'…In his speech at the opening ceremony, Mr. Van Acker, the Belgian Prime Minister, spoke of Belgium's preoccupation with 'the notion that the peoples which can claim to direct the destiny of mankind are not those possessing the most vast and terrible engines of destruction but those whose actions are informed by the spirit of peace and the will to increase the well-being of the whole world'…

"The night-time illuminations form an important feature…Both by day and by night the Atomium forms a sparkling and glittering centerpiece, but it is only at night, when it becomes a galaxy of changing colors, that the water staircase running down the central avenue really becomes impressive."

UNIVERSAL APPEAL Considered a daring wonder when it was opened in 1958, the Atomium has been one of Brussels' most popular tourist attractions ever since.

CN TOWER

WONDER AND INTENSE VERTIGO ARE INSPIRED BY THE VIEW FROM THIS RECORD-BREAKING SPIRE

As the slogan says: "Walk on air—if you dare!" Even with the knowledge that it is strong enough to support the weight of 14 hippopotamuses, it takes some nerve to stand on the Glass Floor of the CN Tower's SkyPod, suspended 1,122 feet above central Toronto. Way below, traffic moves along the city streets like distant silvery streams, and pedestrians appear like granules of sand pushed along by the wind.

Since the final segment of the antenna was lowered into position by helicopter in April 1975, the CN Tower (named after its owner, Canadian National railways) has held the record as the world's tallest freestanding structure. The tip of its spire is 1,815 feet above the ground, 332 feet higher than the tallest skyscraper, the Petronas Twin Towers in Kuala Lumpur.

Catapulted upward at 20 feet per second in glass-fronted elevators on exterior shafts, visitors reach the seven-story "SkyPod" in under a minute. As back-up in case of complete power failure or some other emergency, the hollow interior of the tower contains a metal staircase—the world's longest, with 2,570 steps. The SkyPod consists of a series of observation decks interleaved with floors where the tower's telecommunications work is carried out. The lowest of these contains receiving dishes protected by an inflated cover that resembles a giant inner tube. The Glass Floor forms part of the Outdoor Observation Deck above this. On the next floor is the Indoor Observation Deck and above that is the world's highest revolving restaurant.

The CN Tower took more than three years to build. Unusual for such a daring project, the construction had a 100 percent safety record. This statistic gives a misleading impression of the risks involved, however, and the Glass Floor was installed as part of an exhibition about the construction of the tower, to give the public an unnerving glimpse of the view faced daily by its 1,537 builders.

PIERCING THE SKYLINE The CN Tower was built primarily to transmit TV, radio and communications signals. The best view is from the Space Deck beneath the antenna.

AMUNDSEN-SCOTT STATION, SOUTH POLE

THERE HAS BEEN A PERMANENT RESEARCH STATION AT THE SOUTH POLE FOR MORE THAN 40 YEARS

Every year the inhabitants of the Amundsen-Scott Station celebrate Christmas Eve with a "Race Around the World." Walking, running, jogging, on skis, on snowmobiles, they complete a 2¾ mile course around the South Pole, and as they do so they travel 360° around the globe and through all the world's time zones.

This bit of fun plays on one of the peculiar concepts of living at the apex of the world. There are many other such peculiarities in this topsy-turvy place, some of them testing human endurance to the limits. Here the Sun sets on March 22 and does not rise again until September 22. In the long months of winter darkness, temperatures drop to –116°F, low enough to freeze the lungs and make steel brittle. By contrast, in summer the Sun shines 24 hours a day, but even then the temperature never rises above 9°F. The threat of frostbite is common.

The South Pole stands on a huge plateau, 9,300 feet above sea level. Because of the low air pressure in Antarctica's comparatively shallow atmosphere, the air is even thinner than the height would suggest, making it hard for new arrivals to catch their breath. An endless blanket of ice and snow covers the area, featureless and dazzling in the bright sunlight. It is also one of the driest places on Earth, with very low levels of precipitation. Skin becomes dry and lips crack.

Despite all the factors that make the South Pole one of the world's most intolerable environments, some 130 people live at the Amundsen-Scott Station during the summer, and 28 stay through the winter. Since 1973, overwintering teams have included both men and women.

Laboratory at the end of the Earth

If the inspiration behind the establishment of the Amundsen-Scott Station was science, the timing was political. During the 1957-8 International Geophysical Year (IGY), attention was focused on the Antarctic. International scientists were invited to pool their findings, and in preparation for the IGY, both America and the Soviet Union established Antarctic stations in 1956. When America heard that the Soviet Union was thinking of building a station at the Pole itself, a U.S. Navy plane was dispatched south to forestall it. On October 31, 1956, the experienced polar pilots Lieutenant Commander Conrad S. Shinn and Captain William M. Hawkes used a ski-equipped plane to make the first-ever landing at the Pole. Accompanied by Rear Admiral George J. Dufek, leader of "Operation Deepfreeze II," they effectively laid the foundations for the Amundsen-Scott Station, which has been supplied entirely from the air ever since.

The first buildings were overwhelmed by snowdrifts, and were replaced by a stronger set in 1971-5. The most prominent of the new ones is the aluminum geodesic dome,

JOURNEY'S END For polar explorers and travellers, the entrance ramp leading to the dome represents the last few steps back to the human world after the vast white expanses of Antarctica.

UNDER THE DOME   The scale of the dome becomes apparent on the inside. It shelters three two-story cabins like the one above.

49 feet tall and 164 feet in diameter. This houses a collection of two-story rectangular units containing accommodation, dining facilities, a recreation room, a library, a communications center and a science building. In front of the dome is a line of ribbed metal "arches" housing more research facilities, the power plant, a garage, gymnasium, carpenter's shop and storage areas. During the summer months, the additional staff are accommodated in a series of solar-heated "Jamesway" dormitories, set at some distance from the dome.

Spread out across the site are the numerous scientific posts, perched above the snow-drifts on stilts. The station carries out important research into the atmosphere, sending up helium-filled especially engineered balloons, for example, to measure pollutants and to monitor the hole in the ozone layer that has appeared over the Pole. Because the atmosphere is shallow, the air clean and the sky often clear, the South Pole also offers exceptionally favorable conditions for astronomy.

High-powered instruments, including a 6 ton telescope, look into deep space, probing the distant galaxies. Instruments lowered into boreholes drilled 6,500 feet into the ice cap help research into the origins of the Earth, while seismological studies look at the hidden geology of the continent.

Supplies, equipment and personnel all have to be flown in between late October and mid February, usually from the American base at McMurdo Sound on the fringes of Antarctica, around 800 miles and 3 hours away. The planes land on Teflon-coated skis, touching down on a "skiway" 4,700 yards long, and can ride right up to the entrance of the Dome. Because both the Amundsen-Scott Station and the base at McMurdo Sound are supplied from Christchurch, New Zealand, both have adopted the same time zone as New Zealand. A much-cherished drop of fresh food, mail and equipment direct from Christchurch used to take place around the full moon in mid-winter, but this 3,000 mile round trip has been a victim of budget cuts. As it is, the Amundsen-Scott Station costs $195 million a year to run.

"Great God! This is an awful place!" wrote the bitterly disappointed Scott after he reached the Pole in 1912. He had made the trek on skis, hauling his supplies and tent on a sledge, wearing clothes of canvas, wool, fur and felt, and surviving on a diet of dried food, chocolate, and tea brewed on a little gas stove. The guardians of this lonesome place today enjoy the comforts of heated cabins, snowmobiles, hi-tech clothing filled with synthetic fibers, frozen foods, air links, satellite communications, modern medicines, even a sauna and a pool table. But no one at the Amundsen-Scott Station is complacent: beyond the confines of their bubble of civilization, they know, lies a dangerous and unforgiving environment.

SENSORY DEPRIVATION

Lieutenant Ricardo Ramos was the Station Science Leader at the Amundsen-Scott Station in 1995-6. This is an extract from an e-mail that he sent from the South Pole during the depths of winter:

"During summer (November to February), 'commuting' to the outlying science buildings isn't a problem. In fact, for most of the summer, I don't have to wear my wind pants or heavy boots. As long as I don't linger outdoors too long, I can get by with Levis (with long underwear) and light hiking boots. During the cold, dark winter, I make sure that I don't have any skin exposed. Even skin that is thinly covered by clothes quickly feels the hot, burning sensation of the cold and wind attacking.

"When the full moon isn't out, it's very, very dark out in winter. Once, when I was leaving work, I couldn't see anything... It was so dark I couldn't see my own hand in front of my face. I might as well have been walking with my eyes closed. It took my eyes at least three minutes to adjust enough so that I could see even very faint outlines of nearby buildings.

"My first full-fledged Antarctic storm was great: winds were blowing 23 miles per hour with 35 mile per hour gusts. Snow was blowing everywhere, and visibility was incredibly low. You had to lean into the wind in order not to be blown over. I had to wear my goggles or else my eyelashes would freeze together in a matter of seconds. It was exhilarating! This is what I had thought the South Pole was going to be like. I've never felt more alive.

"The auroral displays [aurora australis, 'southern lights'] have been awesome. Sometimes they stretch from one horizon to the other. Their color is hard to describe. It's an eerie green, sometimes with just a hint of red or pink. The auroras are very active when directly overhead. They twist, turn and oscillate and give us a delightful show. When the auroras aren't out and it's clear outside, the sky is filled with stars.

"According to Nancy, our cook, consumption of chocolate has increased tremendously since sunset [that is, March 22]. Apparently, without sunlight our bodies are deprived of stimuli—and to counterbalance this, we crave chocolate. The chocolate triggers a chemical in our brain that replaces the lost stimulus. My particular desire is for a chocolate shake!

"Also, with no sun around for a visual clue, some people have had a very hard time sleeping. They either can sleep for only a few hours each night or they sleep for 20 or more hours at a time...

"After months of darkness I find myself thinking about what it will be like to see the sun rise above the horizon again. Will I be overjoyed to know that soon a plane will come and take me away? Or will I feel sad knowing that my year at the Pole will be coming to an end? Right now, in order to cope with the darkness and isolation, I find it best to concentrate on day-to-day matters. Thinking about what will happen four or five months from now somehow makes those things seem like an eternity away."

MCMATH-PIERCE SOLAR TELESCOPE

A GIANT TELESCOPE KEEPS A WATCHFUL EYE ON THE ACTIVITIES OF THE NEAREST STAR TO EARTH

Study of the Earth's nearest star is an important branch of astronomy, and the best and safest way to observe and photograph it is to project the image by means of mirrors. The world's largest solar telescope is at the Kitt Peak National Observatory, near Tucson, Arizona, which was founded in 1958 to take advantage of the clear air at 6,775 feet. Named after its chief instigators, Dr. Robert R. McMath and Dr. A. Keith Pierce, it was inaugurated by President John F. Kennedy on October 22, 1962.

The striking design by Skidmore, Owings & Merrill reflects the need to accommodate three specifications. First, an extremely long telescope was desirable, since the focal length of the mirror has a direct relationship to the size and precision of the image produced. Second, the beams of reflected light within the telescope had to be kept cool, as heat distorts light. Third, the exterior shape of the telescope had to be aerodynamic to minimize the impact of high winds.

The telescope is in fact 500 feet long; angled at 32°, 300 feet is below ground and 200 feet above. The summit, resting on a vertical column 110 feet high, supports the primary tracking mirror, called a heliostat, plus two auxiliary heliostats, all protected by a wind fence. The primary heliostat, which is 6 feet 10 inches across, beams a reflected image of the Sun down the 500 foot tube to a concave mirror of comparable size at the base. The image is then reflected back up the telescope to just above ground level, where a 4 foot 8 inch mirror diverts it downward into a subterranean shaft containing the observation room. This vertical shaft, 69 feet deep, permits a broad range of projections for a spectrometer and spectrographs, which produce photographic records of the spectrum. By analyzing these, astronomers can calculate the Sun's temperature, composition, density, pressure and magnetic field, and can monitor the pattern of the Sun's activity: its corona, sunspots and flares. In addition, the facility is used to study the brightest stars, comets and the Earth's atmosphere.

Above ground, the telescope is sheathed in white-painted copper panels, which contain pipes filled with coolant. This keeps the telescope at a constant temperature, while the polygonal shape of the superstructure deflects the wind. A more recent vacuum telescope, creating high-resolution magnetic maps of the Sun, is housed in the 75 foot tower next to the McMath-Pierce Telescope. Together these form a key element of the National Solar Observatory, which has sister installations on Sacramento Peak in New Mexico.

TEMPLE TO THE SUN The telescope is housed in the sloping structure. The tower behind it is the newer vacuum telescope. The tracking mirror (right), mounted on the flat crest, reflects sunlight down the sloping tube to a second mirror beneath the ground.

FUTUROSCOPE, POITIERS

A FUTURISTIC THEME PARK IS THE CENTERPIECE OF A MODEL SCHEME FOR ECONOMIC RENEWAL

Glinting in the sunlight, the giant rock crystal surging out of the bucolic French landscape cuts an unforgettable image. Subtitled "the European Park of the Moving Image," the Futuroscope has a unique

agenda among theme parks. In 20 purpose-built auditoriums, it explores the future and potential of film images: high-resolution, big-screen, 3D, 360° surround, interactive.

The giant rock crystal is one

of these auditoriums. Called Kinémax, it was built in 1987 to house the first giant-screen Imax movie theater in France. Its 420 seats, sharply raked to the contours of its sloping site, face a screen the size of a seven-story building where short, high-definition films are projected to the deep resonances of a state-of-the-art sound system. At the end of a showing, the screen rises on hydraulic hoists to form a gaping exit, releasing the audience into the open air and onto a terrace overlooking the park's lakes.

SCULPTURAL CENTERPIECE
The rock-crystal exterior of the Kinémax is made up of 3,000 panels of reflective glass.

Illusion is a key theme of the Futuroscope. The illusion of film is translated into illusory architecture. It was the development of this concept that appealed to the park's founders when, in 1984, they chose the young French architect Denis Laming (b.1949) as the winner of a competition to design the pavilions for their 173 acre site. As Denis Laming put it: "The buildings must irradiate, discharge energy and put the viewer in a state of questioning, of incertitude." The exterior of the Kinémax is simply a cosmetic casing; it only vaguely corresponds to the interior of the building and is not even watertight.

Near the Kinémax are two other buildings that each make a gesture toward illusion. The Pavillon du Futuroscope, an exhibition hall, is a glass prism based on the dimensions of the golden section, surmounted by a white polyester sphere. The upper, angled surface of the prism looks flat, but in fact it is concave: this optical illusion reminds one that, to compensate for tricks of the eye, the columns in ancient Greek temples actually bulge outward in order to look straight-sided. The large sphere, meanwhile, looks as though it is about to float away, giving a feeling of instability and lightness.

In contrast, the half-buried sphere of the Omnimax nearby appears to have crashed into the ground like a meteorite, and then

been preserved within an angled cube of glass. The sphere in fact contains a movie theater with a huge hemispherical screen that arcs over the heads of the spectators, immersing them in the projected images.

The Tapis Magique (Magic Carpet), built in 1992, is surrounded by clusters of polycarbonate tubes, like organ pipes or a giant handful of optical fibers. This theater—the only one of its kind in the world—contains two huge screens, each the size of two basketball courts, onto which coordinated films are projected simultaneously. One screen is in front of the audience, and the other is beneath them, viewed through glass panels in the floor. The effect is like flying, hence the theater's name. Specially made films carefully exploit this effect, for instance, documenting the flight of migrating monarch butterflies.

The Imax 3D cinema was built in 1996 to show *Wings of Courage*. This was the first fiction film made using the three-dimensional Imax method; viewed through 3D glasses, it tells the story of heroic pioneer aviators crossing the Andes in the late 1920s. The rear façade of the building plays on the 3D theme: a silver sphere floats against a concave disc set into a reflective surface, the image of a cosmic eclipse designed to confuse the eye.

The façade of the Pavillon de la Vienne

OPTICAL ILLUSION At first sight the upper surface of the Pavillon du Futuroscope looks straight, but on closer examination it curves slightly upward.

(1994) is a sheet of water, 52 feet high and 138 feet wide, that pours down from 720 nozzles in front of a flat glass panel. Inside is an auditorium where a show is presented on a bank of 850 video screens; next door is a giant simulator, with computer-controlled seats that swing and turn in accord with the film to replicate the physical sensation of movement.

Further theaters, simulators and exhibition halls—as well as restaurants, a children's play area, lakes and fountains, and evening spectaculars of fireworks, fountains, lasers and film projected onto screens of water—all contribute to the successful formula of the Futuroscope. Ten years after first opening its doors in June 1987, it was drawing nearly 3 million visitors a year.

RIPPLE EFFECT At the Pavillon de la Communication, a giant water droplet and ripples convey the speed and clarity of modern communications.

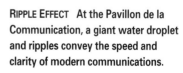

KECK OBSERVATORY

**DARING TECHNOLOGICAL INNOVATION ALLOWS
ASTRONOMERS TO SEARCH DEEP INTO SPACE**

For the astronomers and technicians perched on top of Mauna Kea, Hawaii, December 4, 1990, was a day to remember. The new W.M. Keck telescope captured its first image, and produced a brilliantly crisp picture of a pinwheel galaxy 65 million light years from Earth. It surpassed all expectations —not only because telescopes undergoing trials rarely perform perfectly at first, but also because the new telescope was only one-quarter complete. It was capturing light with just nine panels; when finished it would have 36, and four times the power.

That was achieved 16 months later when, on April 14, 1992, the last segment of the primary mirror was lowered into place. It was the culmination of 15 years of innovation and testing by a team from the University of California and the California Institute of Technology, under the direction of Jerry Nelson, professor of astronomy at Berkeley.

In 1977, a committee of astronomers sat down to address the problem of how to see deeper into space. The key to good optical telescopes is the amount of light that they capture. It was Isaac Newton who discovered in 1668 that a concave mirror does this far more effectively than a lens. The larger the mirror, the more that can be seen. In 1977, the largest reflecting telescope, or reflector, in the U.S. was the Hale telescope on Mount Palomar, California. Built in 1948, it had a mirror 200 inches in diameter. The largest in the world was a Russian telescope on Mount Pastukhov, built in 1974. Its mirror measured 236 inches.

To produce a larger mirror by conventional means presented severe problems. A single mirror would have to be extremely robust, because in the observatory it is constantly on the move as it tracks stars and planets across the sky. This movement has to be conducted with pinpoint accuracy: even if the machinery turning the mirror is supremely smooth, gravitational forces and temperature changes cause unacceptable distortion in the mirror's surface. The manufacturing and engineering costs of a mirror

on this scale were also prohibitive: to look into deep space, mirrors have to be smoothed down, or "polished," to molecular precision; and it would require large-scale machinery to manipulate a mirror of this weight.

Jerry Nelson took a fresh look at the problems and proposed that, instead of a single mirror, a reflector could be made using a series of pliable hexagonal panels. They would be easier to manufacture and would have a much lower combined weight. A mirror twice the diameter of Hale's, and with four times its light-gathering power, could be envisaged. The problem was that each of the panels would have to act in precise harmony with all the others. This is where Nelson produced an ingenious solution. Each panel would be monitored by electric sensors connected to a computer. Any minute distortion —down to 1,000th the width of a human hair—would be registered by the computer, which would then rectify the distortion by

TWIN OBSERVERS From their vantage point on Mauna Kea, Keck I (left) and II (right) can see deep into space. Both can be focused on the same object to produce a clear image.

RESCUE MISSION In 1993, astronauts carried out essential repairs to the Hubble Telescope.

TOIL AND TROUBLE

While Keck I was under construction, the National Aeronautics and Space Administration (NASA) was working on an equally ambitious project. Because the Earth's atmosphere distorts observations of space, NASA planned to put a powerful telescope above the atmosphere. Amid great fanfare, the Hubble Space Telescope was launched by the space shuttle *Discovery* on April 24, 1990, and set in orbit 381 miles above the Earth's surface.

The Hubble Telescope is able to make razor-sharp observations both of our own planetary system, and of objects far deeper in space. Powered by solar panels, gyroscopes position the telescope, which can then be locked onto distant objects.

Instruments on board, including cameras and spectrographs (monitoring electromagnetic emissions), then relay the information back to Earth.

Because of the clarity of its images, the Hubble is able to locate objects that Keck I, with 17 times Hubble's light-gathering power, can then observe in greater detail. Hubble has found thousands of new galaxies in areas of the sky that previously seemed blank.

In 1996 a twin observatory, Keck II, was opened just 280 feet from Keck I. They work in tandem, doubling the light-collecting power, and enhancing the resolution of the images received. They can see objects 10 billion light years into space (one light year is about 6 trillion miles). Because light takes time to reach the Earth, anything seen at this distance happened only a few billion years after the Universe was created. Astronomers can therefore observe stars and galaxies being formed, as others fall to their deaths, and thus learn more about the history of the Universe.

Keck I and II have helped to confirm many observations and theories that were previously based on inadequate data; but they also take astronomy into new realms. As Jerry Nelson put it when Keck I was still on the drawing board: "With this telescope, we might see something completely unexpected out there, and that's the real reason you build a telescope—to see the things you have not anticipated."

PERFECT SITE Standing above 40 percent of the atmosphere, which distorts astronomical observations, and with its dry, unpolluted air, the summit of Mauna Kea provides an exceptional platform for celestial observation and has attracted a cluster of observatories. Keck I and II are to the right of center.

manipulating an ultrasensitive structure, called a "whiffletree," behind each panel.

The construction of a 394 inch mirror was executed. Funding was provided by the W.M. Keck Foundation in Los Angeles, a charitable organization created by the founder of the Superior Oil Company. Over the span of the project, it has donated $140 million, the largest-ever single private donation to a science project.

Roof of the world

The site chosen for the observatory was the top of Mauna Kea, a volcanic peak and, at 13,796 feet, the tallest mountain in the Hawaiian islands. Ground was broken on September 12, 1985, and construction and installation took 6 1/2 years. The observatory building is 98 feet high and 118 feet in diameter. A key feature is its air-conditioning system, which keeps the telescope and its structure cool during the day, in anticipation of nighttime temperatures. The primary mirror and its secondary mirrors, onto which the images are directed, are attached to an array of high-powered equipment, including spectrometers (which measure the wavelengths and the

intensity of the light spectrum), and computer-controlled infrared cameras that can "see" into clouds of galactic gas and dust.

1900

At the Paris International Exhibition, **Art Nouveau** first comes to public attention as a fashionable style of architecture and decoration. The centerpiece of the Exposition is the "**Palace of Electricity,**" celebrating the wonders of this emergent source of power.

The **Paris Métro** is inaugurated, 30 years after the first "tube railway" had been opened in London. The Paris stations are designed in florid, sometimes grotesque Art Nouveau style by Hector Guimard.

The Scottish Art Nouveau architect and designer **Charles Rennie Mackintosh** has a major impact when he exhibits at the Vienna "Sezession" Exhibition.

1901

Belgian Art Nouveau architect Victor Horta designs the **Grands Magasins A L'Innovation** department store in Brussels, bringing a new degree of ornateness and sophistication to an iron construction.

1902

The first **Aswan Dam** in southern Egypt is completed by the British.

1903

The **Flatiron Building** is completed in New York.

The **Williamsburg Bridge** over the East River, New York, is the first large suspension bridge to have steel towers, and carries a span of 1,600 feet.

The Vienna "Sezessionists" Josef Hoffmann and Koloman Moser set up the **Wiener Werkstätte** (Vienna Workshop), combining manufacturing with avant-garde design.

The Spanish architect Antoní Gaudí begins work on the upper transept of his **Sagrada Familia** church in Barcelona.

1904

The French civil engineer Eugéne Freyssinet develops **prestressed concrete**, containing steel wires and cables under tension, which markedly increases the load-bearing potential of reinforced concrete.

FANTASY BUILDING   Gaudí's Casa Batlló in Barcelona introduced a new imaginative freedom into architecture.

Charles Rennie Mackintosh completes his celebrated Art Nouveau **Willow Tea Rooms** in Glasgow.

In the first attempt to generate electricity from **geothermal power**, five electric light bulbs are illuminated at Larderello, Italy.

1905

Work begins on the **Palais Stoclet**, Brussels, a private mansion designed by Josef Hoffmann and completed in 1911.

Frank Lloyd Wright completes his innovative office block, the **Larkin Building**, in Buffalo, New York. Centered on an atrium, it is fully air-conditioned and contains the first metal office furniture.

1906

The **Simplon Tunnel** for the electric railway is opened after eight years' construction. Linking Switzerland and Italy, it remains the world's longest tunnel (12 1/3 miles) until 1982.

1907

Antoní Gaudí completes his idiosyncratic and highly sculptural **Casa Batlló** in Barcelona, Spain.

1908

The **Singer Building**, New York, designed by Ernest Flagg, becomes the tallest building in the world.

The U.S. astronomer George Ellery Hale installs a 60 inch **reflector telescope**, then the largest in the world, at Mount Wilson, California.

Josef Maria Olbrich, Austrian architect and Vienna "Sezessionist," dies.

1909

The **Metropolitan Life Tower**, New York, designed by Pierre L. Lebrun, is completed and becomes the world's tallest building.

Peter Behrens' stylish **AEG turbine factory** in Berlin sets a new standard for industrial architecture.

1910

Frank Lloyd Wright completes his most celebrated "prairie house," the **Robie House** in Chicago.

1911

Henry van de Velde completes his **School of Arts and Crafts** at Weimar, which later forms part of the Bauhaus premises.

1913

The **Woolworth Building**, New York, an elaborate neo-Gothic skyscraper, takes over as the world's tallest building.

New York's **Grand Central Station**, primarily the work of engineers William Wilgus and the

THE WONDER OF CONCRETE   Inside the tiered Jahrhunderthalle was a dome supported by 32 arching ribs of reinforced concrete.

partnership of Charles Reed and Allen Stem, is completed.

The massive dome, 213 feet across, of the **Jahrhunderthalle** in Breslau, Germany, by Max Berg, demonstrates the structural strength of reinforced concrete.

Austrian philosopher Rudolf Steiner begins work on his timber-domed **Goetheanum I**, at Dornach, near Basel, Switzerland, showing how philosophy and imagination can be given architectural form. It was designed as a meeting hall for his "Free High School for Spiritual Science."

Englishman Harry Brearly develops **stainless steel** by adding chromium to steel.

1914

The **Panama Canal** opens to shipping, seven years after construction began.

The **Fagus shoe factory** in Alfeld an der Leine, Germany, points the way toward the glass-walled office block. It is one of the first significant works by Walter Gropius and Adolf Meyer.

The Swiss-born architect Le Corbusier develops his concept of box-like concrete "**Domino**" houses, intended for factory production.

A **Futurist Manifesto**, *L'archittetura futurista*, proclaims that architects should make a virtue of technology, not hide it away.

1916

Irving Gill's stridently rectilinear **Dodge Residence** in Los Angeles

is completed. It is later acclaimed as the first Modernist building.

1919

Walter Gropius founds the **Bauhaus** school of art, architecture and design at Weimar, Germany.

1920

Work begins on William Randolph Hearst's elaborate dream estate, **Hearst Castle**, at San Simeon, California, and continues over the next 18 years.

1921

Erich Mendelsohn completes his highly sculptural **Einstein Tower** at Potsdam, Germany. It causes a sensation and will exert a great influence on architecture.

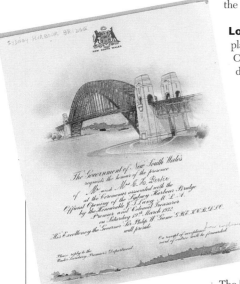

COME TO THE PARTY The opening of the Sydney Harbor Bridge is greeted with a fanfare of celebrations. Background: An airship hangar at Orly, France, designed by Freyssinet.

The short length of dual-track Avus Autobahn in Berlin points to the future of **highways**.

1922

The Dutch **De Stijl** architect Theo van Doesburg has a profound impact when he teaches at the Bauhaus.

1923

Le Corbusier publishes his influential *Vers une architecture*, in which he sets

out his idea that "the house is a **"machine for living in.**"

Eugène Freyssinet's **airship hangars** at Orly, near Paris, 300 feet wide and 197 feet high, are the first major buildings to demonstrate the strength of the parabolic arch, and take reinforced concrete to new heights.

1924

Italy opens the **first highway** of any significant length, linking Milan to Varese (35 miles).

The Dutch *De Stijl* designer Gerrit Rietveld completes his first architectural commission, the **Schroder House**, Utrecht.

The Hungarian-born Bauhaus designer Marcel Breuer designs the **first tubular steel chair**. It is known as the "Wassily Chair."

Louis H. Sullivan, architect who played a key role in the influential Chicago style of skyscrape design, dies.

1925

The Exposition Internationale des Arts Décoratifs et Industriels Modernes in Paris is dominated by the style that will later be labelled **Art Deco**. Le Corbusier's radical **Pavillon de L'Esprit Nouveau** is considered so unsightly it is screened off by the organizers at the opening ceremony.

The **Bauhaus** moves into its new buildings, designed by Walter Gropius, at Dessau.

1926

The Spanish architect Antoní Gaudí dies, having completed only a portion of his masterwork, the **Sagrada Familia** church in Barcelona.

1927

The Australian government relocates to its new capital, **Canberra**, laid out by the architect Walter Burley Griffin.

1928

The first of the influential **CIAM** (Congrès Internationaux

d'Architecture Moderne) conferences takes place in Switzerland. Le Corbusier is among the original founding participants.

Charles Rennie Mackintosh, the Scottish Art Nouveau designer, and **George Washington Goethals**, the U.S. Army engineer who oversaw the construction of the Panama Canal, die.

1929

The **Chrysler Building** in New York becomes the world's tallest building. New York now has 377 buildings with 20 stories or more.

The German architect Ludwig Miës van der Rohe points the way to the International Style with his elegantly simplified **German pavilion** at the International Exhibition in Barcelona.

1930

Ludwig Miës van der Rohe takes over as director of the **Bauhaus**.

1931

The **Empire State Building**, New York, is completed and becomes the world's tallest building.

Le Corbusier's radical **Villa Savoye**, near Paris, is completed.

The statue of **Christ the Redeemer** is erected on the summit of Corcovado Peak overlooking Rio de Janeiro, Brazil.

The **Viceroy's House** in New Delhi is inaugurated after nearly 20 years' work by its British architect, Edwin Lutyens.

The **George Washington Bridge**, New York, is completed. This suspension bridge doubles the record for the world's longest span to 3,500 feet.

1932

The **Sydney Harbor Bridge**, the world's widest long-span bridge, is inaugurated in a ceremony interrupted by a fascist sympathizer.

The architect Philip Johnson coins the term the "**International Style**" to describe radical Modernist

architecture influenced by the Bauhaus school and individual architects such as Le Corbusier.

Plastics, exemplified by **bakelite** and **rayon,** come into widespread use in everything from clothes to radios.

SUSPENDED ANIMATION In 1934, the penguins of London Zoo were treated to a spiral ramp that was soon acknowledged as a design classic.

1933

Under Nazi pressure, the **Bauhaus** at Dessau is forced to close.

1934

The **Penguin Pool** at London Zoo, by the Tecton Group, demonstrates a new sense of spatial flair and elegance in cantilevered concrete technology.

Cass Gilbert, the skyscraper architect of the Beaux-Arts school, dies.

1935

The streamlined Art Deco **Hoover factory** is completed at Perivale, west of London. Factories are now given highest architectural attention.

WORKING FOR THE MOTHERLAND The construction of the first Moscow Metro line attracted volunteers from all over the Soviet Union.

The first line of the **Moscow Metro** is completed.

1936

The largest dam to date, the Boulder Dam on the Colorado River, between Nevada and Arizona, is completed. It is renamed the **Hoover Dam** in 1947.

The **De La Warr Pavilion** opens at Bexhill. Designed by Erich Mendelsohn and Serge Chermayeff, it represents a rare example of Modernist architecture in England.

WATERING THE WEST   The Hoover Dam was part of a program of water management to improve farmland and provide power for industry in the American West.

Irving Gill, the architect who pioneered cubic houses, dies.

1937

The **Golden Gate Bridge**, San Francisco, first opens to traffic. Its central span remains the longest in the world for 27 years.

1938

Fiberglass and **Teflon** are developed, and later adopted by the construction industry.

1939

Frank Lloyd Wright completes **Fallingwater**, a private retreat at Bear Run, Pennsylvania.

1940

The collapse of the **Tacoma Narrows Bridge**, in Washington State, demonstrates the vulnerability of long suspension bridges to high winds.

Peter Behrens, the innovative German architect who influenced Gropius, Miës van der Rohe and Le Corbusier, dies.

1941

The giant sculptures of four presidents at **Mount Rushmore**, South Dakota, are finally completed after 14 years—and seven months after the death of their creator, Gutzon Borglum. The work will go in and out of fashion repeatedly in years to come.

The **Grand Coulee Dam** on the Columbia River in Washington goes into service. It remains the world's largest concrete dam.

1942

In a squash court at Chicago University, Italian physicist Enrico Fermi improvises the first **atomic reactor**, paving the way to the age of nuclear power.

Hector Guimard, the French Art Nouveau architect, dies.

1943

The **Pentagon**, Washington DC, still the world's largest office block, is completed after just 16 months.

1944

The British architect **Edwin Lutyens** dies.

1945

The engineer Palmer Putnam abandons his attempt to produce electricity from his huge **Smith-Putnam Wind Turbine** in Vermont.

1946

The Brazilian architect Oscar Niemeyer completes his Church of St. Francis at **Pampulha**, near Rio de Janeiro, bringing a new sense of plasticity and creative expression to concrete architecture.

1947

Robert Neutra's classic **Desert House** in Palm Springs, California, shows how simplified rectangular forms and large areas of plate glass can be used to integrate domestic architecture with landscape. It was built as a winter house for Edgar Kaufmann, owner of Fallingwater.

The sculptor Korczak Ziolkowski begins work on the statue of **Crazy Horse** at Thunderhead Mountain, South Dakota, a project destined to produce the world's largest sculpture some time in the 21st century.

The Belgian Art Nouveau architect **Victor Horta** dies.

1948

The **Hale reflector telescope** is installed at the Palomar Observatory, California. At 200 inches, it remains

PEOPLE IN GLASS HOUSES   Philip Johnson's Glass House echoes the style of Miës van der Rohe.

the largest telescope in the world for nearly three decades.

1949

Philip Johnson's **Glass House**, New Canaan, Connecticut, takes the domestic use of glass walls to the ultimate extreme. The circular bathroom has the only opaque wall.

1950

Walter Gropius and TAC (The Architects' Collaborative) complete the **Harvard Graduate Center**, Cambridge, Massachusetts.

1951

Le Corbusier begins work on **Chandigarh**, the new capital of the Punjab, India.

Ludwig Miës van der Rohe completes his minimalist **Farnsworth House** at Plano, Illinois, and the first of his **Lake Shore Drive** apartment blocks in Chicago.

Britain marks the centenary of the Great Exhibition with the **Festival of Britain**. Held at the South Bank, London, it features the futuristic "Skylon" monument and the Dome of Discovery, at the time the largest dome in the world, designed by Ralph Tubbs.

1952

Le Corbusier's first **Unité d'habitation** is completed in Marseille, France.

1953

The first "glass-box" office building, the 24 story **Lever House**, is completed in New York. The sterile design contrasts with the elegant Seagram Building across Park Avenue.

Erich Mendelsohn, the German-born British architect, dies.

1954

Richard Buckminster Fuller produces a **prototype geodesic dome** at the Ford Rotunda, Dearborn, Michigan.

ENGINEERING ATHLETICS Nervi's stadium provided a dramatic backdrop to the 1960 Olympics in Rome.

Auguste Perret, the French architect who pioneered the use of reinforced concrete, dies.

1955

Le Corbusier surprises the world with his sculptural chapel, **Notre-Dame du Haut** at Ronchamp, France.

Disneyland, the first of the Disney amusement parks, opens in Anaheim, California.

1956

Calder Hall, the world's first industrial-scale **nuclear reactor**, opens at Sellafield, England.

The **Amundsen-Scott Station** at the South Pole is founded by the U.S.

Josef Hoffmann, Austrian architect and Vienna "Sezessionist," dies.

1957

The Danish architect Jørn Utzon wins the competition to design the **Sydney Opera House**.

Henry van de Velde, the Belgian Art Nouveau designer who created the foundations for the Bauhaus in Weimar, dies.

1958

The **Seagram Building**, Miës van der Rohe's classic International Style office block, is completed.

The centerpiece of the 1958 Exposition Universelle in Brussels is the **Atomium**, a giant model of an iron atom.

The **Wairakei Geothermal Power Station** in New Zealand comes into service.

1959

The **Guggenheim Museum** opens in New York, 11 years after being commissioned, and five months after the death of the architect, Frank Lloyd Wright.

The **Valle de los Caídos**, General Franco's monument commemorating the Spanish Civil War, is inaugurated on April 1, the anniversary of his victory.

The architect **Frank Lloyd Wright** dies.

1960

The **Rome Olympics** use two striking stadiums designed in reinforced concrete by the Italian architect Pier Luigi Nervi.

The Missouri Botanical Garden inaugurates its innovative conservatory, a geodesic dome called the **Climatron**, using a design by MIT's Richard Buckminster Fuller.

1961

Brazil's new capital, **Brasília**, masterminded by Oscar Niemeyer and Lúcio Costa, is inaugurated.

The Finnish-American architect **Eero Saarinen** dies.

1962

Eero Saarinen's **TWA Terminal** is completed at Idlewild (later John F. Kennedy) Airport, New York.

The huge **McMath-Pierce Solar Telescope** on the summit of Kitt Peak, Arizona, is inaugurated.

1963

The **Chinon A1** power station comes into service on the banks of the River Loire, launching France's nuclear power program.

1964

Pedro Ramírez Vasquez's innovative **National Museum of Anthropology** opens in Mexico City on Independence Day, September 17.

For the **Tokyo Olympics**, the Japanese architect Kenzo Tange brings a new dynamic to stadium design.

The **Moscow Rocket Monument**, celebrating the many pioneers of the Soviet space program, is inaugurated.

The **Verrazano Narrows Bridge** across New York harbor takes the record for the longest single span of any suspension bridge.

1965

The **Gateway Arch** in St. Louis, Missouri, is inaugurated. The world's tallest monument, it was designed in 1947 by Eero Saarinen, but was not completed until four years after his death in 1961.

The 620 foot **Post Office Tower** is opened in London. It is the tallest building in Britain.

The Swiss-born, French architect **Le Corbusier** dies.

1966

The world's first **tidal power station** is opened: the "usine marémotrice" on the Rance estuary in Brittany, northern France.

FULLER'S EARTH The U.S. pavilion at Expo '67 in Montreal was a geodesic dome designed by Richard Buckminster Fuller, who described it as an "environmental valve." Background: The vast water-cooling towers of the nuclear reactor at Calder Hall in England.

1967

Richard Buckminster Fuller's geodesic dome housing the U.S. pavilion is the star exhibit of **Expo '67**, the international exhibition held in Montreal, Canada.

Miës van der Rohe completes his **New National Gallery** in Berlin.

The task of excavating, moving and reconstructing the ancient Egyptian temples of **Abu Simbel** is successfully completed in advance of the rising waters of Lake Nasser and the completion of the Aswan Dam.

Work begins on the colossal concrete **statue of the Motherland** outside Volgograd, Russia, to commemorate the Battle of Stalingrad in 1942-3.

1968

The **Oakland Museum**, California, is completed, integrating cascading vegetation and concrete roof terraces. It is one of the most important works of the partnership of John Dinkeloo and Kevin Roche.

1969

The **Odeillo Solar Oven** in the French Pyrenees comes into operation.

The German-American architects, **Ludwig Miës van der Rohe** and **Walter Gropius**, die.

1970

The crown-shaped **Metropolitan Cathedral of Brasília**, designed by Oscar Niemeyer, is completed.

The last section of one of Europe's most ambitious highways, the **Genoa-Livorno autostrada** in Italy, is opened.

1971

The **Aswan High Dam** on the River Nile in Egypt is inaugurated.

1972

The **Transamerica Pyramid** building becomes San Francisco's tallest skyscraper.

The world's largest sculpture, the Confederate Memorial Carving at **Stone Mountain**, Georgia, is finally completed nearly 50 years after work first began.

WORK OF ART   James Stirling's Neue Staatsgalerie in Stuttgart is as absorbing as its contents.

1973

The twin-towered **World Trade Center**, New York, becomes the world's tallest building, taking the 42 year record from the Empire State Building.

The **Sydney Opera House** finally opens to the public, 17 years after the project was initiated.

1974

The **Sears Tower** in Chicago becomes the world's tallest building.

1975

The world's largest dome, the **Louisiana Superdome** stadium, New Orleans, is inaugurated.

The geodesic dome is completed at the **Amundsen-Scott Station** at the South Pole.

The topping out of the **CN Tower** in Toronto, Canada, sets the record for the tallest free-standing structure in the world.

1976

The **National Theatre** on the South Bank, London, is completed. It was designed by the British architect Denys Lasdun.

1977

The new **Pompidou Center**, in the Beaubourg district of Paris, designed by Richard Rogers and Renzo Piano, opens to controversy and acclaim.

The **Trans-Alaska pipeline** is completed, transporting crude oil overland between the wells of northern Alaska and the tanker port of Valdez.

1978

I.M. Pei completes his influential **East Building** for the National Gallery, Washington DC.

1979

The nuclear power station at **Three Mile Island**, Pennsylvania, comes very close to meltdown in an accident that puts a brake on the U.S. nuclear power program.

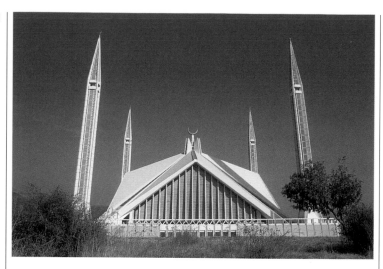

SPACE FOR WORSHIP   The open-sided, tent-like Shah Faisal Mosque in Islamabad was built to accommodate many thousands of worshippers inside and outside.

Pier Luigi Nervi, the Italian architect known for his innovative use of reinforced concrete, dies.

1981

The **Humber Bridge** in northern England opens, taking the record for the suspension bridge with the longest span.

1982

The somber and dignified **Vietnam Memorial**, in Washington DC, is dedicated at an emotionally charged ceremony on Veterans Day, November 11.

1983

The **Sultan of Brunei's Palace**, the largest in the world, is completed in time for Independence Day ceremonies on January 1, 1984.

Richard Buckminster Fuller, designer and inventor of the geodesic dome, dies.

1984

The **Thames Barrier** is officially opened, although it has already successfully defended London from a flood tide in February, 1983.

The **Neue Staatsgalerie** in Stuttgart, Germany, designed by the British architect James Stirling, is opened to the public.

1985

The architect Richard Meier, famed for his white buildings, completes his **Museum of Decorative Arts** in Frankfurt am Main, Germany.

1986

The **Lloyd's Building**, London, designed by the Richard Rogers Partnership, is completed.

Norman Foster's **Hong Kong and Shanghai Bank**, in central Hong Kong, is completed.

The Soviet nuclear power station at **Chernobyl** explodes on April 26—a disaster that confirms a deep public distrust in the nuclear power industry.

The completion of the Eastern Scheldt dam in the Netherlands marks the end of the final phase in the network of sea defenses known as the **Delta Project**.

1987

The **Futuroscope**, France's theme park devoted to the moving image, opens its doors to the public.

1988

The **Seikan Rail Tunnel** goes into service. The longest rail tunnel in the world, it links the Japanese islands of Honshu and Hokkaido.

The new **Shah Faisal Mosque** near Islamabad, Pakistan, becomes the mosque with the greatest capacity in the world, capable of accommodating some 200,000 people in its exterior space.

HEAD IN THE CLOUDS From ground level, visitors to La Grande Arche at La Défense look up to the roof through a structure of fiberglass "clouds." Background: The huge piers of the flood barrier across the River Thames.

1989

La Grande Arche, centerpiece of La Défense, to the west of Paris, is inaugurated on Bastille Day, July 14.

The **Louvre Pyramid**, designed by the American I.M. Pei, is opened in Paris in the courtyard of the famed museum on October 14.

The **Basilique Notre-Dame de la Paix**, a vast replica of St. Peter's, Rome, is completed in Yamoussoukro, the new capital of Côte d'Ivoire.

1990

I.M. Pei's **Bank of China** building in Hong Kong is completed against the backdrop of the 1989 massacre in Tiananmen Square, Beijing, and protests by the construction workers.

1991

Canary Wharf Tower, designed by architect Cesar Pelli, is completed and becomes London's tallest building.

Although operating since 1984, the **Itaipú Dam**, on the border between Brazil and Paraguay, is finally completed with the installation of its eighteenth generating unit.

The tallest structure ever erected, the **Warsawa Mast** in Poland, collapses 17 years after its construction, passing the title to the KTHI-TV Tower in North Dakota, erected in 1963.

1992

The 500th anniversary of Columbus's first arrival in the New World is marked by the opening of the huge and controversial **Columbus Lighthouse** in Santo Domingo, Dominican Republic.

The final segment of the **W.M. Keck Telescope**, on Mauna Kea, Hawaii, is fixed into position, to complete the world's largest reflector telescope.

The **Main-Danube Canal** in Germany is officially opened, 71 years after work first began.

The Chinese government gives the go-ahead for the construction of a massive dam on the Yangtze River. Called the **Three Gorges Dam**, it is scheduled for completion in 2009.

1993

A bronze-coated statue of the **Amida Buddha** in Ushiku, Japan, becomes the world's tallest statue.

Astronauts successfully install equipment in the **Hubble Space Telescope** to rectify the distortions that have blighted it since it was launched in 1990.

The 64th birthday of King Hassan II of Morocco is marked by the inauguration of the **Great Hassan II Mosque** in Casablanca, one of the world's largest and most sumptuous mosques.

1994

The **Channel Tunnel**, linking England to France, is officially opened, six and a half years after construction began.

Renzo Piano's **Kansai International Airport** in Japan is opened.

1995

The **Shri Swaminarayan Hindu temple** in Neasden, London, is completed after the assembly of some 26,300 pieces of stone bought in Europe, carved in India and transported to London.

1996

On completion, Cesar Pelli's **Petronas Twin Towers** in Kuala Lumpur, Malaysia, becomes the tallest building in the world.

1997

The **Tsing Ma Bridge**, Hong Kong, becomes the world's longest road-and-rail suspension bridge.

To mark the year 2000, the new British Labor government agrees to go ahead with the **Millennium Dome** at Greenwich, south London, designed by the Richard Rogers Partnership.

Frank O. Gehry's **Guggenheim Museum** opens in Bilbao, Spain, in October, to widespread acclaim.

Richard Meier's "classic Modernist" **J. Paul Getty Center** opens in Los Angeles in December after 14 years of construction.

1998

Hong Kong's new international airport, **Chek Lap Kok**, opens. With a terminal designed by Foster & Partners, it is said to be the most technologically advanced airport in the world.

The **Akashi-Kaikyo** road bridge is opened. Linking the Japanese islands of Honshu and Shikoku, it takes the record for a suspension bridge with the longest span.

1999

London's **Millennium Dome**, worlds largest domed structure, opens in time for the celebration of the new year and the new century.

STEELING GLANCES Standing by a busy highway, Gormley's steel *Angel of the North* is seen by 100,000 people every day.

INDEX

ACKNOWLEDGMENTS

Abbreviations:
T=top; M=middle; B=bottom;
L=left; R=right

3 Robert Harding Picture Library/ Simon Harris, L; David Noble, LM; Arcaid/John Edward Linden, RM; Arcaid/Richard Bryant, R. 6 Architectural Association/Tony Weller, RM; AKG, B. 7 Corbis/UPI, TR; AKG/Hilbich, BL. 8 Corbis/ Bettmann, TR; AKG, TM, BL. 9 AKG, TR; Arcaid/Ian Lambot, B. 10 View/Nathan Willock. 11 Popperfoto, TL; Mary Evans Picture Library, TR; Tony Stone/ Ragnar Sigurdsson, LM. 12 Network/Salgado, TL. 12-13 Tony Stone/Mark Segal, B. 14 Hayes Davidson, RM, B. 15 Arcaid/ESTO/Scott Frances; Popperfoto, L; Osterreichisches Museum, LM; Getty Images, RM; View/Peter Cook, R. 16 John Parker, TR, B. 17 Osterreichisches Museum. 18 Popperfoto, TR; British Architectural Library/RIBA, L. 18-19 Bridgeman Art Library. 20 John Parker. 20-21 John Parker. 21 Getty Images. 22 Getty Images. 22-23 Arcaid/ESTO/Scott Frances. 23 View/Peter Cook, TL, TR. 24 Magnum/Rene Burri, TR; David Hoffman, B. 25 Getty Images, M; Colorific/Alan Reininger, BM. 26 Bilderberg/S. Elleringmann, LM; Magnum/Abbas, B. 27 Robert Harding Picture Library; Bauhaus Archiv, Berlin/Erich Consemuller, L; Arcaid/Richard Bryant, LM; Arcaid/Nick Dawe, RM; Corbis, R. 28 Culver Pictures Inc. 29 Brown Brothers, TR; Robert Harding Picture Library/Adam Woolfit, BL. 30 Library of Congress, R; Culver Pictures Inc., BL. 31 Brown Brothers, TR; Robert Harding Picture Library, BL. 32 Arcaid/ Dennis Gilbert. 33 Bauhaus Archiv, Berlin/Erich Consemuller, TL, BR. 34 Arcaid/Dennis Gilbert, TR; Corbis-Bettmann, BL. 35 Robert Harding Picture Library/Simon Harris, BL; Roger-Viollet/ND Viollet, BR. 36 Corbis, TL; Arcaid/ Nick Dawe, BR. 37 Julian Cotton Picture Library/Jason Hawkes. 38 Julian Cotton Picture Library/ Jason Hawkes. 39 Arcaid/ESTO/ Peter Aaron, TR; Corbis-Bettmann, BL. 40 Corbis-Bettmann/UPI, TR; Kobal Collection, BL. 41 David Noble. 42 ESTO/Ezra Stoller. 43 ESTO/Ezra Stoller, TL; Arcaid/ ESTO/Scott Frances, BR. 44 Jane MacAndrew, TR, B. 45 Tony Stone, T; Image Library of NSW, BM.

46 David Noble. 47 David Noble. 48 Robert Harding Picture Library. 49 Magnum/Stuart Franklin, TR; Telegraph Colour Library, BL; Corbis, BR. 50 David Noble. 51 Robert Harding Picture Library/ S. Harris, T; Magnum/Rene Burri, BR. 52 Arcaid/Richard Bryant. 53 Colour Telegraph Library, TR; Arcaid/Richard Bryant, BM. 54 Arcaid/Ian Lambot, TL; Foster & Partners, TR; Foster & Partners/ Jens Willebrand; Arcaid/Richard Bryant, BM. 55 Arcaid/Neil Troiano. 56 Cesar Pelli and Assoc., TR: Robert Holmes/ Corbis-Bettmann, L. 57 ESTO; Tony Stone/ Robin Smith, L; Tony Stone/John Lamb, M; Network/Rapho/S. Bios Prevost, R. 58 Arcaid/Richard Bryant, T, B. 59 Corbis/Roger Wood, TR; Tony Stone/John Lamb, B. 60 The Walt Disney Company. 61 The Walt Disney Company, TL; New York, New York Hotel & Casino, BR. 62-63 AKG/Henning Bock. 63 Image Library of NSW, TM, TR. 64 Tony Stone/Robin Smith, TL; Image Library of New South Wales, BR. 65 Corbis/Kelly-Mooney. 66 Corbis/Danny Lehman. 67 Corbis/Robert Holmes. 68 Arcaid/William Tingey, RM; Corbis/Robert Holmes, BL. 69 Arcaid/Richard Einzig, TR; Network/Rapho/S. Bios Prevost, B. 70 John Parker, T; Skyscan Photo Library, BL. 70-71 View/Dennis Gilbert. 72-73 Bilderberg/Thomas Ernsting. 73 Arcaid/Ian Lambot. 74-75 ESTO/Jeff Goldberg. 76 Frank Spooner Pictures/Eric Vandeville. 77 ESTO/Jeff Goldberg. 78 Arcaid/John Edward Linden, TR, B. 79 Architectural Association/Richard Glover; Bilderberg/Wolfgang Volz, L; Image Library of New South Wales, M; John Parker, R. 80 Brown Brothers, TR, BL. 80-81 Corbis/Morton Beebe – S.F. 81 Tony Stone/Will & Deni McIntyre. 82 AKG/Keith Collie, TR; David King Collection, ML; Network/Barry Lewis, BL. 83 AKG/Keith Collie. 84-85 David Noble. 86 Brown Brothers, TL; Getty Images, BR. 87 Image Library of New South Wales, M, B. 88 Getty Images, L. 88-89 Arcaid/ Alan Williams. 90 Gail Mooney/ Corbis-Bettmann, M; Charles Phillip/Corbis-Bettmann, R; Lee Snider/Corbis-Bettmann, L. 91 Honshu-Shikoku Bridge Authority. 92 Societa Autostradà Ligure Toscana, SALT.

93 Illustration by Colin Woodman; Ecoscene, TR; Bilderberg/Wolfgang Kunz, B. 94 Travel Ink/Derek Allan, LM. 94-95 Travel Ink/Derek Allan. 96 Network/Salgado. 97 Bilderberg/Wolfgang Volz, TL; Julian Cotton Picture Library/Jason Hawkes, BR. 98 Illustration by Martin Woodward; Japan Railway Construction, B. 99 View/Dennis Gilbert; Tony Stone/A.B. Wadham, L; Tony Stone/Glen Allison, M; Science Photo Library/Alex Bartel, R. 100 Science Photo Library/Alex Bartel. 101 Popperfoto, TL; Bilderberg/Georg Fischer, RM, BR. 102 Network/Carol Lee. 103 Topham, TR; Julian Cotton Picture Library, B. 104 Eiland Neeltje-Jans. 105 Marc Garange/ Corbis-Bettman 106 Tony Stone/Louis Bencze. 107 Bilderberg/Wolfgang Volz, TR; Science Photo Library/Alex Bartel, B. 108 Tony Stone/Chris Kapolka. 109 NHPA/Patrick Fagot, TR; David Williams Picture Library, RM. 110-111 Tony Stone/Glen Allison. 112 Tony Stone/A.B. Wadham. 113 Tony Stone/A.B. Wadham, TR; Network/Saba/ Robert Wallis. 114-115 Arcaid/ David Churchill. 116 Julian Cotton Picture Library, T; Julian Cotton Picture Library/Jason Hawkes, BR. 117 Frank Spooner Pictures/ Christian Vioujard; Tony Stone/ Thierry Cazabon, L; View/Julie Phipps/Peter Cook, M; Robert Harding Picture Library/P. Craven, R. 118 David Noble. 118-119 David Noble. 120 Brown Brothers, TR, BL. 121 Frank Spooner Pictures/Mazin-Figaro, BL; Arcaid/John Edward Linden, R. 122 Institut Amatller D'art Hispanic/Arixu Mas, TR; Bilderberg/Eberhard Grames, BL. 123 Architectural Association/P. Bond, TR; View/Julie Phipps/Peter Cook, B. 124 Arcaid/David Churchill, T. 124-125 Shri Swaminarayan M. & Y.M. Patel. 126 Tony Stone/Thierry Cazabon. 126-7 Tony Stone/Ary Diesendruck. 127 Frank Spooner Pictures/Kaku Kurita. 128 Architectural Association/ Dennis Wheatley. 128-9 Tony Stone/Peter Pearson. 130 Frank Spooner Pictures/Beltra-Vandeville. 131 Robert Harding Picture Library/P. Craven. 132 David Noble. 133 Tony Stone/Jon Ortner. 134 Popperfoto. 134-5 Hutchison Library/M. Harvey. 136 Arcaid/ Nick Meers, TR; Frank Spooner

Pictures/Christian Vioujard, BL. 137 Arcaid/Nick Meers. 138 Network/Jenny Matthews, TR, L. 139 Science Photo Library/Tony Craddock; Science Photo Library/ Simon Fraser, L; Tony Stone/ Robert Evans, M; Science Photo Library/Phillipe Plailly, R. 140-1 Tony Stone/Robert Everts. 142 Tony Stone/Richard Simpson. 143 Scott Polar Research Institute/ Charles Swithinbank. 144 Scott Polar Research Institute/Charles Swithinbank. 145 Science Photo Library/Phillipe Plailly, RM; Science Photo Library/NOAO, B. 146 Science Photo Library/Tony Craddock. 147 Futuroscope/ M. Vimenet, TR, BR. 148 Science Photo Library/Simon Fraser. 149 Science Photo Library/NASA, TL; Science Photo Library/John Sanford, BR. 150 Arcaid/Paul Raftery, TM; AKG, BR. 151 View/ Chris Gascoigne, TR; Image Library of New South Wales, ML; David King Collection, BR; Architectural Association. 152 Popperfoto, LM; Architectural Association, BR. 153 AKG, TL; Architectural Association/Chris Macdonald, TR; Popperfoto. 154 Frank Spooner Pictures/Heinz Stucke, TR; AKG/Hilbich, LM. 154-5 Arcaid/David Churchill. 155 Arcaid/John Edward Linden/ TM; North News and Pictures, BR.

Front Cover
Top: David Noble
Middle: Science Photo
  Library/Simon Fraser
Bottom: Julian Cotton Picture
  Library/Jason Hawkes

Back Cover
Top: AKG/Henning Bock
Middle: Arcaid/Neil Troiano
Bottom: Tony Stone Images/Robert
  Cameron

The editors are grateful to the following individuals and publishers for their kind permission to quote passages from the publications listed below:
Academy Editions, from *The Great Engineers*, by Derek Walker, 1987.
The Independent, October 18, 1997.
Lonely Planet, from *Antarctica*, 1996, quote by Lt. Ricardo Ramos.
The Illustrated London News, April 19 & 26, 1958.
Jude Sharp.
Times Newspapers Ltd., from *The Times*, February 10, 1931, December 2, 1989.
Yale, from *The Rise of the New York Skyscraper*, by Landau & Condit, 1996.